A Taste of Virginia History

D1411578

Also by Debbie Nunley and Karen Jane Elliott

A Taste of Pennsylvania History
A Taste of Ohio History

John F. Blair, Publisher
Winston-Salem
North Carolina

A Taste of
Virginia History

A Guide to
Historic Eateries
and Their Recipes

DEBBIE NUNLEY & KAREN JANE ELLIOTT

The paper in this book meets the guidelines for
permanence and durability of the
Committee on Production Guidelines for
Book Longevity of the Council on Library Resources.

ON THE FRONT COVER, CLOCKWISE FROM THE TOP—
Maple Hall in Lexington; Inn at Court Square in Charlottesville; Prospect Hill in Trevilians

Library of Congress Cataloging-in-Publication Data
Nunley, Debbie.
A taste of Virginia history / by Debbie Nunley and Karen Jane Elliott.
    p.   cm.
Includes index.
ISBN 0-89587-293-5 (alk. paper)
1. Cookery. 2. Restaurants—Virginia—Guidebooks. 3. Historic buildings—Virginia. I. Elliott, Karen Jane, 1958–
II. Title.
TX714.N865 2004
647.95755—dc22
2004020398

Design by Debra Long Hampton

To our husbands, David and Gordon,
without whose love and support through the years
this book would not have been possible

Contents

Chapter 10
B is for Bistro

Chapter 11
Carry Me Back . . .

Chapter 12
History Repeats Itself

RESTAURANTS FEATURED IN *A TASTE OF VIRGINIA HISTORY*

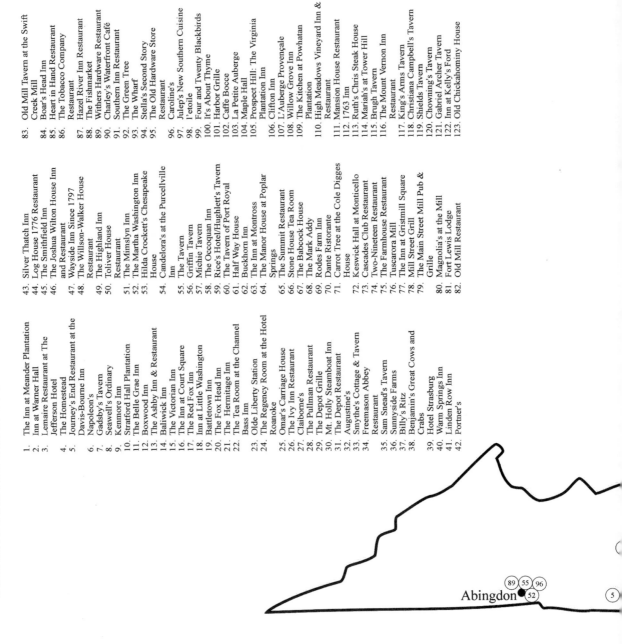

Abingdon 89 55 96 52

5

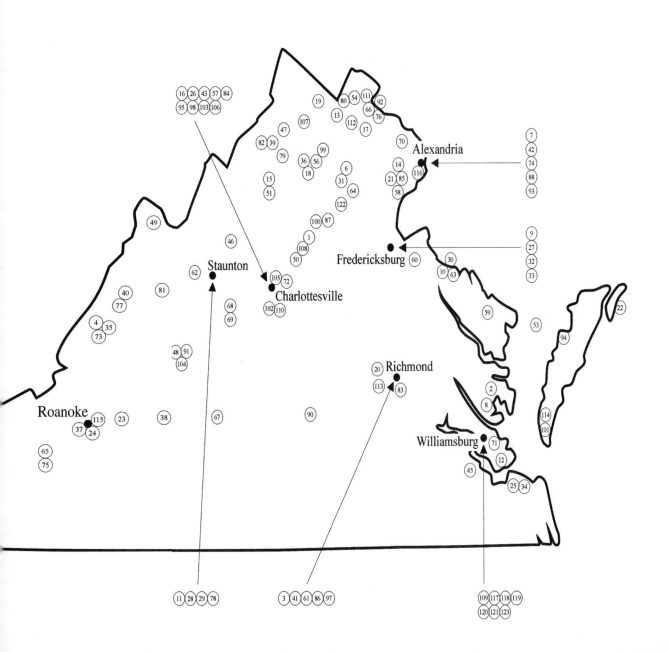

Preface

When we began writing in 1998, we did it because we enjoyed all that our restaurants provided. It wasn't just eating, it was dining. It wasn't just a meal, it was an experience—an experience steeped in history and ambiance. We so enjoyed this that we wanted to share what we had discovered with anyone and everyone who was interested. So we set about the task of researching, compiling, and recording. Somewhere along the way, one of the restaurant owners said to us, "I don't view myself as a restaurateur, but as a keeper of the history for future generations. In my hands, I know the bit of history associated with my restaurant is safe." What had started as a hobby took on greater significance with that statement, and has now evolved into our own two-person crusade in support of local, independent business owners and of maintaining and utilizing historic buildings.

As we scour a state for potential candidates to be featured within the pages of our books, we typically look for buildings of some significance—whether it be local, state, or national—as well as for buildings that have kept at least a portion of their original interior or exterior. Because of the succession of owners through the years, and because of increasingly stringent building codes, maintaining a building's historic appearance can present quite a challenge. And that's not to mention the fires, hurricanes, and other disasters that many of these structures have had to face.

After we completed *A Taste of Pennsylvania History* and *A Taste of Ohio History*, people immediately began to ask what was next. When we told them Virginia, the comments were all similar: "Ooh! That should be fun" or "There's so much history, how will you ever decide what to include?" We started researching the restaurants in Virginia with the same thoughts in our mind. What we discovered was actually somewhat surprising to us. Virginia does have a lot of history and many historic buildings. However, as a state, it has not converted many of those wonderful old structures into restaurants. We drove the highways and byways in search of any inn, tavern, or other historic eatery that may have evaded our notice. We gained new respect for how much was destroyed during the Civil War, as well as how much has been maintained. Virginians, it seems, prefer to utilize those buildings as museums, private homes, and bed-and-breakfasts. With that said, *A Taste of Virginia History* does include more restaurants than our two previous books. This isn't because there were more to choose from, but rather because Virginia restaurant owners on the whole were more accepting of our philosophy and the opportunity to be included.

One of the questions we are frequently asked is, "Do you ever get tired of eating out?" The answer to that is a resounding yes! For that reason, we typically travel for no longer than a week at a time before returning home. That way, we're able to be fresh and unjaded for each meal. What never gets old is the enthusiasm and awe that we experience as we have a bite to eat at a mill that once provided an entire community with grain, as we sit in an old depot that once saw soldiers off to war, or as we savor a meal in the same dining room where individuals such as Thomas Jefferson and George Washington once ate. In this word of hustle and bustle, these experiences give us a sense of connectedness and a sense of time—not the five-minute variety, but the continuum of time and our place within it.

Acknowledgments

We would like to thank the many people at the chambers of commerce, the convention and visitors' bureaus, and other local agencies throughout Virginia. Special recognition goes to Suzanne Pearson of Newport News and Janine Charbeneau of Richmond for their tireless efforts to assist us in our quest to represent as much of the state as possible. We would also like to express our gratitude to the public-relations individuals at the restaurants. Their promptness and professionalism made our jobs easier. Finally, we'd like to thank the terrific staff at John F. Blair, Publisher, for continuing to support us in doing what we so love to do.

On a personal note, I would like to extend my personal appreciation to my good friends the Boretzky family for taking my daughter in as one of their own during my trips to Virginia. I would also like to recognize my daughter, Dori, for her independent spirit and her support of my pursuits.

Debbie

I would like to acknowledge my family, who all took turns to cook while I was away in Virginia. They were unfailingly helpful, especially considering the number of times that I called them to send emergency faxes, or even to mail a spare computer screen to a hotel when I was on the road. I am extremely grateful for the support and the home-cooked meal when I return.

Karen

CHAPTER 1
Officers and Gentlemen

Inn at Warner Hall

Throughout history, many individuals have left their unique
imprints upon the events that unfolded around them. These restaurants reflect
the sentiments of two different quotes, both by Thomas Carlyle:
"The history of the world is but the biography of great men" and "History
is the essence of innumerable biographies." This chapter doesn't retell the well-
known tales of such men but instead gives a glimpse into
some of their lesser-known comings and goings.

THE INN AT MEANDER PLANTATION

2333 North James Madison Highway
Locust Dale, VA 22948
540-672-4912

Turning off US 15 and onto the tree-lined drive that leads to the picturesque white mansion on the knoll, it's easy to imagine the riders on horseback and the carriages filled with gaily dressed women that must have traversed this very path in earlier decades and centuries. The brick herringbone sidewalk takes guests past the dependencies and into the main house. I stood in awe on the porch for a second or two, marveling at the enormous white columns and the wide front porch soaring two full stories. Stepping inside to the entrance hall, I was warmly greeted by innkeepers Suzie Blanchard and Suzanne Thomas.

After chatting with Suzie and Suzanne and enjoying the hors d'oeuvres that were being passed by the friendly wait staff, the other guests and I were invited to dinner. Chef Paul Deigl made an appearance from the kitchen and explained in detail what we would enjoy on the menu for the evening. The atmosphere among the guests assembled in the dining room was as warm

and cheery as the rich red walls. The slate floors, crisp white trim, colonial fireplace, and brass accessories provide an elegant, yet inviting, ambiance.

Our taste buds were first entertained by a Cucumber Grenadine amusé topped with a pickled oyster—just the merest hint of the good things to come. The first course was a delicious Pâté in Puff Pastry accented by caramelized leeks. About the time this course was cleared, Royce and Linda Savelle, who were seated at the table to my right, invited me to join them. Before the smooth Black Bean Soup swirled with Lime Crème Fraiche arrived, we'd rearranged the furniture. We then proceeded through our main courses of Duck with Quinoa Pilaf and Roasted Beets and Turnips; Flank Steak Roulade with Mascarpone, Spinach, and Basil; and Wild Rockfish with Chive Crust and Cumin-Carrot Sauce. Karen arrived to pick me up just as dessert was served, and Suzanne graciously brought a portion of the scrumptious Banana Cream Napoleon for her to enjoy as well.

Meander Plantation began in 1727, when it was patented by Colonel Joshua Fry, a professor at William and Mary and a member of the House of Burgesses. It was Madison County's first plantation to be settled. Fry and his partner, Peter Jefferson, the father of Thomas Jefferson, worked together to survey and draw the first official map of the state of Virginia. Fry commanded the Virginia militia during the French and Indian

War, with George Washington serving as his second in command. When Fry was killed at the Battle of Cumberland, Washington assumed command of his forces. Local legend states that Washington subsequently encamped here for about a month to pay tribute to Fry's widow and children.

Fry's son, Henry, enlarged the manor in 1766. Henry was a lifelong friend of Thomas Jefferson, who visited the plantation often, as did the Marquis de Lafayette. William Wirt, a renowned eighteenth-century lawyer who served as counsel for the prosecution against Aaron Burr in 1807, spent much of his youth here among the plantation's three thousand acres.

Skipping ahead a hundred years, the property was owned by George Shearer and inhabited by his two daughters, Judith and Julia, who lived here their entire lives. The sisters were well-known international horse and dog show judges. Upon their deaths, the house sat vacant for many years. Fortunately, a plan to turn the estate into a country club with surrounding homes never materialized. Suzie and Suzanne came along in 1991, converting the home into a bed-and-breakfast. The restaurant and cooking school came later but have been deservedly well received. Suzie and Suzanne also continue to operate a horse farm, perpetuating Meander's rich history as a working plantation.

 MOROCCAN VEGETABLE SALAD WITH TAHINI VINAIGRETTE

1 eggplant
olive oil
salt and pepper to taste
1 red bell pepper
¼ cup water
¼ cup red wine vinegar
3 tablespoons tahini (sesame seed paste)
2 tablespoons grainy mustard
1 teaspoon honey
1 small clove garlic, minced
¾ cup vegetable oil
4 leaves lettuce
1 cup chickpeas

Preheat oven to 425 degrees. Thinly slice eggplant lengthwise. Brush lightly with olive oil and sprinkle with salt and pepper. Core and cut bell pepper into 6 to 8 large pieces. Brush with olive oil and sprinkle with salt and pepper. Place vegetables on a baking sheet, roast in oven for 15 minutes, and allow to cool. Whisk together water, vinegar, tahini, mustard, honey, and garlic for vinaigrette. Slowly add vegetable oil while whisking. Allow to rest 5 to 10 minutes.

Place lettuce on each of 4 plates. Top with eggplant and roasted red pepper. Sprinkle chickpeas over vegetables and drizzle salad with vinaigrette. Serves 4.

 BUTTERMILK-BLACK PEPPER
PANA COTTA

3 gelatin sheets
1¼ cups heavy cream
¾ cup sugar
¼ teaspoon fresh black pepper, ground coarse
1 vanilla bean, split, seeds scraped out and
    reserved
1¾ cups buttermilk

Place gelatin sheets in a bowl of cold water to bloom. Bring cream, sugar, pepper, and vanilla seeds (with bean) to a boil in a medium saucepan, stirring until sugar dissolves. Turn off heat and let infuse for 30 minutes. Strain mixture through a cheesecloth into another saucepan and reheat gently. Squeeze excess water out of gelatin and add to warm cream mixture. Stir until dissolved. Add buttermilk and whisk together. Spray 6 ramekins or fluted molds lightly with vegetable spray. Divide mixture among ramekins and cover with plastic wrap. Chill until set, at least 4 hours or overnight.

To serve, dip ramekins in hot water for a few seconds, then invert onto center of plates. Serve immediately. Serves 6.

POACHED PEARS

6 D'Anjou pears
2½ cups Cabernet Sauvignon
4½ cups water
¼ cup sugar
juice of 1 lemon

Peel pears, leaving about ½ inch of peel connected to the stem. Bring remaining ingredients to a simmer in a large pot and gently add pears. Bring back to a simmer and cover pears with a paper towel to keep them submerged. Simmer approximately 1 hour until pears are tender but not mushy, checking frequently. Remove pears and refrigerate. Strain the poaching liquid into another saucepan and reduce over medium heat until only ½ cup remains. Refrigerate until cold. Mixture should be syrupy. When ready to serve, plate each pear and drizzle with syrup. Serves 6.

Inn at Warner Hall

4750 Warner Hall Road
Gloucester, VA 23061
804-695-9565

It had been a long, eight-hour day of driving when we arrived at this beautiful inn. Before we could mount the brick stairs, our gracious hostess, Theresa Stavens, opened the wide front door. She quickly soothed our flagging spirits and encouraged us to begin to unwind. Since dusk was approaching, we put on casual clothing and headed down the path to the boathouse, where we lounged in Adirondack chairs and enjoyed the serenity of the river.

When Augustine Warner arrived in Jamestown in 1642, he had with him twelve additional settlers. As compensation for bringing these men, Warner was given a "head grant" of six hundred acres in nearby Gloucester. He was quite a success in the colony, serving in several legal and government advisory roles. He expanded his plantation, Warner Hall, to several thousand acres.

Warner's legacy lives on not only through the land, but also through his lin-eage. He was the great-great-grandfather of George Washington and an ancestor of Robert E. Lee. Through the earl of Strathmore and the Bowes-Lyon family, Queen Elizabeth II is a direct descendant of Augustine Warner.

When the senior Warner died in 1674, Augustine Warner II inherited Warner Hall. He improved the property and the manor house. As successful as his father, he was a member of the King's Council and served as speaker of the House of Burgesses in Williamsburg. He married Mildred Reade, daughter of George Reade, the founder of Yorktown. Warner had to endure not only her death but also the deaths of all of his sons at a very young age. When he passed away in 1681 at the age of thirty-nine, three daughters—Mary, Mildred, and Elizabeth—survived him.

Subsequent generations went on to be quite successful in their own right. Mary's son, Augustine Smith, was a member of the Knights of the Golden Horseshoe, who accompanied Governor Spotswood across the Blue Ridge Mountains in 1716. Mildred married Lawrence Washington and bore a son, Augustine. Young Washington married Mary Ball. It was Augustine and Mary Ball Washington who became the proud parents of a baby boy named George, named in honor of his great-grandfather George Reade. Elizabeth became the wife of John Lewis and inherited Warner Hall. The Lewis family retained possession of the manor home for many generations.

By far the best way to experience the Inn at Warner Hall is as an overnight guest. However, if an overnight stay doesn't fit your travel plans, a prix fixe luncheon is served on Wednesdays or by special arrangement. Dinner on Friday and Saturday evenings is also prix fixe. The menu changes regularly. Amusé offerings include Crab Salad with Chive and Lemon Mosto Oil, as well as Grilled Shrimp with Vidalia Onions and Mango Sorbet. Appetizers range from Roasted Corn Soup with Lump Crab and Crispy Bacon to Stuffed Quail with Spinach and Feta over Wild Rice. The salad course is equally appealing. The chef's creativity continues in entrées such as Veal Chops with Lavender Mushroom Reduction and Grilled Rockfish over Braised Fennel and Onions. Desserts include Orange Pound Cake with Lime Sorbet and Berries, as well as Chocolate Mousse with Caramelized Bananas and Toasted Almond Cream. Surrounded by luxury and steeped in history—there is no better way to enjoy fabulous cuisine.

PESTO CHEESECAKE
WITH MARINATED TOMATOES

1 cup grape or cherry tomatoes
¼ cup olive oil
¼ cup balsamic vinegar
salt and pepper to taste
¾ cup cream cheese, room temperature
½ cup grated Parmesan
½ cup pesto (commercial)
½ cup pine nuts
½ cup fresh herbs (basil, chives, or parsley), chopped
2 eggs
¼ cup sour cream
mixed garden greens
crostinis

Halve tomatoes and place in a small bowl. Add oil, vinegar, and salt and pepper and set aside to marinate. Stir occasionally.

Preheat oven to 250 degrees. In a mixer, cream the cream cheese. Add Parmesan, pesto, pine nuts, and herbs and mix to combine. Add eggs 1 at a time and beat well. Add sour cream and season with salt and pepper. Mix thoroughly.

Prepare a 6-inch springform pan with parchment paper on the bottom. Spray entire pan and parchment paper with nonstick vegetable spray. Spread cheese mixture evenly in pan. Place pan in a water bath and bake for 2 hours. Remove from oven and allow to cool in water bath. Remove from pan and refrigerate overnight.

To serve, slice cheesecake into 8 pieces, place each slice on a bed of mixed greens, and spoon marinated tomatoes over top. Serve with crostinis. Serves 8.

CHILLED WILD RICE SALAD

2 cups wild rice
¼ cup fresh chopped mint
oregano to taste
1 cup peeled and diced cucumbers
1 cup peeled, diced, and blanched carrots
1 tablespoon chopped garlic
1 tablespoon chopped shallots
½ cup rice wine vinegar
salt and pepper to taste

In a 2-quart saucepan, bring 1 quart water to a boil. Add wild rice, cook until tender, and drain. To cool rice quickly, spread it out on a cookie tray and refrigerate. In a large bowl, combine remaining ingredients except salt and pepper. Add cooled rice and season to taste. Let sit for at least 30 minutes. Adjust seasonings as necessary. Serves 8.

CARAMEL CHOCOLATE MOUSSE

4½ ounces dark chocolate
2 cups heavy cream
1½ cups sugar
3½ cups unsalted butter
pinch of salt
1 cup assorted berries
whipped cream for garnish

Melt chocolate in a double boiler and set aside in a warm spot. Whip heavy cream to stiff peaks and set aside in refrigerator. Caramelize sugar by adding a little at a time to a heavy-bottomed saucepan over medium heat. Stir constantly with a wooden spoon until sugar browns, then add a little more sugar. Repeat process until all of the sugar is caramelized. Stir butter, salt, and half of the whipped cream into caramelized sugar. Pour mixture into a warm bowl and allow to sit for 15 minutes. Add chocolate to caramel. Fold in remaining whipped cream a little at a time. Pour into serving cups and refrigerate overnight. Serve with fresh berries and dollops of whipped cream. Serves 12.

The Jefferson

RICHMOND, VIRGINIA

Lemaire Restaurant at The Jefferson Hotel
101 West Franklin Street
Richmond, VA 23220
www.jefferson-hotel.com
804-788-8000

Restaurants are frequently named after presidents or other prominent citizens. In our research, this is the first time we've come across a restaurant named after an employee. The fine-dining restaurant at The Jefferson—a posh, upscale hotel in Richmond—is named in honor of Etienne Lemaire, who served as maître d'hôtel to Thomas Jefferson from 1794 through the end of his presidency.

Lemaire is located in the area originally used as the ladies' parlor. The menu reflects Thomas Jefferson's fondness for light sauces, garden-fresh herbs, and innovative dishes incorporating regional elements with classical European influences. Jefferson also had an appreciation for fine wines. It is Lemaire who is thought to have been the foremost influence in America on the use of wine in cooking.

Breakfast, lunch, and dinner are served in these elegant environs. The breakfast menu is the most traditional, offering Belgian Waffles, French Toast, Pancakes, and an array of egg dishes. However, partaking of a fluffy Salmon and Dill Omelet in these surroundings would get anyone's day off to a good start. The lunch selections include appetizers, soups, and salads such as Beef Tenderloin Cobb Salad. Entrées such as Penne Pasta Gulf Shrimp with Mascarpone Grits and Fennel-Crusted Atlantic Salmon are served, as is a variety of sandwiches, including the SBLT, concocted of smoked salmon, veal bacon, and dill mayonnaise on sourdough toast. For dinner, it would have been so much fun to dine with a group that loved to share. We could have sampled the Mushroom-Dusted Ahi Tuna, served with Roasted Butternut Squash Risotto; or the Butter-Basted Black Grouper, accompanied by Goat Cheese Potato Purée and Root Vegetable and Blue Crab Hash; or the Pumpkin-Seed-Crusted Salmon, served with Polenta, Brussels Sprouts, and Cider Glaze.

The Jefferson Hotel was the vision of Major Lewis Ginter, who arrived in Richmond in 1842 at age eighteen. In the years leading up to the Civil War, Ginter became a millionaire by selling fabric. He served with the Confederate army and later became one of Richmond's most respected citizens. His good fortune as a banker, land developer, tobacco tycoon, and civic leader helped fuel his dream of building the finest hotel in Richmond, maybe even in all of America! Ginter kept a firm hand on the design and construction, spending approximately $8 million on the project. The hotel included modern conveniences such as electric lights, elevators, hot and cold water, and a Teleseme—a precursor to the telephone—by which guests could order room service.

Just two years after the hotel opened, Ginter passed away. The entire dream almost vanished when a fire in 1901 took more than half the building. A portion of the hotel was reopened a few months later. However, the hotel suffered financially in its damaged condition and slowly declined until a group of entrepreneurs formed the Jefferson Realty Corporation with the intent of restoring the dream.

From 1907 through 1980, The Jefferson Hotel hosted numerous celebrities, presidents, and other notables. In 1980, the doors were again closed, the hotel having suffered a steady decline since a second fire in 1944. After a $34 million restoration, it rose again. In 2003, The Jefferson became one of only twenty-two hotels in North America to hold AAA's Five Diamond rating and Mobil's Five Star rating simultaneously. The quality and service at The Jefferson Hotel are without a doubt something of which Major Ginter would be proud.

 ROASTED RACK OF LAMB

2 whole racks lamb
salt and white pepper to taste
1 cup whole-grain mustard
½ cup Jack Daniel's whiskey
2 cups fresh breadcrumbs
6 tablespoons clarified butter
Mint-Cherry Chutney (recipe below)

Preheat oven to 450 degrees. Season all sides of lamb with salt and white pepper. In a small bowl, combine mustard and Jack Daniel's. Place a thin coating of mustard mix on front and back of meat and dredge in breadcrumbs. Place clarified butter in a hot sauté pan and put front side of lamb into hot pan. Allow to brown for 2 to 3 minutes. Turn when golden brown. Finish in oven about 18 to 20 minutes for medium-rare. Remove from oven and allow to rest for 8 to 10 minutes. Carve 4 bones per person. Serve with Mint-Cherry Chutney. Serves 6.

Mint-Cherry Chutney

1 cup dried Bing cherries
½ cup plus 2 tablespoons port wine
1 shallot, minced
1 tablespoon red wine vinegar
1 tablespoon sugar
2 tablespoons mint, cut into very fine strips

Place all ingredients except mint in a small, nonreactive saucepan over low heat. Cook for 25 to 30 minutes until cherries are rehydrated and flavorful. Fold in mint. Yields 1 cup.

 STONE-GROUND GRITS

1½ cups stone-ground grits
2 cups chicken stock
3 cups whole milk
¾ cup butter
½ cup fresh mascarpone cheese
salt and white pepper to taste

Place grits, stock, milk, and butter in a large, heavy-bottomed pan. Gently simmer for approximately 4 hours until grits are soft and creamy, stirring occasionally. Remove from heat and gently fold in cheese. Season with salt and pepper. Serves 6.

 BUTTERMILK-CHIVE CORNBREAD

1¾ cups all-purpose flour
1¾ cups cornmeal
6 tablespoons sugar
2 tablespoons baking powder
1 tablespoon kosher salt
4 eggs, beaten
2¼ cups buttermilk
1 tablespoon corn syrup
1½ cups butter, melted
1 bunch chives, minced

Preheat oven to 400 degrees. Line an 8-by-11-by-2-inch baking pan with parchment paper and lightly grease. Place flour, cornmeal, sugar, baking powder, and salt in a large bowl and combine. In a smaller bowl, combine eggs, buttermilk, corn syrup, and butter. Add wet mixture to dry mixture and fold to combine thoroughly. Fold in chives. Pour into prepared pan and bake for 25 to 30 minutes. Serves 12.

THE HOMESTEAD. 1766

Hot Springs, VA 24445
www.thehomestead.com
540-839-1766

Knowledge of the natural mineral springs in this area was fairly widespread among the educated and socially elite citizens of colonial America. While he was commander of the Virginia militia, George Washington is thought to have sought respite in the curative spring waters after his arduous journeys assessing the system of forts in the region. During that time, Washington got to know Thomas Bullett, a lieutenant in the militia and a surveyor commissioned by the College of William and Mary to map out the area. Bullett's bravery soon became renowned, resulting in his promotion to captain. In 1758, Washington praised Bullett as one of the bravest officers at the Battle of Fort Duquesne. It was common practice in those days for militia officers to be compensated for their service with land grants. Bullett and fellow officers Thomas and Andrew Lewis managed to obtain three hundred acres of land that included all seven of the mineral springs at Hot Springs. Today, that grant forms the core of The Homestead's fifteen-thousand-acre resort.

Of the three, Bullett took the lead in developing the land. He encouraged other militia members and their families to homestead on his property. This gave him a work force to improve the springs, add cabins, and construct a one-story, fifteen-room lodge named The Homestead, honoring the homesteaders who had helped improve his land.

Decades later, after meeting with James Madison and others to finalize plans for the University of Virginia, Thomas Jefferson spent twenty-two days at the springs as he sought comfort from his rheumatism. Upon Jefferson's recommendation, James Madison came to the area two years later to enjoy the spa. The pools at Warm Springs were later named in Jefferson's honor. Nineteen other presidents have also visited The Homestead.

Around the same time as Jefferson's visit, another Thomas was enjoying the springs. Thomas Goode quickly came to love The Homestead and wanted to own it. Alas, it was not for sale, and he had no capital. He went off to medical school, returned to the area to practice, and ultimately realized his dream of owning the spa. Goode began his tenure by demolishing the old buildings one by one, replacing them with structures of classical proportions crafted out of local timber. That architecture forms the basis of The Homestead's style today. Dr. Goode had a prescription for guests at The Homestead. Partaking of the springs was first. Another facet of the experience was romance, with the first ballroom being built during his tenure. The third was a menu that established The Homestead as a destination for fine dining.

While Karen was back in Pittsburgh, I was fortunate to experience The Homestead with Eileen Judah, the director of marketing. We chatted over breakfast, a buffet that includes many more appealing selections that anyone could possibly sample. The dinner menu changes daily. Its selections are something of which Dr. Goode would be very proud. Appetizers such as Tricolor Vegetable Terrine and Pineapple and Mango with Passion Fruit Coulis are as beautiful as they are delicious. Follow that with entrées of Chicken Breast with Pistachio Nut, Citrus, and Wild Rice Stuffing and Allegheny Mountain Trout with Grapes and Almonds and diners are in gastronomic heaven.

Even though much has happened between then and now, The Homestead today is much as it was those many years ago. A place of elegance and gentility, it offers much to guests beyond the soothing springs that spawned its success—golf, tennis, historic tours, fine dining, and, most importantly, a place apart from everyday life.

 FETTUCCINE FRUITS DE MER

2 tablespoons salt
¼ cup olive oil, divided
1 pound fettuccine
4 cups whipping cream
2 stalks celery
½ medium carrot
½ bunch broccoli
1 medium zucchini
1 medium red bell pepper
6 ounces mushrooms
½ pound bay scallops (or sea scallops cut up)
½ pound lobster, fresh or cooked
½ pound small shrimp, peeled and deveined
1 tablespoon chopped shallots
½ teaspoon pesto
salt and freshly ground white pepper to taste
dash of cayenne
4 ounces snow peas
¼ cup grated Parmesan

Bring 7 quarts of water to a boil in a covered stockpot. Add 2 tablespoons salt and 2 tablespoons of the olive oil, then add fettuccine. Re-cover pot, return to a boil, and adjust heat so pasta cooks at a slow boil. Cook until al dente, stirring occasionally. Remove pot to sink and let cold water run briskly into it for about 30 seconds, then drain pasta in a colander and reserve.

Add whipping cream to a 3-quart saucepan. Over medium heat, reduce to slightly less than half, stirring occasionally. Cut celery into match-sized sticks, removing strings. Peel carrot and cut into strips about 2 inches long and ⅛ inch thick. Wash broccoli and break off buds so they are 2 inches long. Reserve. Clean zucchini and cut into match-sized sticks. Wash bell pepper, cut in half to remove seeds, and cut into match-sized sticks. Wash mushrooms and cut into thick slices. Wash scallops under cold running water and drain. Cut lobster into ½-inch cubes. Add remaining olive oil to a 12-inch sauté pan over medium-high heat. When oil is hot, add shrimp and cook for 2 minutes, stirring with a wooden spatula. Add shallots, celery, carrots, broccoli, zucchini, bell pepper, and mushrooms. Saute for 3 minutes, stirring occasionally. Add scallops, lobster, and pesto. Sauté, stirring, for 2 minutes. Stir in reduced cream and season with salt and white pepper and cayenne. Remove pan from heat and reserve.

When ready to serve, trim snow peas and blanche them briefly in boiling water in a small saucepan. Drain and reserve. Stir fettuccine into vegetables in the sauté pan and simmer over medium heat for 2 minutes. Stir in snow peas. Remove pan from heat and blend in Parmesan. Serve immediately on warm plates or in pasta bowls. Serves 6 to 8.

 FASSIFERN TOMATOES

28-ounce can whole tomatoes
½ cup sugar
salt and freshly ground black pepper to taste
1 tablespoon cornstarch
¼ cup cold water
2 cups ½-inch bread cubes
½ cup butter, melted

Put tomatoes and juice into a 3-quart saucepan. Add sugar and salt and pepper and bring to a boil over medium-high heat. While tomatoes are coming to a boil, mix cornstarch with cold water in a small bowl and set aside. When tomatoes are boiling, remove saucepan from heat and slowly pour cornstarch mixture into tomatoes, stirring constantly with a wooden spoon. When well blended, set saucepan over medium heat and bring tomatoes to a simmer. Adjust heat so tomatoes will cook gently for 10 minutes. Stir occasionally.

Preheat oven to 300 degrees. While tomatoes are simmering, place bread cubes on a baking sheet and put them in the oven for 5 to 10 minutes until lightly browned. When done, remove from oven and reserve. When tomatoes have finished simmering, pour them into an 8-by-8-by-2-inch baking dish. Arrange bread cubes over top and drizzle with melted butter. Place baking dish on middle rack of oven and bake for 20 minutes. Serves 10.

Journey's End Restaurant

119 Journey's End
Independence, VA 24348
www.davisbourneinn.com
540-773-9384

Maple, oak, and black walnut trees have spread their roots for long enough to see this Queen Anne-style home endure many changes through the years. The large wrap-around porch invites visitors to relax the Southern way before setting off to sightsee or to retire to one of the inn's four bedrooms. The home was constructed around 1865 by Alexander Davis, a colonel with the 145th Regiment of the Confederate army. The colonel was a local attorney who went on to become a congressman. He had three sons.

Upon his father's death, James Garnett Davis inherited the property. He embellished the home with beautiful woodwork. Like his father, James was a legislator. He was also the man responsible for building the mill and the electric powerhouse at Peach Bottom Falls that brought the first electricity to town. The younger Davis was in the process of further improving the home when his wife died giving birth to their fourth child. In his grief, he left the home, not even allowing the Washington, D.C., decorator to complete his tasks. This is particularly noticeable in the incomplete tiling around the fireplaces, which today is nearly the same as when Davis departed and rented the place to a local physician.

J. Simon Bourne, another local attorney, purchased the homestead in the 1930s. Unfortunately, he passed away shortly after buying it, but his two daughters remained in the home until the 1970s. Like her father, Pauline Bourne was an attorney. Mary was the home-economics teacher at the local high school. It was they who affectionately named the house Journey's End.

Grayson County purchased the property at auction in the mid-1970s and built a new county courthouse on a portion of the land in 1980. The home fell into a state of disrepair until 1996, when Mary Lucy and Eddie Copenhaver took ownership and began renovations. A year later, the Davis-Bourne Inn opened. Edd and Elsie Cole, the owners since 2001, have expanded the gracious hospitality here by incorporating a full-service restaurant. They've managed to create a fine-dining experience while maintaining the comfortable, friendly atmosphere of a hometown eatery.

Seafood is featured prominently on the menu. Smoked Trout Canapés, Seafood Bisque, and Coconut Shrimp are but a few of the selections. The Breast of Chicken Parisienne with Champagne Cream Sauce sounded delicious. Many of the other guests on the evening of our visit enjoyed the New York Strip Imperial, topped with crabmeat and Swiss cheese. We enjoyed chatting with Edd Cole as we savored our salads. These were followed by Crab Cakes and the Filet Tower, which consisted of a perfectly prepared Filet Mignon with tasty Mashed Potatoes. Too full to partake of dessert, we ordered a piece of Almond Amaretto Cheesecake to go, which we enjoyed at midnight when we finally arrived at our hotel. Another tasty dessert choice would have been the Cookie Pie.

The name Journey's End is appropriate for a variety of reasons. Located in an area of Virginia quite removed from the fast-paced interstates, this is definitely not somewhere you just happen by. But now that you're here, why would you want to go anywhere else?

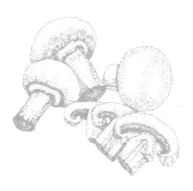

MADEIRA-WILD MUSHROOM SAUTÉ WITH HERB-ENCRUSTED PITA

3 tablespoons clarified butter, divided
1 portabello mushroom, diced
6 shiitake mushrooms, diced
6 oyster mushrooms, diced
2 silver dollar mushrooms, diced
1 clove garlic, minced
2 tablespoons Madeira wine
¼ cup demi-glace
fresh rosemary to taste, chopped fine
fresh thyme to taste, chopped fine
1 tablespoon unsalted butter
salt and pepper to taste
1 pita bread
fresh herbs and seasoning salt to taste

Heat a sauté pan over medium-high heat. Add 2 tablespoons of the clarified butter. Add mushrooms and sauté for about 1½ minutes. Add garlic. Immediately add Madeira. Add demi-glace, rosemary, and thyme. Allow to simmer. Add unsalted butter and cook for about 2 minutes over high heat until mixture reaches desired thickness. Add salt and pepper. Brush remaining clarified butter over pita. Sprinkle with fresh herbs and seasoning salt. Toast pita and serve with mushroom mixture. Serves 2 as an appetizer.

67 Waterloo Street
Warrenton, VA 20186
www.napoleonsrestaurant.com
540-347-4300

In 1978, a restaurant called 67 Waterloo was established to provide the citizens of Warrenton with a fine-dining experience. It was located in a home built in the 1830s. After the death of Charles E. F. Payne, the property was transferred to Payne's father-in-law, James Vass Brooke. Brooke was a successful attorney, a member of the Secession Convention, and a signer of the Ordinance of Secession. Ultimately, he served in Stonewall Jackson's corps.

During the Civil War, the house was owned by Judge William H. Gaines, who later became the presiding justice of the Fauquier County Court. At some point, General Eppa Hunton resided here. At the onset of the Civil War, Hunton was a colonel in the Eighth Virginia Infantry. He rose to the rank of brigadier general during the war. After the conflict, he served in the United States House of Representatives and the Senate.

Not all of the property's owners were soldiers and politicians. Alexander Hunter, a nineteenth-century journalist, called 67 Waterloo home for a time. His *Women of the Debatable Land* was a book that paid homage to the matrons of Fauquier County. It hailed their efforts in keeping the community together and the Yankees at bay during the strife.

The restaurant known as 67 Waterloo and a neighboring property—a casual, relaxed eatery called Napoleon's Café—eventually joined forces to become the Napoleon's of today. Upstairs, in the dining rooms fashioned from the old house, layers of paint have gradually been scratched away to the original wide-plank floorboards. Upholstered chairs in a quiet green, pulled up to tables covered in white linen, blend nicely with the burgundy-patterned window treatments and the pale pink walls. An occasional statue or painting of Bonaparte himself reminds guests of where they are. If dining in this section is important to you, we strongly suggest double-checking to make sure Napoleon's will be seating here during your visit.

The lunch menu reflects the casual, tavernlike atmosphere in which it is served. Soups, sandwiches, and home-style entrées such as Meat Loaf are available. I opted for a house salad and the soup of the day, Southwestern Chicken Tortilla, which wasn't nearly as spicy as I'd expected. When Karen joined me a little later, we shared the Blueberry Bread

Pudding, which came highly recommended by the staff. It was terrific.

There is some crossover from the lunch menu to the dinner menu. The restaurant is well known for its She-Crab Soup, which makes an appearance at both meals, as does the Chicken Fettuccine Pesto entrée. Considering the restaurant's moniker, other entrées seem appropriately named—Fruits de Mer Provençale, Wellington's Mixed Grill, and Chicken Alsace, made with pears, walnuts, and Brie. The pork, lamb, venison, veal, fish, and beef choices offer something for every palate. Napoleon's is proud to be a part of Warrenton's past and future.

SMOKED SALMON CHEESECAKE

1 cup Parmesan, grated or shredded
1 cup dried breadcrumbs
½ cup unsalted butter, melted
2 tablespoons Cajun seasoning
1 tablespoon olive oil
1 cup finely diced onion
⅓ cup finely diced red pepper
2 teaspoons finely chopped garlic
4 8-ounce packages cream cheese
4 large eggs
½ cup heavy cream
2 teaspoons salt
1 teaspoon ground black pepper
1 cup grated smoked Gouda
½ cup smoked mozzarella, grated
1 pound smoked salmon
¼ cup finely chopped parsley
¼ cup finely chopped basil
Orange Horseradish Sauce (see next recipe)
balsamic reduction

Preheat oven to 350 degrees. In a 10-inch springform pan, thoroughly combine Parmesan, breadcrumbs, and butter. Add Cajun seasoning. Firmly press into bottom and up sides of pan. Heat oil in a sauté pan. Sauté onions, peppers, and garlic about 2 minutes until cooked through. Remove from heat and cool completely. Process cream cheese in a food processor until smooth. While processing, add eggs 1 at a time until fully incorporated. Add cream, salt, and pepper.

In a separate bowl, combine vegetables with Gouda and mozzarella. Fold in cream cheese mixture, salmon, parsley, and basil. Pour into crust. Bake on middle rack of oven for about 1 hour and 15 minutes until set in the center. Remove from oven and cool completely. Slice and serve with Orange Horseradish Sauce and a balsamic reduction. Serves 16.

Orange Horseradish Sauce

½ cup sour cream
½ cup mayonnaise
¼ cup half-and-half
zest of 1 orange
juice of 1 orange
2 tablespoons horseradish
2 teaspoons chopped garlic

Combine all ingredients in a mixing bowl until well incorporated. Yields approximately 1½ cups.

138 North Royal Street
Alexandria, VA 22314
703-548-1288

The town of Alexandria was founded as a seaport in 1749. Taverns quickly popped up, providing travelers a place to rest, eat, and catch up on the latest news. These hostelries also were the setting for many business deals, political discussions, and enjoyable entertainments. The site known today as Gadsby's Tavern actually consists of two early buildings—a tavern built around 1770 and the City Hotel, constructed in 1792. Entrepreneur John Gadsby leased the two buildings from 1796 to 1808, creating a haven that was the center of Alexandria's economic, political, and social life.

So successful was the tavern that George Washington, Thomas Jefferson, John Adams, James Madison, and James Monroe were all patrons. In 1798, Gadsby's hosted a celebration of Washington's birthday. As a matter of fact, it was from the steps of Gadsby's that George Washington held his last military review, and it was here that he gave his last military order in November 1799.

Today, the original tavern houses a museum, and the City Hotel functions as a restaurant. The buildings are noteworthy examples of Georgian architecture saved from demolition in the early twentieth century by the efforts of Post 24 of the American Legion. The city of Alexandria acquired Gadsby's in 1972, and further restoration was done for America's bicentennial celebration in 1976. In addition to maintaining its historical appearance both inside and out, the restaurant strives to duplicate the food, serving pieces, furnishings, and costumes of its original era. The illumination indoors is provided by single tapers inside hurricane globes.

After an active day of sightseeing, our party of fourteen was famished, so the Sally Lunn Bread disappeared from its basket as soon as it arrived. Tales abound as to how the bread came to be named. One story tells of a girl selling bread on the streets, crying *"Soleil-lune!"* to advertise her wares. *Soleil-lune,* French for the sun and the moon, was to be imagined in the golden tops and the white bottoms of the buns. As *soleil-lune* evolved in America, it became Sally Lunn and was no longer a bun, but baked bread in a Turk's-head mold.

We enjoyed Artichoke Cheese Fritters and Baked Brie en Croute, stuffed with blackberries and walnuts. The Venison Chops, coated in pommery mustard, herbs, and Wild Mushroom Sauce, were equally satisfying. The Chicken Saltimbocca, a pan-fried breast layered with Smithfield ham, tomato, and cheese and covered with Mornay Sauce, was given approval by those who'd ordered it. And in one quick bite, the Virginia Ham Steak, served with fried apples and a puff pastry dumpling, sent us back two hundred years!

As we exited through the crowded dining room and the accompanying buzz of conversation, it was easy to imagine Gadsby's as the hub of Alexandria. Reservations are in order here, because the place is certainly as popular as ever.

 COLONIAL PYE

1 package frozen pastry dough
½ cup butter
½ cup flour
8 cups milk
1 cup clam juice
¼ cup diced celery
¼ cup diced onion
¼ cup diced potato
2 cups chicken, cooked and chopped
1 cup salad shrimp, cooked
Old Bay seasoning to taste
parsley to taste

Preheat oven to 350 degrees. While preparing the rest of the recipe, let pastry dough thaw at room temperature. In a large saucepan or stockpot, melt butter over low heat. Gradually stir in flour to make a roux. Whisk in milk and clam juice until smooth. Slightly

increase heat. Continue cooking, whisking frequently, until thickened. Steam celery, onions, and potatoes until tender but not mushy. Add to thickened sauce. Stir in chicken and shrimp. Season with Old Bay and parsley. Cool slightly, then pour into individual serving crocks. Roll out pastry dough. Cut 8 to 10 circles from the dough, depending on how many crocks you filled with the sauce mixture. Cover each crock with a circle of dough and bake for about 15 minutes until crust is browned and filling is heated through. Serves 8 to 10.

POTATO, CABBAGE, AND COUNTRY BACON HASH

1 tablespoon butter
2 strips bacon, diced fine
½ head green cabbage, julienned
1 onion, diced fine
2 potatoes, skin on, diced small
1 tablespoon black pepper

Melt butter in a medium skillet. Add bacon and cook until done but not overly crisp. Add remaining ingredients and cook about 7 to 10 minutes until vegetables are tender. Serves 2.

Seawell's Ordinary

3968 George Washington Memorial Highway
Ordinary, VA 23131
804-642-3635

According to local lore, it was at Seawell's Ordinary that George Washington supped with the Marquis de Lafayette and planned the maneuvers to encircle Cornwallis. A charred section of the floor in the original building has been blamed on the Marquis, who is said to have been careless with his pipe. Records show that French officers stationed on the ships anchored at nearby Gloucester Point frequented a public house and billiard tables owned by Joseph Seawell.

It was 1712 when the oldest part of the building was constructed. Joseph Seawell, son of an English merchant, added to the structure in 1757 and subsequently established an ordinary. The distinction between an ordinary and an inn was that both served food but only inns provided overnight lodging. The farmland surrounding the ordinary was used for horse racing. Advertising in a 1739 edition of the *Virginia Gazette* tells of a subscription meet to be held at Seawell's. There are those who believe that the inspiration for much of Virginia's current love of horses grew from this area of Gloucester County.

The establishment continued as an ordinary until 1871, when Richard Henry Hogg purchased it as a residence. It passed from hand to hand until 1948, when extensive renovations were undertaken and it became a restaurant again. In 1959, the structure was moved back a hundred feet to accommodate the expansion of US 17. It was again renovated and redecorated in the fall of 1984, when the current owners took over.

We were seated in the dining room to the right of the entry hall. It was painted burgundy and had white wainscoting and a white mantelpiece. An old broom leaned in a corner nearby. Hunt-club pictures hung throughout, intermixed with brass double sconces. Across the hall, the walls were washed in a hunter green and accented by a variety of paintings of ships.

The oil lamp on our table flickered quietly on the rainy evening we visited. Karen ultimately chose the Oyster Volcano, made by stacking fried, breaded oysters atop White Wine Cream Sauce. The serving was plentiful and the flavor fresh. It was preceded by a salad of mixed greens tossed in a flavorful homemade Ranch Dressing. Debbie also started with a salad, her choice being the house specialty, the Ordinary Salad. It was one of the most deliciously unusual salads she's tried. It was made by topping mixed greens with melted Brie and toasted almonds, then drizzling the entire salad with the robust Sesame Honey Salad Dressing. The combination was superb. Debbie also tried the Baked Phyllo Cigars, featuring lump crab, herbs, and mixed cheeses, served with White Wine Cream Sauce. It was another winner. The dessert choices ranged from the banana-flavored Cheesecake Zango to Blueberry Peach Cobbler. The chef had also prepared Dark Rum Crème Brûlée, but Karen couldn't resist the Chocolate Pâté with Raspberry Sauce.

Thomas Jefferson's early maps displayed the location of Seawell's Publick House. Now that we've visited, it's on our map for great food.

 SMITHFIELD HAM AND POTATO SOUP

1 large onion, chopped
1 bunch celery, chopped
2 pounds Smithfield ham, chopped
1 tablespoon parsley
1 tablespoon thyme
1 tablespoon crushed garlic
10 Idaho baking potatoes, peeled and chopped
4 cups water
2 tablespoons chicken base
2 quarts heavy cream
salt and pepper to taste

In a stockpot, combine first 7 ingredients and cover with water. Bring to a boil. Reduce heat and continue cooking about 15 minutes until vegetables and potatoes are very tender. Do not drain. Place entire contents in a blender and purée until very smooth. Return to pot. Add chicken base and heavy cream. Heat through, bringing just to a simmer. Reduce slightly. Add salt and pepper. Serves 8 to 10.

 ONION CUSTARD

2 cups onions, sautéed
1½ cups grated fontina cheese
1½ cups sour cream
9 eggs
3 cups heavy cream
1 tablespoons fresh chives
2 tablespoons chopped shallots

Preheat oven to 350 degrees. Combine all ingredients in a large bowl, then pour into a greased casserole dish. Bake in a water bath for 40 minutes until set. To serve, cut into squares if you used a square or rectangular casserole or into wedges if you used a round casserole. Serves 8.

SESAME HONEY SALAD DRESSING

1 cup balsamic vinegar
1½ cups honey
1 cup sesame oil
1 cup salad oil

Place all ingredients in an airtight container, shaking well to combine. Serve over any type of salad. Yields 4½ cups.

Kenmore Inn

1200 Princess Anne Street
Fredericksburg, VA 22401
www.kenmoreinn.com
540-371-7622

The property where the Kenmore Inn stands was on the original boundary line of Fredericksburg, as surveyed in 1757. From this location, you can still walk across adjacent Lewis Street to see the corner marker that was laid establishing this demarcation. Colonel John Lewis, father of respected patriot Fielding Lewis, originally purchased the property. Historical accounts are unclear as to which man built the house across the street at 1201 Princess Anne. It is known, however, that Fielding Lewis brought his bride, Catherine, to the dwelling in 1747. Sadly, Catherine perished in 1750, leaving behind an infant son. Later that year, Fielding was wedded to George Washington's only sister, Betty. For his new bride, Fielding built a mansion known as Kenmore atop a hill several blocks away from his previous home. Kenmore Inn's name honors that mansion.

Fielding Lewis was a wealthy planter and businessman who owned ships that traded between Virginia and England. He was also a staunch patriot who sacrificed his personal fortune to arm the Revolutionary War effort, most notably the Fredericksburg gunnery. In a sad irony, he died just weeks after the British surrendered to his brother-in-law.

The lot at 1200 Princess Anne was sold in 1776 to the William Champe Carter family. It was again sold in 1794, along with the property across the street at 1201, this time to the William Stanard family. Interestingly enough, both the Carters and the Stanards were direct descendants of the Lewis and Washington families. In 1807, during the great Fredericksburg fire, the house at 1201 Princess Anne burned. City records indicate that it was rebuilt in 1812, its interior details modeled after the dwelling across the street. This account is the first official record of a home at 1200. Historians differ as to when that house was actually constructed. The property passed from the Stanards to Rebecca Taylor Lomax in 1819.

Many years later, the house, although heavy shelled, survived the Battle of Fredericksburg. Evidence of the bombardment is still evident in some of the roof supports. Union soldiers housed their horses in the lower level. After the Civil War, the structure continued to be used as a private residence. Some of Virginia's most prestigious families—including those of Alexander Phillips, Thomas Knox, and Samuel Gordon Wallace—called 1200 Princess Anne home.

In 1931, the house passed into the hands of James T. Horton, who made major additions, including the rear wing and an underground garage. He then opened a small hotel known as Kenmore Tavern. Two years later, Horton sold the property to his sister

Harriet Hall. Mrs. Hall ran the small hotel for many years. She also leased the lower level to Charles Lakey, who used it for his Kenmore Coffee Shop from 1939 until 1978.

The elegance of yesteryear continues in today's décor. The main dining rooms are appointed with lovely linens and furnishings. Federal-style window treatments allow the sun to pour through. In a small dining room just off the bar area, the décor is more rustic, with an old crossbow saw hanging on the wall.

Appetizers like Roaster Red Pepper Soup and Roasted Asparagus with red peppers and melted blue cheese are a terrific way to start a scrumptious meal here. You can follow those with entrées like Champagne Trout and Portabello Pasta Purse. The Kenmore Inn has won the "Taste of Fredericksburg" award many times, so it's a safe bet that whatever your menu choice, it will be sure to please.

 ROASTED RED PEPPER SOUP

7 red bell peppers
4 cups hot water, divided
¾ cup butter
1¼ cups flour
3 tablespoons chicken base
4 cups heavy cream
4 cups half-and-half
4 dashes hot sauce
chipotle powder to taste
salt and white pepper to taste

Preheat oven to 375 degrees. Cut peppers in half and remove seeds. Place peppers cut side down on a lightly oiled sheet pan. Oven-roast for about 30 minutes until skins begin to blacken. Remove peppers from oven and run under cold water. This should allow you to easily remove skins. Place peppers in a food processor and purée with ½ cup hot water.

In a large stockpot, melt butter and add flour to make a roux. Add chicken base, then gradually whisk in remaining water. Once mixture is thick, add puréed peppers and whisk to combine. In another saucepan, heat cream and half-and-half over medium heat. When creams are very warm, gradually add mixture to pepper base. Turn heat down to low and add spices. Serve immediately. Serves 16.

Stratford

Stratford Hall Plantation
485 Great House Road
Stratford, VA 22558
www.stratfordhall.org
804-493-8038

The history of Stratford Hall Plantation is really that of the Lee family itself. Thomas Lee and his wife, Hannah, were the proud parents of six sons and two daughters, the majority of whom made an indelible mark on the history of early America. Thomas was a founder of the Ohio Company, a member of the governing council of the Virginia colony, and acting governor of Virginia. A successful tobacco planter and land speculator, he purchased this property in 1717 but did not begin construction of his lovely Georgian home until between 1730 and 1738. Ultimately, his vast landholdings encompassed sixteen thousand acres in Virginia and Maryland.

At Stratford Landing on the Potomac River, Thomas Lee built a wharf and a gristmill. This allowed him to create a plantation home that was really a "towne in itself," as one visitor described it. The Lees owned an interest in several sailing vessels, which allowed them to trade directly with England. Tobacco, the family's principal crop,

soon depleted the land at Stratford. For a while, it was grown on outlying farms, but by the mid-1750s, Thomas Lee needed to find other sources of trade. Shops of many kinds along the wharf kept trained craftsmen busy. The Lees employed wheelwrights, distillers, smiths, furniture makers, and others to see to the needs of the plantation.

The family's eldest son, Philip Ludwell Lee, eventually inherited the home. Like his father, he was a member of the governing council. Well known for his interest in entertaining, he made several changes to the home to incorporate that pursuit. Philip's younger brothers, Richard Henry and Francis Lightfoot Lee, were the only brothers to sign the Declaration of Independence. Yet another brother, Thomas, helped to write the Virginia Resolves and was one of the first judges elected to the Virginia Supreme Court. The other two brothers, William and Arthur, were diplomats who worked to secure European support during the Revolutionary War. Political pursuits were not left just to the Lee brothers. Daughter Hannah Corbin Lee was a strong proponent of women's rights. Her sister, Alice, married Dr. William Shippen, who served as chief physician and director general of the Continental Army hospitals. All in all, the Lees were a very prominent, highly successful family.

The history of this fine edifice didn't end with Thomas and Hannah's offspring. Soon after the death of Philip Lee, ownership of Stratford Hall was transferred to his eldest daughter, Matilda. Matilda married her cousin, Revolutionary War hero Light Horse Harry Lee. Upon Matilda's death in 1790, her husband was given a life interest in the plantation. Three years later, he married Ann Hill Carter of Shirley Plantation. Robert E. Lee, the future general of the Confederate army, was born at Stratford Hall Plantation in 1807. He was the son of Light Horse Harry Lee and his second wife, Ann.

A log-cabin dining room located in a wooded setting provides a dining opportunity for visitors to Stratford Hall Plantation. The menu includes such perennial favorites as Fried Catfish, Chicken Pot Pie, Virginia Ham, and Fried Oysters. As we enjoyed a midafternoon snack of Ham Biscuits, Coleslaw, and Peach Cobbler, we found ourselves absorbed in the fascinating history of this place. In today's world of interdependency, we marveled at the self-sufficiency that succeeded here so long ago.

 GINGER COOKIES

1½ cups margarine, softened
½ cup dark molasses
2 cups sugar
2 eggs
4 cups flour
4 teaspoons baking soda
2 teaspoons cinnamon
1 teaspoon ground ginger
1 teaspoon ground cloves
½ cup brown sugar

In a medium bowl, combine margarine, molasses, sugar, and eggs. Beat well. In another bowl, combine flour, baking soda, cinnamon, ginger, and cloves. Mix well. Add flour mixture to margarine mixture. Stir together until dough is formed. Wrap dough in plastic wrap and refrigerate for several hours.

Preheat oven to 350 degrees. Remove dough from refrigerator and roll into 1-inch balls. Roll balls in brown sugar and place on a cookie sheet. Bake for 8 to 10 minutes until firm and light brown. Yields 4 dozen cookies.

QUICK BUCKWHEAT CAKES

4 cups buttermilk
2 teaspoons baking soda
2 teaspoons baking powder
1½ teaspoons salt
1 cup flour
2 cups buckwheat flour
1 to 2 teaspoons vegetable oil

In a large bowl, combine buttermilk, baking soda, baking powder, and salt. Stir in flour and buckwheat flour. Beat until thoroughly mixed. Heat oil in a medium skillet. Pour ¼ cup batter at a time into skillet. Cook until bubbly. Turn with a spatula and cook other side. Remove to a warm plate. Yields 16 cakes.

CHAPTER 2
The *Inn*side Story

The Belle Grae Inn

For weary travelers, an inn provided welcoming solace
from the elements and the evils that befell them during an arduous journey.
While the accommodations of yesteryear may not pluck an appreciative chord in
modernity, the gratitude felt by those early sojourners has been written about
over and over. Some of the inns featured in this chapter existed to provide just
such comforts, while others have been converted from previous uses to meet the
needs of modern wayfarers. Regardless, the hospitality
extended is sure to be enjoyed by all.

515 West Frederick Street
Staunton, VA 24401
www.bellegrae.com
540-886-5151

The town of Staunton is a remarkable tribute to Victorian architecture. Boasting more than eighteen hundred restored buildings, this community has more such structures than any other community of its size in the country. More than a few of those buildings belong to Belle Grae's owner, Michael Organ.

The Victorian mansion that houses Belle Grae was built around 1870 and has been carefully restored. It's hard to imagine that this property, located within blocks of downtown, was once part of a two-hundred-acre farm at the edge of town. During the years following the Civil War, the home was flanked on either side by Victorian-style houses. These varied in size from large three-story properties owned by prominent ministers, doctors, and businessmen to smaller versions that housed the laborers who worked in local pajama and furniture factories.

Today, this lovely brick home boasts seventeen guest rooms furnished with antiques, period reproductions, and keepsakes. Visitors

can while away the hours playing chess or backgammon in the Garden Room or curl up in a wicker rocker on the veranda to delve into a good book, enjoy some idle conversation, or marvel at the view of Betsy Bell Mountain and Mary Gray Mountain. It was from these that the name of the inn was derived. The Museum of American Frontier Culture, lovely Mary Baldwin College, Woodrow Wilson's birthplace, and the boutiques and antique shops of Staunton's historic district are all within easy access of the inn. If theater is to your liking, you'll enjoy Staunton's replicas of Shakespeare's Globe Theater and Black Friar's Theater.

For those interested in a light dinner, The Belle Grae Inn offers the Garden Room. This lovely café has seating both indoors and outdoors when weather permits. For fine dining, a three-course or four-course meal is offered in the main house, also referred to as the Old Inn. Unlike many prix fixe meals, a variety of options are available to dinner guests. Choosing one dish from each of the courses is the most common approach, but if the fancy strikes, choosing all three appetizers on the menu and a dessert would be equally acceptable.

Subtly painted walls and lovely Oriental carpets enhance the subdued atmosphere. Diners can begin with choices like Artichoke Hearts Stuffed with Herb Cream Cheese, Shiitake and Smoked Gouda Tarts, and Crab Puffs with Lime Aioli. Homemade dressings such as Buttermilk Dill and Honey Poppy

Seed augment salads of baby greens. Choosing an entrée is difficult when the options include Roast Pork Loin in Blackberry Sauce, Chicken Roulade Stuffed with Spinach and Boursin Cheese, and Pecan-Encrusted Tilapia. Not surprisingly, the dessert offerings are every bit as tempting. We reveled in the Pumpkin Cheesecake, made by Ken Hicks. In one of our previous books, the Pumpkin Cheesecake recipe was extremely good and very popular. Ken's creation is even better.

Excellent food and interesting attractions abound in Staunton, and the Belle Grae Inn provides effortless access to it all.

HONEY POPPY SEED DRESSING

1 cup poppy seeds
1/3 cup salt
3 cups sugar
3 cups cider vinegar
3 cups Dijon mustard
5 pounds honey
1/2 cup finely chopped onion
1 gallon vegetable oil

Combine first 7 ingredients in a large container. Add vegetable oil and mix with a hand mixer for 4 to 5 minutes until dressing is completely blended. Yields 1½ gallons.

Note: Dressing keeps well in refrigerator. This recipe is great for hostess gifts. It will fill approximately 12 two-cup Mason jars.

SOFT AND CREAMY CHOCOLATE PIE

1½ cups sugar
3 eggs
12-ounce can evaporated milk
1 heaping tablespoon flour
3 tablespoons cocoa
1 tablespoon vanilla
9-inch pie shell

Preheat oven to 325 degrees. In a large bowl, combine first 6 ingredients. Prick bottom of pie shell to keep it from bubbling or shrinking. Pour filling into crust. Bake about 25 minutes until set. Yields 1 pie.

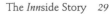

The Boxwood Inn

10 Elmhurst Street
Newport News, VA 23603
www.boxwood-inn.com
757-888-8854

There is so much to see at the Boxwood Inn, it's difficult to know where to begin. Built in 1896, the house was originally the home of Simon Curtis, the "bossman" of Warwick County. Mrs. Curtis was known as a gracious hostess, and the house was used for many political gatherings and social events. She was reputed to have saved a guest room especially for the tea and coffee salesman. No doubt, she was well supplied with tea and spices in return.

Over the years, the house has served as the Warwick County Hall of Records, a general store, a post office, and even a hotel for officers stationed at nearby Camp Eustis during World Wars I and II. In the late 1990s, it was scheduled to be torn down in order for a fast-food place to be built. But current owner Barbara Lucas stepped in, and today this charming inn has been restored to its former glory. The delightful guest rooms are filled with antiques. They're decorated with an interesting collection of old military uniforms, petticoats, dress forms, and old photos discovered in the attic. An old spinning wheel sits in the corner of one of the rooms.

We wandered around the house looking into each nook and cranny. The elegant rooms have fourteen-foot ceilings, arched fireplaces, and wooden floors. The original kitchen is no longer in use. You can visit Simon Curtis's office, which has its own entrance at the side of the house. The glass-enclosed porch where the Curtis family held dancing parties is still there. The country store, with its original shelving all around the walls, conjures up days when deeds were filed, wedding licenses were obtained, and taxes were paid across the counter. On the day we visited, staff members were packing box lunches for a local school—and jolly good they looked, too!

The inn serves lunch and dinner in addition to the popular box lunches. We enjoyed lunch with Barbara Lucas and Suzanne Pearson, who is the media-relations manager for the Newport News Tourism Development Office. We sat in the delightful Blue Willow Tea Room to sample a few of the delicious treats on the menu that day. As you would expect from the name, the room has a large collection of Blue Willow china displayed on shelves around the walls.

The creamy Broccoli Soup was very tasty, as was the Chicken Salad with red and green grapes and toasted almonds. We tasted the Bran-Raisin Muffins and loved the moist texture. The Boxwood Inn is known for the quality of its desserts and cookies, and rightly so. We sampled the Blueberry Bread Pudding and the Teacup Brownie. Both were fabulous. And we also received what Barbara called "two hunks of love" to take with us—a Butter Pecan Bar and a Mounds Candy Bar Cookie. What a wonderful reminder of a lunch to remember!

 FRESH PEACH BREAD PUDDING

1 tablespoon butter
4 ripe peaches, peeled and sliced
2½ cups brown sugar, packed, divided
1 tablespoon peach schnapps
1 small loaf white bread, cubed
¼ teaspoon cinnamon
1 quart half-and-half
12 eggs
vanilla ice cream

Preheat oven to 325 degrees. In a medium sauté pan, melt butter and sauté peaches until lightly browned. Sprinkle with 2 tablespoons of the brown sugar and schnapps. Stir well, remove from heat, and set aside. Spray a 9-by-13-inch Pyrex pan with oil and cover bottom with 1 pound of brown sugar. Arrange peaches over top of sugar. Evenly distribute bread over top of peaches and very lightly dust bread with cinnamon.

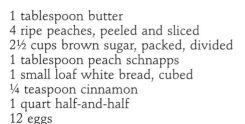

In a separate bowl, beat half-and-half together with eggs. Pour mixture over bread cubes and let sit for 15 minutes. Bake for about 1 hour until knife inserted in center comes out clean. Cut into squares to serve. Serve with vanilla ice cream if desired. Serves 12.

 TEACUP BROWNIES

1 package rich brownie mix
½ cup half-and-half
1½ cups semisweet chocolate chips
4 scoops vanilla ice cream

Prepare brownie mix according to package directions. Make sure ingredients are mixed very well. Spray 4 large café au lait cups with oil and fill about ⅓ full of brownie mix. Refrigerate until ready to bake.

Place half-and-half and chocolate chips in a small bowl and microwave for about 1 minute on high until chocolate chips have melted. Stir well to create chocolate sauce.

To bake, place cups 1 at a time in microwave and heat for 1 minute on high. Center of brownie will still be moist. Top with 2 tablespoons chocolate sauce. Add a scoop of vanilla ice cream and drizzle with an additional tablespoon of chocolate sauce. Serves 4.

THE
ASHBY
INN
& Restaurant

692 Federal Street
Paris, VA 20130
www.ashbyinn.com
540-592-3900

Restaurant critiques that we read about The Ashby Inn prior to our evening there said it was "regarded as one of the best restaurants in Northern Virginia," that it served "delightful Sunday brunches," and that "it's been consistently terrific." Our experience paralleled these fine claims.

Karen ordered the Grilled Filet Mignon with Au Poivre Sauce. Although the server brought a steak knife, it was superfluous, since the beef was almost tender enough to cut with a fork. Debbie opted for something that appears regularly in Virginia but rarely elsewhere. She thoroughly enjoyed the Grilled Quail, served with Oven-Roasted Rosemary Potatoes. On another evening, our choices could have easily been the Pan-Seared Catfish accompanied by a side of White Bean and Pepper Stew and the Raisin- and Jalapeño-Stuffed Pork Loin on Cinnamon Rice. Of course, in an establishment where all the breads and desserts are homemade, how could we evade dessert? The Chocolate Molten Cake, served with Cof-

fee Ice Cream, deliciously employed one of Karen's favorite flavor combos. One of her other all-time favorites is Bananas Foster. It, too, was on the menu—in the form of Bananas Foster Cheesecake, that is. Since this wasn't an occasion for two desserts, Debbie tried it, forgoing the Raspberry and Mango Napoleon with Grand Marnier Cream and Raspberry Coulis.

The Ashby Inn was forged from a farmhouse built at the east end of this hamlet around 1829. It is situated directly across the street from the original Ashby Tavern, frequented by George Washington in his early days as a surveyor. During the Civil War, control of Paris changed many times. When its proximity to the Ashby Gap, not more than a mile away, is considered, this isn't surprising. The gap was a focal point for both the North and the South during the conflict because whichever side controlled the gap also controlled eastern access to the northern end of the Shenandoah Valley. "The Gray Ghost," Confederate colonel John S. Mosby, staged many of his famous raids around these parts. During a period of Confederate control, Stonewall Jackson is said to have slept on the front porch of this farmhouse while his troops were bivouacked nearby.

When John and Roma Sherman abandoned their Washington, D.C., lifestyle in 1984, they purchased this property with a strong sense of what they wanted—a village inn. With Paris's current population standing at right about fifty, that's certainly what they've created. The guest rooms are unique, each decorated with its own special flair. Several are situated in the farmhouse, while others are just a few steps away.

The Ashby Inn is a perfect place to get away from the hustle and bustle of modern life. But with all the inn has to offer, we prefer to think of it as a "get away to" destination. Getting away to lovely surroundings and great food sounds great to us.

 PARMESAN-CRUSTED PORK LOIN

5 pounds boneless pork loin, sliced into 12
   two-inch slices
salt and pepper to taste
2 cups grated Parmesan
2 cups dry seasoned breadcrumbs
flour for coating
6 eggs, lightly beaten
reduced pork stock or demiglace for sauce

Preheat oven to 450 degrees. Season pork with salt and pepper. Combine Parmesan and breadcrumbs. Set aside. Roll pork in flour, then egg wash, and finally in breadcrumb mixture, coating well each time. Quickly deep-fry to set crust and to brown. Bake about 8 minutes for medium. Remove and keep warm. Serve with demiglace, if desired. Serves 6.

 CAPONATA

kosher salt
2 medium eggplants, diced into ½-inch pieces
3 tablespoons olive oil, divided
1 cup red onion, diced
1 cup celery, diced
salt and pepper to taste
1 cup peppers (combination of red, yellow, and
   green), diced
½ cup capers, drained
½ cup niçoise olives, pitted and chopped coarse
¾ cup red wine vinegar
1 tablespoon sugar
4 tablespoons tomato paste
1 tablespoon basil, chopped
1 tablespoon thyme, chopped
1 tablespoon oregano, chopped
1 tablespoon garlic, chopped

Lightly salt eggplant and place in a colander for 1 hour. Heat 1 tablespoon of the olive oil in a large skillet. Sauté onions and celery quickly, but do not brown. Season with salt and pepper. When crisp but tender, add peppers. Cook until tender but not mushy. Reserve. Rinse eggplant and squeeze dry. Sauté eggplant in small batches in remaining olive oil. Combine eggplant with onion mixture in a large pot. Add capers and olives. Whisk together vinegar, sugar, and tomato paste and add to eggplant mixture. Heat gently. Add herbs and garlic and adjust seasonings. Serve warm or at room temperature with Parmesan-Crusted Pork Loin. Serves 6.

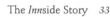

THE BAILIWICK INN

4023 Chain Bridge Road
Fairfax, VA 22030
www.bailiwickinn.com
703-691-2266

The word *bailiwick* in its oldest form means "area around the court." Since the Fairfax County Courthouse stands directly across the street, the name seems appropriate for this lovely Federal-style structure. Joshua Gunnell constructed the house sometime between 1800 and 1812. A large addition in 1832 doubled its size, paving the way for the luxury of today.

At the onset of the Civil War, Joshua Coffer Gunnell, once sheriff of the county, and his family were living in the home. The Battle of Fairfax Courthouse took place across the home's property and resulted in the first Confederate officer casualty, as Captain John Quincy Marr died on the front lawn. According to legend, former Virginia governor William Smith was a houseguest at the time. When he learned of the casualty, he dashed across the street to assume command, thus beginning his military career at age sixty-four. The next year, during their midnight raid and capture of the courthouse, John Mosby's raiders searched the Gunnell house. Lore has it that the house was successfully defended by Mrs. Johnstone, wife of Union colonel Robert Johnstone, from her strategic position in the privy. During roof repairs made in the 1900s, medical instruments and bandages were discovered, indicating that the house was used as a hospital during the fray.

Confederate spy Antonia Ford was also a frequent houseguest here, since her family home still stands just one block north of the inn. Miss Ford was eventually captured and put in jail by Union troops. During her incarceration, she fell in love with her jailer. In order to marry, she was forced to renounce the Confederacy. The bridal suite at the Bailiwick Inn, dedicated to her love story, includes a reproduction of her marriage certificate.

Whether arriving for tea, breakfast, lunch, cocktails, or dinner—all of which are open to the public—or as an overnight guest, visitors enter the Bailiwick Inn by ringing the doorbell. In this manner, they're greeted individually and welcomed with the personal attention they'd receive when visiting someone's home. It's a genteel touch that sets the tone for the manner in which the staff sees to the needs of the guests.

The fourteen guest chambers of the Bailiwick Inn have their own personalities. Aided by the staff of the Virginia Room at the Fairfax County Library, a team of decorators furnished the rooms with antiques and reproductions reflecting the personalities and time periods of the individuals for whom they're named. For example, the Thomas Jefferson Room, just off the main hall, is festooned in rich burgundy and gold and contains an adaptation of his famous "whirligig" chair. In the James Madison Room, the wallpaper is called "Dolly Madison damask" and was copied from a red fabric used on her bed.

If arriving for a meal at the Bailiwick Inn, guests are ushered into the parlor before being called to the table. Prior to dinner, hors d'oeuvres are passed as if at a cocktail party in someone's home. This European style of service allows guests to separate themselves from the hustle and bustle of today's world and enjoy the leisurely service and excellent cuisine.

We visited for lunch, which was a tremendously enjoyable experience. Karen loves watercress and was thrilled to begin with the Watercress and Frisse Bouquet, while Debbie savored the Poached Pear and Endive Salad. Our entrées of Wild Boar Chop with Cranberry Bean Ragout and Sautéed Grouper were equally good. We ended by sharing a portion of the warm-centered Almond Chocolate Fondant Cake. In fact, we wished we'd each gotten one all to ourselves. Go and enjoy. We certainly did.

 WILD MUSHROOM AND BRIE SOUP

¼ cup plus 2 tablespoons butter
1 finely diced onion
2 tablespoons finely minced garlic
2 pounds shiitake mushrooms, chopped rough, stems removed
2 pounds crimini mushrooms, chopped rough
2 cups dry sherry
3 tablespoons porcini mushrooms, powdered
2 tablespoons fresh thyme, chopped
7 cups chicken stock
2 cups heavy cream
10 ounces Brie
salt and pepper to taste

Melt butter in a large pot. Add onions and garlic and brown slightly. Add shiitake and crimini mushrooms and sauté. Add sherry and reduce. Add porcini, thyme, chicken stock, and cream. Simmer and skim. In a blender or food processor, purée Brie and a small amount of liquid from the soup. Add this to the soup. Add salt and pepper and simmer to reduce. Skim before serving. Serves 12.

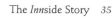

Woodruff Inns & Restaurant

The Victorian Inn
138 East Main Street
Luray, VA 22835
www.woodruffinns.com
540-743-1494

The warm yellow exterior trimmed with crisp white Victorian accents offers a great deal of curb appeal. Add to that a picturesque picket fence and The Victorian Inn has you smiling at first glance. A wide flagstone path leads from the street toward the inviting front porch, where many a guest, both from this century and last, has decided to "sit a spell." The front door opens to a grand entry hall with a highly polished hardwood floor, Oriental rugs, and a crystal chandelier. It is this ambiance that has created the inn's reputation as "the fantasy Victorian."

"Prepare to be pampered" is the mantra of Lucas and Deborah Woodruff, owners and operators of the collection of getaways known as the Woodruff Inns. The Victorian Inn is just one of several properties they own. Guests can also relax at the Rose House, the Woodruff House, The Shenandoah River Cabin, and the Shenandoah River Cottage. Built in the

1800s, The Victorian Inn is the most recent addition to the Woodruffs' collection of Victorian homes. Deborah gave us a personal tour of the inn's three lovely suites, each created to provide comfort, luxury, and a touch of romance for its guests. The décor is distinctly Victorian. We were particularly intrigued by the many unusual windows throughout the inn. Some were filled with marbles, while others had been garnered from old churches. As we admired the leaded-glass windows in the dining room, Deborah confessed that they were actually doors hung horizontally. She uses and reuses accessories, finding new and creative purposes for them. As Deborah told us, "It's Victorian. You can never overdecorate."

The inn offers five dining rooms. Breakfast for inn guests and afternoon tea are served in the sumptuous Fireside Drawing Room. Lunch and dinner are open to the general public, although lunch is by reservation only. We stopped in for a late midweek luncheon. Karen chose the Tropical Tomato Salad, created from mesclun lettuce, pineapple, and mango and topped with Japanese Ginger Dressing. Debbie enjoyed the Baked Crab and Shrimp Cakes, accompanied by Cajun Remoulade Sauce. Both were delicious. The dessert choices—which included Caramel Apple Pie, Ultimate Chocolate Cake, Bourbon Street Pecan Pie, Crème Brûlée Cheesecake, and Wild Berry Ice Cream—were quite tempting.

Several of the menu items are available

for both lunch and dinner. The Brie with Berry Sauce and the Garlic Chicken Skewers sound intriguing. Among the entrées are Pasta with Rose Sauce, Filet Mignon with Shallot and Roasted Garlic Wine Sauce, Prime Rib with Jack Daniel's Demi-Glaze, and Pork Tenderloin with Spicy Rub and Barbecue Mop. Having been featured in *Food & Wine* and *Gourmet* in 2000 and 2001, respectively, Lucas Woodruff has a longstanding reputation of excellence in the kitchen.

 JAPANESE GINGER DRESSING

1 cup minced onion
¼ cup minced celery
¼ cup minced ginger root
1½ tablespoons tomato paste
¼ cup soy sauce
½ cup water
½ cup rice vinegar
1 cup peanut oil
1 tablespoon lemon juice
1½ tablespoons sugar
1 teaspoon salt
1 teaspoon pepper

Place all ingredients in a glass jar with a tight-fitting lid. Close lid firmly and shake well to combine. Yields about 2½ cups.

 BAKED CRAB AND SHRIMP CAKES

1 cup finely chopped onions
1 cup finely chopped celery
4 cloves garlic, minced
1 cup chopped green onions
6 tablespoons butter
1½ pounds lump crabmeat
1 pound small shrimp
4 tablespoons fresh parsley, minced
1½ cups mayonnaise
2 teaspoons dry mustard
2 teaspoons salt
½ teaspoon cayenne
½ teaspoon freshly ground black pepper
4 saltine crackers, crushed

Preheat oven to 400 degrees. Sauté onions, celery, garlic, and green onions in butter. Remove from heat and stir in crab, shrimp, and parsley. Combine mayonnaise, mustard, salt, cayenne, pepper, and crackers in a bowl. Fold in crab mixture. Form into 8 patties and place on a baking sheet. Bake 8 to 10 minutes. Serve with a Remoulade Sauce. Serves 4.

THE INN AT COURT SQUARE

410 East Jefferson Street
Charlottesville, VA 22902
434-295-2800

Through sheer will power, we passed on the tempting dessert choices of Raspberry Cheesecake and Chocolate Torte with Orange Sauce. We had just enjoyed a delicious luncheon in the dining room of The Inn at Court Square. The seating is at round tables for two or four. Our favorite table was across the room, nestled with a corner settee. Oil paintings and mirrors in gilded frames added to the formal atmosphere, while the fire crackling in the fireplace gave the room a homey touch. The day was brisk, and most of the guests took a moment or two to warm themselves in front of it before sitting.

The inn functions primarily as a bed-and-breakfast with five lovely guest rooms, each with a working fireplace. Owner Candace DeLoach also has an antique shop just around the corner, so the common rooms and guest rooms of the inn are filled with treasures from the store.

Karen thoroughly enjoyed the Herb-Roasted Pork Tenderloin Sandwich, topped with roasted red peppers and smoked Gouda. Debbie's Lime-Chipotle Chicken Salad Wrap was also delicious. Other diners enjoyed the Panini, topped with chicken and Genoa salami on that particular occasion. The chef changes the toppings, coming up with unique combinations daily. The Stilton Salad, topped with Fuji apples and D'Anjou pears and dressed with Port Wine Vinaigrette, also made frequent appearances around the dining room. Since the first hint of winter was in the air, the Onion Soup was quite popular, in combination with a salad or sandwich.

The home in which the inn is located is considered to be Charlottesville's oldest. It was built by Edward Butler around 1785. Sixteen years later, Butler conveyed the property to his son, James, and his wife, Susannah. The younger Butler sold the property in 1808 to John Kelly, who then gave the home to his son-in-law Opie Norris. Known to some as the Butler-Norris House, it has through the years housed a law firm, a slate company, the Church of Christ, and a real-estate office. It stands as the only extant example of eighteenth-century architecture in the Court Square area. The exterior displays Flemish bond brickwork and the only molded brick cornice in the city. Inside are examples of eighteenth-century woodwork, including Georgian mantels with pilasters and dentils.

The inn is situated in a lovely part of Charlottesville, surrounded by "newer" construction from the nineteenth century. Across the street are the old Albemarle County

Courthouse and Stonewall Jackson Park. The focal point of the park is a statue of the general sitting astride his horse. The work is considered by many art historians to be one of the finest equestrian statues in the world. With many of the area's historic destinations just a few miles distant and the pedestrian mall just two blocks away, the inn is ideally situated to let guests enjoy the past and the present at the same time.

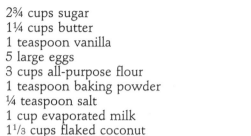 PORTABELLO ROASTED RED PEPPER QUICHE

3 medium to large portabello mushrooms, chopped
1 large red pepper, roasted and chopped
1/3 cup chopped onion
1 unbaked piecrust
1 cup grated Gruyère cheese
4 large eggs
3/4 teaspoon salt
freshly ground pepper to taste
2 cups heavy cream

Preheat oven to 425 degrees. Layer mushrooms, red peppers, and onions in piecrust and top with cheese. In a medium bowl, whisk together eggs, salt, and pepper. Add cream and whisk well to combine. Pour egg mixture over top of cheese. Bake for 15 minutes, then lower temperature to 300 degrees for a further 30 to 35 minutes. Serves 8.

ORANGE-COCONUT POUND CAKE

2¾ cups sugar
1¼ cups butter
1 teaspoon vanilla
5 large eggs
3 cups all-purpose flour
1 teaspoon baking powder
¼ teaspoon salt
1 cup evaporated milk
1⅓ cups flaked coconut
3 tablespoons shredded fresh orange peel

Preheat oven to 350 degrees. Grease and flour a 12-cup Bundt pan or tube pan. In a large bowl, beat together sugar, butter, vanilla, and eggs on low speed, scraping bowl constantly. Beat on high speed for a further 5 minutes, scraping occasionally. Beat in flour, baking powder, and salt alternately with milk on low speed. Fold in coconut and orange peel. Pour batter into pan and bake for 70 to 80 minutes until toothpick inserted in center comes out clean. Allow cake to cool for 20 minutes before turning out. Serves 12.

The Red Fox Inn
Estab. c.1728

2 East Washington Street
Middleburg, VA 20118
540-687-6301

Middleburg is an adorable town with interesting shops lining the streets. Although it wasn't chartered until 1787, the village derives its name from the fact that it is situated midway between Alexandria and Winchester, considered a frontier town in the 1720s. Taking advantage of that fact, Joseph Chinn built a tavern out of local fieldstone in 1728. The surrounding territory at that time was part of the vast estate of Thomas, sixth lord of Fairfax and baron of Cameron. Lord Fairfax, a bachelor, was not particularly interested in a privileged lifestyle, preferring instead his log cabin situated on the Shenandoah River. Chinn's Ordinary quickly became a popular stopping point for colonists, including a young surveyor by the name of George Washington, who is believed to have visited in 1748.

In 1787, the tavern and the surrounding fifty acres were sold to the town of Middleburg for $2.50 per acre. The area grew and prospered, gaining a reputation as a premier locale for fox hunting, thoroughbred breeding, and horse racing. Chinn's Ordinary was the center of social and economic activities.

In 1812, the inn underwent extensive remodeling and a name change, becoming the Beveridge House. During the Civil War, the Beveridge House was the site of a meeting between General Jeb Stuart and Colonel John Mosby. At the beginning of the Gettysburg Campaign, fierce battles raged in and around Middleburg. The inn served as both a headquarters and a hospital for the Confederates. The pine service bar still used today was crafted from the field operating table used by the army surgeon serving with Stuart's cavalry.

Some years after the war, the Beveridge House became the Middleburg Inn, which continued the tradition of providing fine food and accommodations. In 1937, the name changed again, to The Red Fox Inn. From the early years until today, the inn has remained a destination for those seeking the pleasures of hunt country.

Just as little has changed in the philosophy of service, the same can be said of the tavern's décor. We entered the dining room and felt as if we'd joined another century. The low, beamed ceilings are supported by solid, rough-hewn posts. Simple wooden plank tables are flanked by Windsor chairs. Pewter tankards hang from the rafters, while pewter dinnerware is displayed on shelves throughout.

We were seated at what must have been a coveted spot in days of yore. Cozied up to the fire, we perused the menu, trying to choose among the Spinach and Leek Salad, the Wild Mushroom Ravioli, the Mango Chicken Salad, and the Peanut Soup. Ultimately, our choices reflected the history of our surroundings. Debbie enjoyed the thick Butternut Squash Soup, while Karen enjoyed the Game Stew, which had a hint of curry and was served over yellow rice. The dinner menu features a wide variety of interesting dishes. Among the appetizers, the Basil Cheese Terrine and the Asparagus Citronee are unique. The entrées include several seafood and beef options, as well as pork, lamb, and duck.

After our meal, when we stepped outside and reentered the twenty-first century, we were glad to have visited the 1800s for a while.

BRIE IN PHYLLO WITH PISTACHIO NUT BUTTER

2 ounces raw pistachios, shelled and peeled
½ cup unsalted butter, softened
salt and white pepper to taste
2 sheets phyllo dough
2 tablespoons clarified butter
4 ounces Brie

Preheat oven to 275 degrees. On a cookie sheet, roast pistachios 6 to 8 minutes until golden brown. Process in a food processor or blender with a steel blade until finely ground. Combine pistachios with butter, add salt and pepper, and set aside. Increase oven temperature to 450 degrees. Lay out phyllo and brush with butter. Place 2 ounces Brie on each phyllo sheet. Spread butter mixture over Brie. Fold phyllo into thirds and seal edges with butter. Place on a greased cookie sheet and bake for about 5 minutes until golden brown. Be careful not to overcook. Slice while hot. Serves 4.

BLACK BEAN AND SAUSAGE SOUP

1 cup chopped carrot
1 cup chopped onion
1 cup chopped celery
⅛ cup garlic, minced
salt and pepper to taste
⅛ head thyme, chopped
⅛ cup fresh basil, chopped
⅛ head marjoram, chopped
2 tablespoons oil
1 cup red wine
½ gallon chicken stock
10-ounce can black beans
1¼ pounds Italian sausage, cooked

In a large skillet, sauté vegetables, garlic, and spices in oil. Deglaze pan with wine, then reduce by ⅔. Add chicken stock, beans, and sausage. Cook slowly for about 1 hour until vegetables are tender. Serves 12 to 16.

INN AT LITTLE WASHINGTON

Middle and Main Streets
Washington, VA 22747
540-675-3800

In 1749, an apprentice surveyor by the name of George Washington laid out the streets for the village of Washington, Virginia.

In 1978, there was a plain two-story building at the corner of Middle and Main Streets in Washington. The building was used as a small country garage that advertised Standard Gas and Atlas Tires. Who knew that this unadorned building would go on to become one of the most famous restaurants in America?

When current inn owners Patrick O'Connell and Reinhardt Lynch first rented the building, it is said that the three most important things they did were to move in a fire-engine-red cookstove to serve as a sideboard, wrap baskets in pink silk and hang them upside down as lamps to create atmosphere, and write the menu in French!

Within months, the Inn at Little Washington was being called one of the finest restaurants within 150 miles of Washington, D.C. Two years after the inn opened, guests were still consuming their predinner drinks in their cars before dining, since Rappahannock County was dry. Determined to change the county's attitude, the inn's wait staff dressed up as pilgrims and petitioned the town to amend its dry laws. They succeeded in persuading the county to grant the inn the area's very first liquor-by-the-drink license.

It was in 1985 that the inn actually became an inn, opening eight guest rooms above the dining room. As time passed and the inn's fame grew, more rooms were added. In 1991, it became the first establishment in history to receive two Mobil Five Star ratings—one for the restaurant and the other for the accommodations. And the rest, as they say, is history!

The service at the inn is impeccable. And the elegant dining rooms still have pink silk lampshades hanging low over each table. The owners are passionate about using the finest local produce, and every dish is a feast for the eyes and the palate. Dinner is prix fixe, and reservations are most definitely required.

Debbie was elsewhere the day I visited. I began my dinner with three tiny mouthfuls served on a strip of green gingham ribbon: a Smoked Salmon Roulade, a Mini BLT, and a Ham Biscuit, all of which were delicious. A "warm sip" came next—an espresso cup of Red Pepper Soup with a dollop of Sambuca Cream. I chose the Charred Fresh Blue-Water Prawns and Onions with Mango Mint Salsa, followed by Cucumber Sorbet with Cucumber-Dill Salsa and the inn's Steak and Kidney Pie with Button Mushrooms and Pearl Onions. All three courses were fabulous, yet still left me with enough room to consider a dessert.

There are many unusual offerings on the dessert menu here. I was tempted by the Molten-Centered Chocolate Cake with Roasted Banana Ice Cream and the Checkerboard Terrine of Pistachio and White Chocolate Ice Cream with Blackberry Sauce. The irresistible Selection of Cheeses is presented on the back of a small plaster replica of Faira, a Jersey cow that came up a winner at the 1996 Iowa State Fair. Faira is pushed along on her tiny wheeled hooves. While mooing, she proudly displays a selection of some of the most delicious cheeses from around the world. Eventually, I opted for the inn's signature dessert, the Seven Deadly Sins. Served on a large, square plate, the seven miniature versions of the most delectable desserts imaginable were indescribably good. And the end of the meal was still not in sight! To finish, I was presented with a tiny picnic basket containing a fuzzy bee, tiny cookies, dried fruits, crystallized orange peel, and candied nuts.

The Inn at Little Washington has been a popular dinner destination for more than twenty-five years. Long may it reign!

CRAB AND SPINACH TIMBALE

½ pound backfin crabmeat
¾ cup heavy cream, divided
1 teaspoon lemon juice
½ teaspoon mustard
½ teaspoon celery salt
dash of cayenne
1½ teaspoons salt, divided
½ teaspoon pepper
5 eggs, divided
1 pound fresh spinach
3 tablespoons unsalted butter
2 tablespoons flour
¾ cup milk
⅛ teaspoon nutmeg, grated
pimentos cut into stars

In a medium bowl, combine crabmeat, ¼ cup of the cream, lemon juice, mustard, celery salt, cayenne, ½ teaspoon of the salt, and pepper. Beat 2 of the eggs in a small bowl. Add beaten eggs to crabmeat mixture. Stir to blend. Refrigerate.

Boil spinach in salted water. Drain, then cool in cold water. Drain again and chop fine. In a small saucepan, make a roux with butter and flour. Add milk, remaining cream, remaining salt, pepper, and nutmeg. Bring mixture to a boil. Remove from heat and stir in spinach. Allow mixture to cool slightly, then beat in remaining 3 eggs.

Preheat oven to 375 degrees. Half fill 8 buttered molds or muffin tins and place tins in a shallow pan of cold water. Bake for 25 to 30 minutes until set. Cool. Run a knife around the edges to free from molds. Place on serving plates. Spoon crabmeat on top and garnish with pimentos. Serves 8.

COEUR À LA CRÈME
WITH RASPBERRY SAUCE

8-ounce package cream cheese, softened
²/₃ cup powdered sugar
1¼ cups heavy cream
1 teaspoon vanilla
1 teaspoon lemon juice
1 teaspoon framboise or kirsch
Raspberry Sauce (recipe follows)
whole raspberries for garnish

In a large bowl, beat cream cheese until smooth. Blend in powdered sugar a few tablespoons at a time. In a chilled bowl, whip cream until stiff. Gently fold half of whipped cream into cream cheese mixture. Add vanilla, lemon juice, and framboise or kirsch and gently fold in remaining whipped cream. Line 6 half-cup coeur à la crème molds with a double thickness of dampened cotton cheesecloth. (These molds have tiny holes in the bottom to allow liquid to drain from the cheese.) Fill with mixture and refrigerate overnight.

Remove cheesecloth and free mixture from molds by inverting onto serving plates. Spoon Raspberry Sauce over each dessert. Garnish with whole berries. Serves 6.

Raspberry Sauce

2 pints raspberries, hulled and washed
½ cup sugar
1 tablespoon framboise or kirsch
1 teaspoon lemon juice

In a blender, purée berries, sugar, framboise or kirsch, and lemon juice. Strain through a fine sieve to remove seeds. Yields about 2 cups.

Battletown Inn

102 West Main Street
Berryville, VA 22611
www.battletowninn.com
540-955-4100

We came across Battletown Inn one day quite unexpectedly. As usual, we were starving, so we quickly reached an agreement to stop for lunch. The menu choices all sounded delicious, among them Smoked Pork Salad, consisting of field greens tossed with pears, walnuts, and smoked pork loin in Honey Mustard Dressing, and Walnut-Crusted Chicken Salad, in which the chicken tenders were crusted with walnuts, laid on top of mixed greens, and topped with Creamy Apple Dressing. Burgers, sandwiches, and soups were available, as was the interesting Black Bean and New York Sirloin Chili. Alongside these offerings were main courses such as Dry-Cured Baked Virginia Ham, Shepherd's Pie, Oven-Roasted Smothered Chicken, and Chicken Blanquette.

Before making our selections, we asked our server to tell us about the dessert menu. She described the virtues of the homemade Sweet Potato Flan, the Chocolate Coffee Torte, the Blueberry Apple Crisp, and the Walnut Bourbon Pie, among the large list of choices available that day.

We ate by the fireplace in the first of three dining rooms. The simplicity of the room was very appealing, the plain painted walls supporting just a few portraits. The wide-plank flooring, simple wooden tables, and Windsor chairs added to the simplicity. We both admired the large antique sideboard against the wall. Needless to say, we enjoyed all of our selections. The delectable food was served promptly and at a very reasonable price.

After lunch, we wandered the ground floor of the inn and took in the atmosphere. Each of the dining rooms has its own flavor. In the second room, the low beam ceiling and the large rugs create a cozy, intimate feel. The room features a brick fireplace with pots displayed on the fender. Small oil lamps are on each table. In the third dining room, ivy grows on the walls and hunting prints are on display. There are in fact seven dining rooms at the inn. The garden patio and the Gray Ghost Tavern upstairs offer informal dining and casual fare.

The original building was constructed in 1809 for Sara Stribling, the only daughter of Benjamin Berry, the founder of Berryville and the man for whom the town was named. Although this lovely old building stared life as a house, it wasn't long before it was turned into an eating establishment. Visitors could always find good food and hospitality here. Back in the early 1900s, the restaurant was known as The Sign of the Motor Car Inn. The proprietor had a large sign constructed with a picture of an automobile on it.

Before the town was named after Benjamin Berry, it was known as Battletown. Local legend has it that the name came about because of the almost continuous brawling at the local tavern. So when new owner Mary Murray renamed the restaurant Battletown Inn in 1946, it seemed appropriate. Murray is also credited with creating the restaurant's reputation for fine Virginia cuisine. Many of her recipes are still served on a daily basis here at the inn.

BAKED SQUASH PUDDING

7 yellow squash
1 small onion, chopped fine
4 tablespoons butter, divided
½ cup cream
¼ cup crushed crackers
½ cup breadcrumbs

Preheat oven to 400 degrees. Slice squash and bring to a boil in a saucepan of salted water. When cooked, drain and mash squash. Drain again to remove excess liquid. In a small sauté pan, sauté onions in 2 tablespoons of the butter until golden. Remove onions from pan and place in a large bowl to cool. When onions are cool, add cream and crackers and stir thoroughly to combine. Add squash and stir well. Pour mixture into a greased 9-by-13-inch casserole. Melt remaining butter in a small saucepan. Add breadcrumbs and stir to combine. Scatter buttered breadcrumbs on top of squash mixture and bake for 30 minutes. Serve immediately. Serves 8 to 10.

THE FOX HEAD INN

1840 Manakin Road
Manakin-Sabot, VA 23103
804-784-5126

Down a rural road in Virginia's horse country sits this white farmhouse with black shutters. Because of the area's pastoral beauty and the home's nineteenth-century air, it once served as the Hartford House, a set for the soap opera *Search for Tomorrow*.

The house was built at the end of the Civil War by an infantryman named William Ira Mills. Mills was a mere nineteen years old at the time. He and his bride, Luticia, raised their family here. In the front two rooms, William and Luticia operated a storehouse they called the Farmers Alliance. There, they sold kerosene, stick candy, fabrics, and even specialty items like cologne. As was the case with many rural general stores, it also served as the local post office. The two rooms at the back of the building functioned as the kitchen and bedrooms. They were heated by potbelly stoves that are still in use today.

During the early 1900s, a second story was added to the home, creating an elegant facade not found in traditional farmhouses. Some say the additional space was needed because of the family's seven youngsters. However, just after the expansion, the farmhouse began hosting thirsty stagecoach travelers, local fox hunters, and the sheriff of Hanover. Probably not coincidentally, the sheriff was a partner in the inn before and during Prohibition. Some locals remember "brown-bagging" in the private parlors upstairs well into the 1970s, until liquor by the drink was finally legalized in this area.

The original upstairs bar has been preserved, as has the private parlor and its discreet exit. However, today's décor is far removed from that of the building's gin-joint days. Hunter green and burgundy are used throughout the restaurant. In honor of the local horse tradition, prints of fox hunting and similar activities decorate the staid walls. Polished brass adds a bit of sparkle to the quiet elegance of the dining rooms.

We arrived more than an hour early for our reservation. The whole eastern portion of the United States was preparing for an incoming storm, and we'd decided to try to leave the area before it arrived. The staff of The Fox Head Inn was kind enough to accommodate us. The unobtrusive service and quiet atmosphere allowed us to relax.

The appetizer choices that evening were Low Country Grilled Shrimp, Crispy Fried Duck over French Lentils, Blue Crab and Crayfish Cake, and Serviche of Scallops. Our entrées of Salmon in Chilled Cucumber

Sauce and Lamb with Rosemary and Red Wine Sauce were highly enjoyable. And our Dark Chocolate Truffle Pâté and Cobbled Apple desserts ended the meal the way it began—deliciously. For many locals, The Fox Head Inn is synonymous with special occasions, and there's no doubt as to why.

 LOBSTER CAPPUCCINO

6 lobster hulls
sea salt and pepper to taste
1 onion, diced
1 tablespoon oil
handful of peppercorns
1 bay leaf
8 cups half-and-half
2 tablespoons dry sherry or cognac

Preheat oven to 350 degrees. Place lobster shells and claws on a baking sheet and sprinkle with salt and pepper. Bake for about 10 minutes until bright red in color. Remove from oven and set aside.

In a large sauté pan, sweat onions in oil. When onions are translucent, add baked lobster shells, peppercorns, bay leaf, and half-and-half. Bring mixture to a boil, then simmer over low heat for 45 minutes. Remove from heat and strain contents of pan, reserving liquid.

Warm coffee cups and set aside. Over a double boiler, fill a stainless-steel or glass mixing bowl halfway with lobster liquid. Whisk rapidly to create a froth. Add sherry or cognac and whisk again. Ladle mixture into cups. Serve with Parmesan biscotti or cheese straws. Yields 12 cups cappuccino.

 SABAYON SAUCE

8 egg yolks
1 cup plus 4 tablespoons sugar
2 tablespoons Grand Marnier
4 cups heavy cream

In a medium stainless-steel or glass bowl, combine yolks, sugar, and Grand Marnier. Place bowl over a double boiler and whisk continuously over medium heat. Do not curdle eggs. When mixture forms ribbons, remove from heat and let cool to room temperature. In a separate bowl, whip cream until soft peaks form. Fold whipped cream into egg mixture. Chill until ready to serve. Yields 6 cups.

Note: The Fox Head Inn serves this sauce with fresh berries in season.

THE HERMITAGE INN

7134 Main Street
Clifton, VA 20124
703-266-1263

In the late 1800s, Clifton was the largest community in Fairfax County. At that time, the building that now houses The Hermitage Inn was known as the Clifton Hotel. Through the years, its graceful hospitality greeted a wide range of guests. Built by Harrison Otis, it offered healthy mineral waters from its Paradise Spring. Seventeen daily trains stopped here from as far away as Philadelphia and New York City. Serving as a rural retreat from the pressures of life in Washington, D.C., the hostelry accommodated the likes of Ulysses S. Grant, Rutherford B. Hayes, Chester A. Arthur, and Theodore Roosevelt.

A rebirth occurred in 1987, when renovations were undertaken to return the hotel to its previous grace. Today, The Hermitage Inn continues the tradition of fine food and service that began long ago.

As Karen savored dinner at a restaurant down the road, I enjoyed my three-course meal. The staff here is excellent, providing just the right balance between attention and privacy. My waiter, Bo, was quite personable and incredibly knowledgeable about the menu. Since I was there early in the evening, I was able to chat with him before the throng arrived.

The cuisine is described by the restaurant as French Mediterranean. I would simply say it's wonderful. I started off with a bowl of Asparagus and Spinach Soup, served piping hot. Other options were the sherry-laced Lobster Bisque, Herbed Pheasant Pâté, and Mediterranean Beggar's Purse Stuffed with Shrimp.

Since my meal came on the last day of a five-day road trip, I almost decided to watch the calorie intake when making my entrée selection. The Marinated Chicken Breast comes with Roasted Garlic Madeira Risotto and Provençale Vegetables. Instead, I opted for the Pan-Roasted Fillet of Salmon with Pistachio Herb Crust.

Having recently enjoyed a very pleasant experience with Orange Crème Brûlée at another establishment, I chose it again here, hoping for an encore performance. I wasn't disappointed.

The food at the inn speaks for itself, but the ambiance makes dining here all the more enjoyable. On the second floor, a serene dining room has been fashioned from the space once occupied by the guest rooms. The muted shades of peach and green and the French Country furniture provide an elegant, yet relaxed, atmosphere. The paintings lining the walls caught my attention. When I asked Bo about them, he informed me that the artists, Paul and Gerald Hennessy, are close personal friends of the owners.

Standards have certainly changed over the years. The original guest rooms at the inn were large enough for just a bed and chair. The former Presidential Suite was off to one corner near where I was seated. Today, it's used as a private dining room. When I peeked in, I was taken aback. It was about the size of a standard hotel room at any of today's chains. As I descended the main staircase on my way out, I paused to reflect on the footsteps of those who had been here long ago.

 MEDITERRANEAN BEGGAR'S PURSE STUFFED WITH SHRIMP

18 16-20 count shrimp
1 medium onion
2 tablespoons crushed garlic
¾ cup sliced mushrooms
¾ cup goat cheese
24 sheets phyllo pastry
1 cup butter, melted
6 sticks bamboo

Preheat convection oven to 350 degrees or regular oven to 400 degrees. Coarsely chop shrimp and onion and set aside. In a saucepan over medium-high heat, sauté garlic until golden brown. Add shrimp and sauté until shrimp are opaque. In a separate pan, caramelize onions and sauté mushrooms. Add shrimp and garlic. Sauté briskly over high heat for 1 to 2 minutes, then let cool. Add goat cheese, mixing well.

Lay out 1 sheet of phyllo and brush with butter. Place another sheet of phyllo on top of the first. Continue to layer pastry and butter until you have 4 sheets of phyllo. Cut out a 14-inch circle and discard rest of phyllo. Set aside. Using the rest of the phyllo, make 5 more circles of 4-layer pastry. Spoon shrimp mixture into center of each pastry circle. Be sure not to put too much; you must be able to make a nice bundle. Fold edges of pastry, crimp into a fan, and hold together with a bamboo stick. Bake for 7 minutes until pastry is golden brown. Remove bamboo sticks before serving. May be made up to 3 days beforehand and stored in refrigerator or freezer. Serves 6.

Note: This is excellent served on warm plates with a pool of sauce such as a pesto cream sauce. Crabmeat, ground beef, or pork may be substituted for chicken. You can make purses small for appetizers or larger for entrée servings.

The Channel Bass Inn

The Tea Room at the Channel Bass Inn
6228 Church Street
Chincoteague, VA 23336
www.channelbass-inn.com
757-336-6148

"A taste of England" was the phrase that caught our interest when we were on the internet checking out historic places to visit. We were not disappointed.

The Channel Bass Inn, a three-story Victorian house built in 1892, is located on Chincoteague Island. Once the home of longtime Chincoteague mayor John W. Winder, it is now owned and run by Barbara and David Wiedenheft, who moved from England and Chicago, respectively, to become innkeepers in 1992. They created a tearoom in what was a four-star restaurant and became instantly renowned for Barbara's "world-famous scones."

Our taste of England most certainly did not disappoint. We arrived at the inn at three-thirty one afternoon, just in time for a real English afternoon tea. It was a most enjoyable treat to sit down with several other guests at one of the large tables in the spacious dining room. Karen had Earl Grey tea poured from a large silver teapot lovingly encased in an enormous tea cozy to keep the tea from getting cold, while Debbie settled for the more American iced tea. On the table

were Date, Prune, and Dark Raisin Scones, Apricot and Golden Raisin Scones, Cranberry and Golden Raisin Scones, and Karen's favorite, Ginger Scones. We were instructed to spread each scone with butter and jam and then with a large dollop of fresh whipped cream—the traditional English way. Each bite melted in the mouth. Just when we thought we ought to preserve our dignity by stopping before we were too full to rise from the table, we were presented with a slice of Apple Cake and a slice of Pound Cake with Strawberries, Blueberries, and Whipped Cream.

We retired from the table determined to take a long walk around the town later that day. Chincoteague is full of delightful little houses and cottages, all painted in various pastel hues. Although we saw lots of tourists, the town is still the very peaceful fishing village that it always has been. The island has long been known for the quality of the salty oysters farmed from the surrounding bays. Visitors can still see the commercial oyster boats off-load the day's catch. Many guests also cross to nearby Assateague Island to walk on the long, sandy beaches, to bird-watch, and to see the wild horses made famous by Marguerite Henry's children's classic, *Misty of Chincoteague*. We walked a fair distance that day and were glad to return to the comfortable Channel Bass Inn and our cozily furnished guest room, where we slept the sleep of the well fed.

While at the inn, we read that the Native Americans who lived on the mainland nearby called the island Gingo-teague. Translated into English, this means "beautiful land across the water." We encourage you to visit Chincoteague and make some beautiful memories of your own.

🌸 BRAN BREAD 🌸

4 cups Fiber One cereal
2 cups sugar
4 cups milk
4 cups combined dates, raisins, and chopped walnuts
4 cups self-raising flour

Preheat oven to 250 degrees. In a large bowl, combine cereal, sugar, milk, dates, raisins, and nuts. Allow to sit for 1 hour. Add flour and stir well. Grease 2 loaf pans and divide mixture between them. Bake for 2½ to 3 hours. Yields 2 loaves.

Note: This makes a wonderful breakfast bread. Everyone loves its moistness and the fact that it contains no eggs and very little fat. If you replace the milk with soy milk, it's a perfect bread for vegetarians and vegans.

🌸 CHEESE SCONES 🌸

2 cups self-rising flour
2 teaspoons baking powder
¼ teaspoon salt
¼ teaspoon fresh black pepper
⅓ cup unsalted butter
1½ cups grated sharp cheddar
3 tablespoons shredded Parmesan
⅓ cup cold milk
2 large eggs
¼ cup half-and-half

Preheat oven to 400 degrees. In a medium bowl, combine flour, baking powder, salt, and pepper. Cut in butter until thoroughly combined. Add cheeses and mix well to combine. Set aside. In another bowl, beat together milk and eggs. Add liquid to dry ingredients and stir to combine. Handle carefully, as dough will be very soft. Roll out dough on a floured cutting board and cut into scones. Place scones on a cookie sheet and brush tops with half-and-half. Bake for 15 to 20 minutes. Yields 1 dozen scones.

CHAPTER 3
Here to There . . . and Back Again

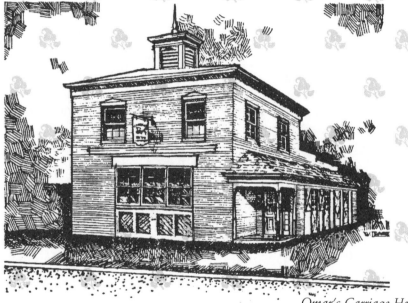

Omar's Carriage House

The speed of the locomotive, the swiftness of the steamboat, and the luxury of the carriage—all speak to the American preoccupation with growth and expansion. In earlier days, access to transportation was synonymous with success. Only wealthy citizens could afford to travel. And the railroads and shipping lines were owned by the wealthiest of them all. These pages salute the technology, entrepreneurship, and pure American idealism of that age.

BEDFORD, VIRGINIA
— Est. 1905 —

515 Bedford Avenue
Bedford, VA 24523
540-587-9377

In the early 1850s, a bridge of locally quarried stone was built in the community then known as Liberty. The arch constructed at its base was not only artistically pleasing but functional as well, being large enough to allow for the passage of trains. The first train station here was built around that same time. Twenty years later, another station was constructed east of the bridge. At the time, the new station was described as "spacious and handsome," as befit the prospering town.

When the Norfolk and Western Railroad emerged in 1881 from a long series of expansions and consolidations, the Bedford station was part of its territory. Through the 1920s, numerous passenger, freight, and mail stops meant activity at the station twenty-four hours a day. The Depression of the 1930s caused a downturn, which was reversed with the onset of World War II. Supplies, ammunition, and troops were all transported through Bedford's station. From here, the men of the 116th Infantry went off to war. Their heroics have been immortalized as part of the National D-Day Memorial.

Today's depot, built in 1905, was originally on the western side of the bridge, across from Randolph Macon College. It was moved to its present site in 1907. Passenger service was terminated in Bedford in 1971, after a long, steady decline brought on by the increasing popularity of automobiles and air travel. The building continued in use through the years, housing a variety of different services. Today, as Olde Liberty Station, it is a full-service, locally owned and operated restaurant listed on the National Register of Historic Places.

Thanks in part to its handsome Colonial Revival style, the station is a popular spot for lunch and dinner. The entertaining décor includes mannequins dressed in the uniforms of railroad employees. A large mural of Virginia scenery graces one end wall. At the other end of the restaurant is an incredibly lifelike mural of a train yard.

On the day we visited, guests lingered over coffee and iced tea, chatting away the afternoon at many of the tables and booths. Many were also enjoying a slice of cheesecake, for which the restaurant and its owner, Harry Leist, are widely known. We started our meal with a piece of Strawberry Swirl Cheesecake. Incredibly creamy and quite flavorful, it quickly disappeared. Of course, we asked what other varieties were served. The lengthy list includes Margarita Cheesecake,

Nuts and Berries Cheesecake, and the After-Dinner Cheesecake, made with Kahlua, Chambord, Frangelico, and Baileys Irish Cream. Showing unusual restraint, we decided to wait until our next visit to try another flavor.

The tasty Salt and Pepper Catfish we sampled was Karen's first experience with this popular regional dish. Catfish is always a pleasant choice for Debbie, bringing back memories of Sunday dinners at her grandmother's. The menu offers a wide range of choices including eight appetizers, five salads, pizzas, pasta, seafood, and more. Each item in the "Station House Steaks" section has been given a railroad moniker, such as the Rock Island Rib Eye and the Albuquerque Express, Olde Liberty's version of fajitas. The restaurant's specialties include Pepper Jack Cheese Sticks and Garlic Shrimp Scampi. We can certainly understand why the Bruschetta and the Raspberry Chicken are local favorites. We may have arrived by car, but we'll be happy to pull into this old train station anytime!

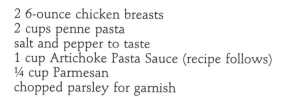 CHICKEN AND ARTICHOKE PASTA

2 6-ounce chicken breasts
2 cups penne pasta
salt and pepper to taste
1 cup Artichoke Pasta Sauce (recipe follows)
¼ cup Parmesan
chopped parsley for garnish

Grill chicken until just done. Remove from heat and dice into ½-inch pieces. Heat pasta in water seasoned with salt and pepper. Do not overcook. Drain well. Divide pasta between 2 bowls and top with chicken. Top with hot Artichoke Pasta Sauce. Sprinkle with Parmesan and top with parsley. Serves 2.

Artichoke Pasta Sauce

½ cup sliced mushrooms
2½ teaspoons chopped garlic
½ cup sliced black olives
1 cup artichoke hearts
1½ cups diced tomatoes
½ cup plus 2 tablespoons white wine
1¼ cups chicken stock
1 tablespoon dried basil
2 tablespoons butter
2 tablespoons flour

In a large skillet, sauté mushrooms and garlic. Add next 6 ingredients and simmer briefly to heat through. Melt butter in a small saucepan. Whisk in flour to make a roux. Add roux to artichoke mixture and simmer at least 5 minutes to thicken sauce. Serve over pasta. Yields 4 cups.

THE HOTEL ROANOKE & CONFERENCE CENTER
A DOUBLETREE HOTEL

The Regency Room
110 Shenandoah Avenue
Roanoke, VA 24016
800-222-8733

I enjoyed a lovely summer breakfast in The Regency Room while in the area with my daughter. Looking at the lunch menu, I was sorry my schedule wouldn't allow for me to choose among the Peanut Soup, the Mint Julep Melon Balls, the Macadamia Chicken Salad, and the Shrimp and Snow Pea Salad later in the day. Had Karen been along, I'm sure she'd have chosen the Ratatouille Tartlette, a delicious concoction of eggplant, zucchini, squash, tomatoes, olives, and two cheeses, all baked in a phyllo shell. And I certainly would have stolen at least one bite! As it was, I didn't have to share my tasty Apple Pecan Pancakes. I lingered over every bite as I perused the restaurant's remarkable background.

In 1881, Frederick J. Kimball opted for the town of Big Lick as the point at which his north-south rail system, known as the Shenandoah Valley Railroad, would intersect the east-west line of the Atlantic, Mississippi & Ohio Railroad. Ultimately, the two companies combined to become the Norfolk and Western Railroad, and the town changed its name from Big Lick. Many wanted the new

name to honor Kimball, but he declined. Instead, Roanoke, an Indian word meaning "money," was chosen. This was an apropos selection, as everyone new that bringing the railroad to town was synonymous with fiscal growth. As expected, a building boom began that saw the construction of the many houses and shops the town would need to support its thriving rail business.

Kimball's vision went beyond his involvement in the railroad. He commissioned a well-known architect of the day to build a grand hotel for the comfort and enjoyment of businessmen and passengers of leisure. The structure was originally to be thirty-four rooms, but an annex of an additional thirty-five was added before the hotel opened in October 1882.

After a fire destroyed much of the hotel in 1898, it was feared that it would be forced to close its doors. However, after only a few months of major repairs, the facility opened again. Over the next sixty years, the hotel redefined itself as automobile excursions overtook train travel. During that time, it became known not only for its modern conveniences but also for its superb dining. Guests such as Joe DiMaggio, Ethel Merman, Jack Dempsey, William Jennings Bryan, and Dwight Eisenhower partook of The Regency Room's cuisine.

Despite this tradition of excellence, the hotel began a decline so typical of such properties in the 1980s. Eventually, then-owner Norfolk Southern donated the hotel to nearby Virginia Tech as a location for conferences and continuing education. This in no way diminished the financial concerns surrounding the building, as the university and the city of Roanoke struggled to finance the necessary updates. Through fund-raising efforts and the eventual involvement of the Doubletree Hotels Corporation, The Hotel Roanoke—"the Grand Old Lady on the Hill"—was able to open its doors again.

Recently, The Regency Room became one of only 768 restaurants worldwide to merit the prestigious DiRoNA award.

BROILED CRAB CAKES

1 cup mayonnaise
1 egg
2 teaspoons Worcestershire sauce
½ teaspoon hot sauce
1 teaspoon lemon juice
1 teaspoon paprika
1 teaspoon dry mustard
½ teaspoon pepper
2 teaspoons Old Bay seasoning or lemon
    pepper
¾ cup breadcrumbs
1 pound crabmeat

Combine first 9 ingredients in a bowl, mixing until smooth. Mix in breadcrumbs and let stand. Pick through crabmeat and remove any shells. Place crabmeat in a separate bowl. Fold mayonnaise mixture into crabmeat a little at a time, using just enough to bind crabmeat together. Shape 4 crab cakes and dredge in breadcrumbs. Broil until heated through and golden brown, carefully turning halfway through. Yields 4 crab cakes.

CHICKEN SALAD À LA RAY

8 to 10 ounces chicken, cooked
1 red bell pepper, roasted
2 stalks celery
1 small onion
1 teaspoon paprika
2 tablespoons whole-grain mustard
¼ cup mayonnaise
salt and pepper to taste

Dice chicken, pepper, celery, and onion and put into a bowl. Add remaining ingredients and mix thoroughly. Taste and adjust seasonings. Refrigerate for a couple of hours to allow flavors to blend. Serves 2.

OMAR'S
Carriage House

3131 West Bute Street
Norfolk, VA 23510
757-622-4990

We pulled up in front of Omar's Carriage House in the middle of a storm that had just shut down the local airport. We were soaking wet and not very happy. But it took us less than two minutes to soak in the delightful atmosphere at Omar's and relax over one of the most delicious meals we've had. Debbie opted for a bowl of hot and tasty Spinach with Feta Cheese Soup, served with hot, crusty bread. Karen tried the Ginger-Spiked Shrimp Gazpacho, which was so delicious she refused to swap with Debbie, though we usually do when we're on the road together. Monday is Moroccan Night at Omar's, so we both sampled the Bastilla, which consists of phyllo stuffed with chicken, almonds, and eggs and sprinkled with powdered sugar and cinnamon. It proved a wonderful combination of sweet and savory tastes in the same mouthful.

Omar's Carriage House can only be described as adorable! The brick walls have been painted white and are covered in vividly colored artwork. The chairs feature a range of brightly colored fabrics, which are accented by the bright blue and yellow of the paint work. The china at each table is a unique collection of plates gathered over the years. The original carriage-house doors are still there at the front of the building. And if you look up at the ceiling, you'll see the original hay drop in the center of the room. This is the kind of unusual place you'll always remember. In fact, owner Omar Boukriss told us several stories about guests who have returned to dine at the place where they got engaged or had their first date!

Although this place has been a restaurant of one kind or another since the 1940s, the building itself dates all the way back to the early 1840s. Once inhabited by horses, carriages, riding equipment, and even a sleigh, it has always been a busy place. The carriage house and its mansion, which was located a block south of the restaurant, were bought just after the Civil War by Captain John L. Roper. It was one of his granddaughters who, once the mansion was demolished, started the idea of a tearoom. It proved extremely popular and became well known for its excellent food. Local celebrities frequented the quaint and unusual tearoom. Imagine sitting down to lunch with the likes of Mrs. Douglas MacArthur, Walter P. Chrysler, Jr., or Imogene Coca.

We didn't spot anyone famous when we

visited, but we did hear tell of a playful ghost that is supposed to inhabit the second floor of the building. She is reputed to be a young pre-Civil War slave child who mischievously mixes up things in the kitchen. Whatever your pleasure—ghosts, history, or simply good food—Omar's Carriage House will brighten your day.

POTATO CHIP-ENCRUSTED FLOUNDER

1 cup all-purpose flour
2 large eggs
1 cup milk
3 cups crumbled potato chips
2 pounds medium flounder fillets
½ cup vegetable oil

Preheat oven to 350 degrees. Place flour in a shallow container. Beat eggs and milk together in another shallow container. Place potato chips in a third shallow container. Dredge fillets in flour, then dip in egg mixture. Place fillets in potato chips and press into both sides.

Place oil in a large sauté pan over medium heat. Add flounder and cook until golden brown on both sides. Finish in oven for 6 to 7 minutes. Serve immediately. Serves 4.

GINGER-SPIKED SHRIMP GAZPACHO

3 cucumbers, peeled, seeded, and diced
2 large tomatoes, diced
1 medium onion, diced
1 large bell pepper, diced
4 cups tomato juice
¼ cup lemon juice
2 tablespoons chopped fresh cilantro
2 tablespoons grated fresh ginger
2 teaspoons cumin
¼ pound shrimp, steamed
sour cream or crème fraiche

Place all ingredients except shrimp and sour cream or crème fraiche in a large bowl. Mix well and place in refrigerator to chill for at least 3 hours. Serve in chilled bowls or glasses. Top with shrimp around edges of bowls. Top with dollops of sour cream or crème fraiche, if desired. Serves 6.

The Ivy Inn RESTAURANT

2244 Old Ivy Road
Charlottesville, VA 22903
804-977-1222

Angelo Vangelopoulos traces his culinary exploits to age five, when he began helping in the kitchen of the family restaurant. His father, Thomas, grew up in the family bakery in Greece before operating his own restaurant for thirty years. And Angelo's mother, Judie, has a reputation as a talented baker in her own right. So their son comes by his interests and talents naturally. After graduating from the Culinary Institute of America in 1990 and having his skills honed under the tutelage of many renowned chefs, he decided to make The Ivy Inn his home.

The Ivy Inn features what it describes as "extraordinary American cuisine," utilizing fresh ingredients from central Virginia. Starters like the Borscht with Duck and Beef, the Warm Medley of Wild Mushrooms, and the Butter-Poached Shrimp with Cornbread Pudding and Country Ham certainly got our attention. Entrée choices include Angus Beef Tenderloin with Caramelized Onion Tartlet and Pan-Seared Wild Rockfish with Coconut Rice. The Vegetable Wellington, concocted of phyllo dough stuffed full of fresh

vegetables and goat cheese, was certainly something we'd order again and again.

The desserts, many of which incorporate homemade ice cream, are equally unique. The traditional Southern Pecan Tart is served with Wild Turkey Ice Cream, while the Warm Chocolate Waffle is coupled with Banana Mousse and Chocolate Crunch Ice Cream.

The restaurant, located just down the road from the University of Virginia, was once part of a larger estate owned by William Faulkner, the well-known author and distinguished writer-in-residence at the university. The original building on the property was constructed in the early 1700s but succumbed to fire in 1815. Jesse Pittman Lewis added several structures when he rebuilt the estate the following year, one of which was the farmhouse that serves as the restaurant today. The kitchen, situated at the back of the house, was formerly a tollhouse that collected five-cent fares from travelers making their way between Richmond and Staunton.

Many years later, the university acquired much of the property, including the outbuildings, for guest housing and dining facilities. James Kiblin purchased the house and just over eleven acres of land in 1893 for the sum of three thousand dollars. Eight years later, the property again changed hands, this time going to an English attorney and engineer by the name of William H. Barlow. The Barlows' ownership continued until 1939, when the youngest son of the family sold the home to a University of Virginia biology professor. In 1973, The Ivy Inn was established to allow area residents and visitors an opportunity to experience rich history and fine dining. Today, thanks to Angelo Vangelopoulos and his creative staff, The Ivy Inn's past is secure, its future is bright, and its present is absolutely delicious.

ROAST PORK TENDERLOIN

2 whole pork tenderloins (approximately 2 pounds)
1 tablespoon paprika
1 teaspoon cayenne
3 sprigs fresh thyme, chopped rough
4 leaves fresh sage, chopped rough
2 teaspoons fresh cracked black pepper
salt to taste
3 tablespoons vegetable oil

Clean and trim tenderloins and set in a container to marinate. Combine paprika, cayenne, thyme, sage, and pepper and pour over tenderloins. Place in refrigerator overnight.

Preheat oven to 325 degrees. To cook, place a large skillet on high heat until very hot. Season tenderloins well with salt. Add enough vegetable oil to coat pan. Gently lower tenderloins into pan and sear all sides. Remove from skillet and place in a roasting pan; use a pan with a rack, if possible. Roast tenderloins in oven for 20 to 25 minutes until an internal temperature of 140 degrees is reached; the time will vary based on size of meat, oven calibration, etc. Remove tenderloins from pan and let rest for 15 to 20 minutes covered with a clean towel. Slice in pieces about ½ inch thick. Serve with Autumn Fruit Chutney (recipe below). Serves 4 to 6.

AUTUMN FRUIT CHUTNEY

2 tablespoons butter
1 Pippen or Granny Smith apple, peeled, cored, and cut into ½-inch cubes
¼ cup apple brandy or sherry
3 dates, pitted and cut into large chunks
3 dried apricots, quartered
¼ cup dried cranberries
¼ cup golden raisins
½ cup chicken stock
salt and pepper to taste
1 tablespoon fresh sage leaves, sliced thin

Heat butter in a medium skillet over medium heat until melted and foaming. Add apples and raise heat to high. Sauté apples, stirring occasionally; let them brown a little. Remove pan from heat. Carefully add brandy and flame. Add remaining fruits and stock. Simmer gently for 10 minutes. Season with salt and pepper, then add sage. Serve warm or at room temperature. May be made a couple days ahead of time and stored in refrigerator in an airtight container. Yields about 2 cups.

CLAIBORNE'S™

200 Lafayette Boulevard
Fredericksburg, VA 22401
www.claibornesrestaurant.com
540-371-7080

When you visit Claiborne's website, you'll hear a train whistle in the background. The hint is quite apropos, since the restaurant is situated in an old depot. A newspaper article from the *Fredericksburg Free Lance Star* dated Saturday, November 12, 1910, said the following: "The new R., F. & P. R.R. depot was opened to the public Thursday afternoon." It went on to detail the transition from the old terminal to the new structure and to praise the depot as the "handsomest and best equipped" in the state. Among the features it mentioned were the highly polished chestnut, the terrazzo floors, the antique bronze furnishings, the electric and gas lights, and the "automatic and self-winding" electric clock.

Today, the outside of the building remains almost exactly the same, the handsome red and gray bricks forming their distinguished checkerboard pattern across the front of the building. The inside, however, has changed quite a bit, while continuing to reflect the station's honored past. Attractively arranged around the three dining rooms are large photographs of trains, together with the original floor plans and elevation of the station. To the right of the main entrance is the bar. We loved the look of the wine racks at the far end, surmounted by a large collection of assorted baggage. The beautiful gas lanterns at either side of the bar add a touch of times gone by. To the left of the entrance is the main dining room, and beyond it is a smaller, more private room. We dined next to the fireplace in the far room, elegant in its simplicity. The walls are paneled in dark wood and topped with small mirrors. The table linens are an unusual black, topped with small oil lamps. Four large, domed-shaped light fixtures complete the look.

The menu here is lengthy, so it took us awhile to make our decisions. The Shrimp and Grits, one of Claiborne's signature items, caught Karen's eye, as did the Blackened Ahi Tuna. Coconut Shrimp is always popular with Debbie, although the Calabash Shrimp Po' Boy was also appealing. Several local favorites such as Pork Barbecue and Low Country Crawfish Casserole also merited consideration. Ultimately, the Shrimp and Avocado Wrap won the debate, and was duly enjoyed.

Every item on the dessert menu tempted our taste buds. The difficulty was in deciding among Chocolate Turtle Cake, Chocolate Pecan Pie, Crème Brûlée, New York Cheesecake, Key Lime Pie, Southern Fruit Cobbler, and more. Karen has long been intrigued with American strawberry shortcake, since it's prepared in so many different ways and is usually so different from the English variety. Claiborne's offered yet another variation on the theme, topped with Grand Marnier Whipped Cream. It was a touch of summer on a bleak winter's day. Debbie rarely passes up coconut pie. She proclaimed Claiborne's Southern-Style Coconut Custard Pie one of her top dessert experiences in Virginia.

SHRIMP AND GRITS

¼ cup clarified butter
6 large shrimp
8 to 10 pieces sausage, seared
¼ cup sliced mushrooms
1 tablespoon Cajun seasoning
2 tablespoons chopped green onions
1 tablespoon minced garlic
¼ cup white wine
1 tablespoon cold butter
2 cups cheese grits, cooked soft
2 sprigs rosemary

Heat clarified butter in a pan. Add shrimp, sausage, mushrooms, Cajun seasoning, green onions, and garlic. Saute for 1 to 2 minutes. Deglaze pan with white wine. Reduce. Add cold butter and swirl until sauce forms. Place grits on each of 2 plates and gently pour contents of pan onto grits. Garnish with rosemary sprigs. Serves 2.

LOUISIANA SAUCE

½ red onion
½ red pepper
2 tablespoons chopped garlic
1 cup hot sauce
½ cup Heinz 57 Sauce
2½ tablespoons Worcestershire sauce
1/8 cup white wine
1/8 cup fresh chopped rosemary
1 tablespoon blackening seasoning
¼ cup cocktail sauce
1½ tablespoons grated Parmesan

Place onion, red pepper, and garlic in a blender and purée. Pour purée into a medium bowl. Add remaining ingredients and mix thoroughly. Store in an airtight container in refrigerator until ready to use. This sauce is great mixed with chicken and shrimp over pasta. Yields 8 cups.

36 Middlebrook Avenue
Staunton, VA 24401
www.thepullman.com
540-885-6612

If Coconut Shrimp appears on the menu, I typically don't look any farther. However, since Karen was elsewhere and this was a research luncheon, it was necessary for me to peruse the menu. The End of the Line Sample Platter, consisting of wings, ribs, chicken tenders, and shrimp, would certainly please a wide variety of palates. The Chattanooga Cheddar Fries were popular with some of the local college students seated at a table nearby. Many of the menu items have names with a railroad theme, including the Train Trax Chicken Wrap, the Pullman Club Car, and the Black Angus Boxcar Burger. The salads range from the Staunton Station Steam Engine (a grilled chicken salad) to the Mediterranean Line (greens topped with black olives, cucumbers, anchovies, onions, and feta cheese) to the C & O Chicken Caesar to the Orient Express. The latter salad's combination of greens topped with grilled ginger chicken, cashews, pineapple chunks, water chestnuts, and spicy Peanut Dressing sounded so appealing that I chose to enjoy it for lunch instead.

The menu isn't limited to sandwiches.

There are five steak selections, Prime Rib, Rack of Lamb, and several pork and chicken entrées as well. All are served with a salad, the vegetable of the day, and a choice of side dishes that range from French Fries to Onion Straws to Coleslaw.

Guests enter the restaurant through the bar area, which was once the station's main waiting area. The unique chandeliers once hung in the lobby of a Milwaukee passenger station. The ornate Victorian backbar testifies to the building's turn-of-the-twentieth-century origin. Lunch and dinner guests are taken to what used to be the platform, now enclosed with large arched windows along the back wall facing the tracks. Old benches and marble-topped tables provide seating throughout. I was fortunate enough to secure a booth right at the edge of the line. From the carpeting to the knickknacks to the period lighting, everything comes together to create the atmosphere of yesteryear.

The Pullman Restaurant is located in the heart of downtown Staunton, one of the most charming places I've visited through the years. Much of the town has been refurbished, so it's only natural that the hustle and bustle of its train station has been restored as well. The original station was destroyed by a serious train derailment in 1890. Twelve years later, the current structure, designed by architect T. J. Collins, was built. Considered Collins's most significant commercial project, it exhibits the Bungalow style popular at the time. The depot quickly became the center of Staunton's economic growth through the early part of the twentieth century. Among those who utilized the depot in their travels were soldiers off to the Mexican border and World Wars I and II.

As I finished my meal, an unusual rumbling began. Before I was completely aware of what it was, a whistle sounded and a train whizzed past. In that brief moment, I felt as if I were watching the past link itself to the present.

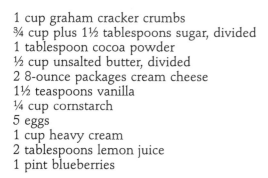 BLUEBERRY CHEESECAKE

1 cup graham cracker crumbs
¾ cup plus 1½ tablespoons sugar, divided
1 tablespoon cocoa powder
½ cup unsalted butter, divided
2 8-ounce packages cream cheese
1½ teaspoons vanilla
¼ cup cornstarch
5 eggs
1 cup heavy cream
2 tablespoons lemon juice
1 pint blueberries

Preheat oven to 350 degrees. Combine graham cracker crumbs, 1½ tablespoons of the sugar, cocoa, and ¼ cup of the butter. Press into a 9-inch springform pan to make a uniform ¼-inch crust. To prepare filling, cream remaining butter and cream cheese in a large bowl. Add vanilla, remaining sugar, and cornstarch. Beat in eggs 1 at a time. Slowly add cream and lemon juice. Pour into pan and bake for about 50 minutes until

toothpick or straw comes out clean. Cool. Clean, rinse, and drain blueberries. Top cheesecake with berries just before serving. Serves 12 to 16.

 APPLE NUT CAKE

4 apples, peeled, cored, and chopped
2 cups sugar
2 eggs
1 cup butter, melted
3 cups all-purpose flour
2 teaspoons baking soda
2 teaspoons cinnamon, ground
½ teaspoon allspice, ground
1 cup pecans, chopped

Preheat oven to 350 degrees. Place apples in a large bowl. Pour sugar over top and allow to sit for 10 minutes. Add eggs and butter. In a separate bowl, combine remaining ingredients. Add to apple mixture. Place batter in a greased and floured 10-inch tube pan. Bake for 50 to 60 minutes until a toothpick or knife comes out clean. Serves 12.

THE DEPOT GRILLE

Staunton Train Station
42 Middlebrook Avenue
Staunton, VA 24401
www.depotgrille.com
540-885-7332

The Depot Grille is situated in what was once the freight depot of the Staunton Train Station. This was the earliest of five significant structures comprising the C & O Train Station complex. Built prior to the Civil War, it is of brick construction with open truss roof framing. Unlike passenger depots, it was designed for function rather than comfort. However, it did serve as a haven for wounded troops during the conflict, since Staunton had no permanent hospital at that time.

Both the one- and two-story additions were added between 1894 and 1904 to handle the increase in goods shipped during the railroad's heyday. Much of the city's economic growth was directly tied to the railroad. When the tracks were laid in the mid-1800s, Staunton, once a rural village, was opened up to commerce, communications, and travel. A thriving commercial trade area known as "the Wharf" sprang up around the train station. The freight depot was the destination for a wide variety of goods, and hence the site of a great deal of hustle and bustle.

Not surprisingly, railroad memorabilia abounds in the décor of this restaurant. Even the kitchen is immersed in the theme, having been fashioned from an old boxcar. Railroad photographs and hurricane lamps hang on the walls.

One of the restaurant's most impressive features has nothing to do with the railroad. The bar, more than forty feet long, was once a fixture in the Ten Eyck Hotel in Albany, New York. A 1921 postcard brought to The Depot Grille by a customer described the Ten Eyck as "the finest hotel in Albany." Some years later, in the mid-1940s, Albany's city directory included a full-page ad for that luxury retreat, boasting of "circulating ice water in every room" and two restaurants. By the 1950s, the hotel had become part of the Sheraton chain. Fortunately for Virginia diners, the bar was saved from the Ten Eyck prior to its demolition and transported intact here for future generations to enjoy.

This place can be enjoyed by young and old alike. The bar area was full of local businessmen enjoying a quick bite in the middle of a busy day. It was in the main restaurant that all the children were having lunch. On every table, the brown-paper tablecloths and the flowerpots holding a selection of crayons encouraged each child to create his or her own masterpiece. There's always a chance that your picture will be pinned with the myriad others in the entrance to the restaurant. It's a chance that few can resist.

The menu also gives everyone something to savor. There are so many offerings, in fact, that it is difficult to choose just one. The Pesto Grilled Tuna Salad sounded unusual and delicious. The Bison Burger was quite tempting because of its low fat content. The Veggie Wrap, served on an Herb Tortilla, would have nicely satisfied a lunchtime appetite. For something heartier, there are plenty of seafood, beef, and chicken entrées. The Ginger Sesame Shrimp Lo Mein and the Fettuccine Middlebrook, made with chicken, shrimp, bacon, and broccoli in homemade Alfredo Sauce, both got strong consideration. Ultimately, the Veggie Chessie's Pasta got the vote. Given all the wonderful choices at The Depot Grille, it's always going to be difficult to choo-choo-choose!

 VEGGIE CHESSIE'S PASTA

6 ounces penne pasta
2 ears Silver Queen corn
2 tablespoons extravirgin olive oil, divided
1 clove garlic, minced
2 medium tomatoes, diced large
¼ cup white wine
2 tablespoons fresh basil leaves, chopped
2 tablespoons capers
salt and pepper to taste
½ cup Parmesan, grated

Cook pasta according to package directions and set aside. Lightly brush corn with 1 tablespoon of the oil and roast on grill until cooked. Remove from grill, carefully cut corn from ears, and set aside. Heat remaining oil in a medium sauté pan. Add garlic and sauté for 2 minutes. Add corn and tomatoes and cook for an additional 2 minutes to blend flavors. Add wine and bring to a boil, stirring frequently until liquid is reduced by half. Remove from heat and stir in basil, capers, and pasta. Add salt and pepper. Toss. Divide between 2 plates and top with Parmesan. Serves 2.

 SESAME SOY VINAIGRETTE

1 teaspoon honey
¼ cup soy sauce
¼ cup lime juice
½ cup sesame oil
pinch of cayenne
1 teaspoon fresh ginger, minced
1 teaspoon garlic, minced

Place all ingredients in a container with a tight lid. Shake vigorously to mix. Yields about 1 cup.

Mt. Holly Steamboat Inn

Est. 1876

3673 Cople Highway
Montross, VA 22520
www.mthollysteamboatinn.com
804-472-9070

The Mt. Holly Steamboat Inn was constructed in 1876. Originally called the Mt. Holly House, it was built to serve the needs of travelers, merchants, and businessman utilizing the steamboat routes in and out of the nation's capital. Hurricane Isabel in 2003 wasn't kind to the inn. Luckily, a portion of the original white clapboard building remained intact, and the owners were able to refurbish what was damaged. Situated atop a bluff overlooking Nomini Creek, the inn still serves boaters who pull up to the dock to enjoy the bar area along the waterfront, as well as diners who come to enjoy the seafood selections in one of the several dining rooms above.

Fresh seafood is what the restaurant does best. Appetizers such as Mini Crab Cakes, Imperial Crab Dip, The Big Chill, and The Steamboat—the last two of which feature a combination of shrimp, oysters, lobster, and clams—are but a beginning. The entrée listings include chicken and steak but focus on local seafood like Soft-Shell Crab, Crab-Stuffed Portabello Mushrooms, Shrimp Imperial, Catfish, and Lobster Ravioli. At the staff's suggestion, I started off with a soup sampler, which allowed me to taste the New England Clam Chowder, the Manhattan Clam Chowder, and the soup du jour, Cream of Crab. All were delicious, but the Clam Chowder was undoubtedly the best I've ever had!

Karen was elsewhere the evening I visited. I savored my view of the sun setting across Nomini Creek. While I watched the sunlight dancing on the water, I anticipated my entrée of Sea Bass in Coconut Curry Sauce, accompanied by Rice Pilaf and Steamed Asparagus. I felt fortunate to experience this entrée, since the restaurant doesn't serve sea bass very often, due to its having been overfished. Though I didn't have room for dessert, the Peanut Butter Silk Pie, the Key Lime Pie, and the Margarita Pie were all tempting.

There are many interesting pieces of memorabilia throughout the dining rooms. In the room used for private parties, a very old piano sits opposite the wall where one of the original fireplaces was once located. In the dining room where I ate, old shipping bills from the steamboat company are displayed in a frame along one wall. At the other end of the room was a copy of an old flyer advertising new schedules and fares for 1885. The cost was fifty cents for a one-way first-class fare, while round-trip fare was a bargain at seventy-five cents.

You'll notice two vivid watercolor paintings in one of the dining rooms, one of a waterside building and the other of a trawler. Owner Cindy Brigman told me that her aunt Mary painted them. It makes sense, because it's a family kind of restaurant. The inn's brochure says this is "a place to enjoy beautiful sunsets, good food, and a friendly staff." I'd have to agree.

 CLAM CHOWDER

3 stalks celery, diced small
3 carrots, diced small
1 onion, diced small
1 tablespoon thyme
6 slices bacon, chopped into pieces
1 cup sherry
16 cups clam stock
2 cups clam juice
½ cup butter
½ cup flour
4 cups heavy cream
3 small red potatoes, cubed
dash of cayenne
freshly ground black pepper to taste
2 pounds clams, chopped

Sweat first 5 ingredients in a stockpot. Add sherry and clam stock. Add clam juice and bring to a boil. Melt butter in a medium saucepan. Whisk in flour to make a roux. Incorporate roux into stockpot liquid to achieve desired thickness. Add cream and potatoes. Season with cayenne and black pepper. Simmer 30 minutes. Add clams last to avoid having them become chewy. Return to a simmer to heat clams through. Remove from stove and serve. Allow to cool before refrigerating. Serves 8 to 10.

THE DEPOT
RESTAURANT

65 South Third Street
Warrenton, VA 20186
540-347-1212

The old train station in Warrenton looks just as it did when it was updated in 1908. The building was completed in 1852 to serve the Warrenton Branch, which operated trains from nearby Calverton into Warrenton. During the Civil War, it served as a supply line and as a result was involved in the action several times. After the war, the line was put to use by several other railroad companies. It became part of the Southern Railway in 1896. It was in 1908 that the station underwent a renovation and became the handsome building visitors see today.

In June 1941, the last passenger train stopped in Warrenton. The decline of the railroad had begun. Freight trains were still in use through the early 1970s, but with less and less frequency. Finally, in the mid-1970s, the trains ceased to run through Warrenton. In 1976, Karen and Behruze Dorbayan renovated the small red brick-building with blue trim and turned it into a very successful restaurant.

Thanks to its plum-painted walls and white woodwork, the interior is warm and welcoming. There are three major rooms at The Depot. Each of the original segregated waiting rooms is now a dining room. Wherever you look, little touches of the past are present in the train pictures on the walls and the old signal lights. Most interesting of all is the clever way in which the original platform has been covered, leaving the gables that hold up the roof exposed. This room now features fourteen sets of French doors overlooking the garden beyond. Guests can even dine outside when the weather permits.

Chef Behruze has prepared meals at The Depot for over two decades now. He concentrates his efforts on using local, seasonal items to provide the freshest cuisine possible. We thought that the Roasted Fennel and Tart Apple Salad with Citrus Dressing and the Apple-Smoked Bacon and Tomato Salad both sounded interesting. The entrées range from Mnazzaleh, a roasted eggplant dish with sautéed lamb, onions, and pine nuts in Tomato Sauce, to Pan-Seared Salmon with Lemon and Spinach. The menu also includes steak, chicken, and tuna selections, as well as the restaurant's heralded Jumbo Lump Crab Cakes.

Guests can enjoy a drink from the quaint little bar or sip a delicious cup of coffee with one of the restaurant's homemade desserts. Karen would choose the Chocolate Mousse Truffle Cake every time she ate here. However, Debbie prefers the Stolen Orange Cake and the Coconut Rum Cake. Whatever your selection, you're sure to enjoy being transported back in time at this fine restaurant.

SPICY MINCED BEEF KABOBS

1¼ pounds ground beef, minced fine
1 large onion, grated
½ teaspoon cumin, ground
½ teaspoon coriander, ground
2 teaspoons paprika
¼ teaspoon cayenne
1 teaspoon salt
small bunch flat-leaf parsley, cleaned and
     chopped fine
small bunch fresh coriander or cilantro,
     chopped fine
Chickpea Purée (recipe follows)

Mix beef with next 8 ingredients. Knead mixture well or put in a food processor and blend until thoroughly mixed. Place in a covered dish and allow to sit for 1 hour. Divide mixture into 6 portions and mold around 6 metal skewers. Mixture should resemble a fat sausage on the end of each skewer. Heat broiler to hottest setting and broil kabobs for 4 to 5 minutes on each side. Serve on a bed of Chickpea Purée. Serves 6.

Chickpea Purée

16-ounce can chickpeas, drained
¼ cup olive oil
juice of 1 lemon
3 cloves garlic, crushed
2 tablespoons tahini
4 tablespoons plain yogurt
salt and pepper to taste

Preheat oven to 375 degrees. Place all ingredients except crackers or pita chips into a food processor. Purée until thoroughly blended. Place purée in an ovenproof dish and bake for 20 minutes. Remove from oven and serve immediately. Serves 6.

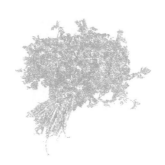

CHAPTER 4
My Hometown

Smythe's Cottage & Tavern

Each of us has one—a hometown, that is. Whether we left long
ago or still reside there, reflecting on that life carries with it
memories of churches, schools, and other institutions where citizens
carry out their daily existences. The eateries in this chapter have had a rebirth.
While still maintaining their original aura, they manage to provide gourmet
dining, home cooking, and everything in between.

AUGUSTINE'S

525 Caroline Street
Fredericksburg, VA 22401
540-310-0063

Although this regal building once served as a private residence, it is perhaps best known as the longtime meeting space of the Benevolent and Protective Order of Elks. The Elks came into existence in 1868, but to understand more fully the history of the group, you must back up to 1867 and the arrival in America of Englishman Charles A. S. Vivian. Vivian was a twenty-one-year-old singer and entertainer who came to the States seeking his fortune. Upon his arrival, he wandered up Broadway and into John Ireland's Star Chop House and gave an impromptu performance. The manager of the nearby American Theater heard Vivian and signed him to a six-days-a-week contract. However, Vivian wanted to work Sundays as well, so he looked for a way to circumvent New York's blue laws. He persuaded some of his new friends to provide refreshments, and the group met for a convivial session in the attic of Mrs. Giesman's boardinghouse, where many performers of the day lodged.

Those Sunday gatherings soon became a regular occurrence. The friends quickly realized the need for some sort of dues-collecting organization, so funds would be readily available for refreshments. They called themselves the Jolly Corks, elected Charles Vivian to the position of Imperial Cork, and gave him the authority to levy fines for all sorts of imagined infractions. Membership expansion forced them out of the attic and into other accommodations. It also gave new purpose to the group, which began to take on loftier goals. To reflect this change, it was felt that the organization needed a new name. Vivian, a member of the Royal Antediluvian Order of Buffaloes back in England, lobbied for "the Buffaloes," but others wanted something more American. Barnum's Museum on Broadway was displaying a magnificent elk head at the time, which impressed many of the members. When they were put to a decision, the elk won out over the buffalo by just one vote. Thus it was that on February 16, 1868, the B.P.O.E. came into being.

Fredericksburg Lodge 875 first met in June 1903. A year later, it moved its headquarters into this structure. Then, in 1905, it began buying the surrounding land. It undertook its most significant construction project, the present lodge, in 1924. The ballroom was built in 1936. The entire cost of the addition was defrayed by leasing space to the United States Post Office for ten months at a rate of a thousand dollars per month. From just eight founding members, the Fredericksburg Elks grew to a membership of 550 in 1968, with assets of over a hundred thousand dollars. That success helps explains the luxury of the structure today.

The menu is equally elegant, offering appetizers such as Rabbit Ravioli and Baby Octopus and entrée choices like Tsar-Cut Norwegian Smoked Salmon Salad and American Rack of Lamb. The menu is five-course prix fixe, but dinner guests have considerable flexibility within that format. I'm sorry Debbie had to miss out on what was a superb meal. I sampled the Smoked Trout with Apple Beets and Horseradish Crème Fraiche, the Roasted Beet Salad with Blood Orange-Cumin Vinaigrette, the Herb-Laced Monkfish with Butternut Purée and Brussels Sprouts, and the Pan-Seared Pheasant with Wild Mushroom Ragout and Sauce Foie Gras. The presentation was as superb as the forkfuls were divine, and the wait staff was knowledgeable, efficient, and attentive. If elegance and fabulous food are what you desire, then Augustine's is a taste of heaven!

ROASTED BEET SALAD WITH BLOOD ORANGE-CUMIN VINAIGRETTE

salt and pepper to taste
4 baseball-sized beets
1 teaspoon extravirgin olive oil
3 blood oranges
4 tablespoons blood orange juice
1 shallot, peeled and minced
2 tablespoons rice wine vinegar
ground cumin to taste
4 tablespoons salad oil
2 ounces pine nuts
1 tablespoon chopped chives

Preheat oven to 350 degrees. Salt and pepper beets, brush with olive oil, and wrap in tinfoil. Bake for about 3 hours until tender. Remove from oven and cool completely. When cool, peel and slice beets into thin disks and arrange in a circle on 4 plates. Separate oranges into segments and arrange on plates between beet disks. Place orange juice, shallot, wine vinegar, cumin, salad oil, and salt and pepper in a blender. Blend ingredients for approximately 1 minute to thoroughly combine flavors. Drizzle enough vinaigrette to just coat beets and orange segments. Sprinkle with pine nuts and chives. Serves 4.

PAN-SEARED PHEASANT WITH RAGOUT OF WILD MUSHROOMS AND SAUCE FOIE GRAS

1 whole pheasant hen
7 tablespoons vegetable oil, divided
1 mild Spanish onion, peeled and diced
2 stalks celery, diced
1 large carrot, peeled and diced
4 cloves garlic
4 springs thyme
1 sprig rosemary
4 sage leaves
1 bay leaf
2 ounces foie gras
salt and pepper to taste
2 shallots, peeled and minced, divided
¼ cup brandy
2 tablespoons unsalted butter, divided
1½ cups wild mushrooms
1 clove garlic, peeled and minced
2 sprigs thyme for garnish

Break down pheasant into breast and legs. Chop carcass into pieces and set aside with giblets. In a 4-quart pan, heat 2 tablespoons of the vegetable oil. Add onions, celery, and carrots. Cook until slightly browned and caramelized. Add 4 cloves garlic, chopped carcass, and giblets. Cover with 12 cups water. Bring to a boil and simmer for 2 hours, skimming any foam or fat that comes to the surface. Remove from heat and strain. Place in a smaller pan. Add thyme, rosemary, sage, and bay leaf and simmer over medium heat until liquid is reduced by ¾. Remove bay leaf and any stems and set sauce aside.

In a smaller sauté pan, heat 1 tablespoon of the vegetable oil. Season foie gras with salt and pepper. Add to pan and brown on both sides. Add 1 of the minced shallots and brandy and remove from heat. Place sauce, foie gras, and 1 tablespoon of the butter in a blender and blend until smooth. Strain into a small pot and set aside until ready to serve.

Preheat oven to 375 degrees. Season breast with salt and pepper. In a large oven-proof sauté pan, heat 2 tablespoons of the vegetable oil until smoking. Place breasts skin side down in oil and immediately place in oven for about 10 minutes until meat thermometer registers 150 degrees.

While pheasant is cooking, remove all dirt from mushrooms using a clean paper towel. Heat remaining 2 tablespoons vegetable oil in a large sauté pan. Add mushrooms and cook for about 5 minutes until brown and crispy. Add remaining minced shallot, minced garlic, and remaining 1 tablespoon butter and stir to combine. Place mushrooms momentarily on a plate lined with a paper towel. To plate, place mushroom ragout in the center of 2 plates and position pheasant on top. Drizzle with hot sauce and garnish with thyme sprigs. Serves 2.

Smythe's Cottage & Tavern

303 Fauquier Street
Fredericksburg, VA 22401
540-373-1645

We spent a delightful lunchtime at Smythe's Cottage & Tavern in the company of Jim and Jessica Frakes and their seven-month-old daughter, Emily. Emily gurgled and smiled the whole time we sampled the cuisine and chatted with this charming couple. The Frakes obviously love what they do, and it shows both in the attention to detail in the cottage and in the delicious food prepared in the tiny kitchen.

This little cottage has two dining rooms, as well as a taproom on the ground floor and a room upstairs that is used as an office. Even the small, bricked back garden is pressed into service in the summer months, when guests can sit outside in the shade of the crab apple tree.

Built in 1835 as a private residence, the cottage is reported to have been a blacksmith shop at one time. It was built on ground that was formerly used for stables. The floors inside the cottage are both wooden and brick and are quaintly uneven. There's an old wood-burning stove in the larger of the two dining rooms. The blue napkins at the brightly polished wooden tables for two, four, or more match the blue-painted wood trim. The floral pattern in the swags at the windows is repeated in stencil work over the top of the window frames. It's the sort of place where you feel immediately at home. Around the rooms, visitors can find family photographs and some really fine pen-and-ink drawings by Jim. He told us that he tries to create at least one each year and has them printed onto note cards for guests to purchase.

Having perused the menu on our way to lunch, we had already decided to sample the Pumpkin Soup and the Virginia Ham Biscuits. However, the ever-generous Frakes offered us samples of many other items on the menu. Both the Peanut Soup and the Pumpkin Soup were hot and delicious. We sampled the Banana Nut Bread and the Cornbread. Both were tasty, but the Cornbread was outstanding. The Ginger Beef, a favorite among frequent guests at Smythe's Cottage, was also a favorite of ours. Debbie loved the Chicken Salad Biscuits, while Karen favored the Virginia Ham Biscuits. We couldn't leave without a spoonful of dessert. We loved the Pecan Pie and know that you'll enjoy making the recipe included here. Smythe's offers a slightly more extensive dinner menu.

Guests enjoy returning time and again to eat their favorite dishes at their usual tables. A little-known secret about Smythe's is that it doesn't close on holidays. And each day here is a family affair. At Christmas, for example, carriage tours depart right from the front door, and guests also enjoy the carolers and the cookie decorating for children in the taproom. The Frakes' eldest two sons even bus tables when they are out of school and all their homework has been completed. Each visit to Smythe's combines a little taste of history with a delicious homemade meal. What an incredible value for the money!

PUMPKIN SOUP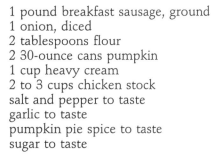

1 pound breakfast sausage, ground
1 onion, diced
2 tablespoons flour
2 30-ounce cans pumpkin
1 cup heavy cream
2 to 3 cups chicken stock
salt and pepper to taste
garlic to taste
pumpkin pie spice to taste
sugar to taste

In a large pan, sauté sausage for 5 to 6 minutes until thoroughly cooked. Add onions and cook until translucent. Add flour and stir well. Add pumpkin, cream, and 2 cups of the stock. Bring to a full boil, stirring constantly. Season with salt and pepper, garlic, pumpkin pie spice, and sugar. If soup is too thick, add a little more stock. Serves 8 to 10.

PECAN PIE

1 cup pecan halves
9-inch prepared piecrust
3 eggs
½ cup sugar
2 tablespoons butter, melted
2 cups dark Karo syrup

Preheat oven to 375 degrees. Place pecan halves in bottom of crust. Combine remaining ingredients in a medium bowl. Pour mixture over pecans. Bake for 45 minutes. Cool completely before serving. Yields 1 pie.

RESTAURANT

209 West Freemason Street
Norfolk, VA 23510
757-622-3966

The stone edifice that sits at the corner of Freemason and Boush Streets in Norfolk was dedicated as a church in 1873. At that time, it was the spiritual home of Second Presbyterian Church. It operated as such for almost thirty years until it was sold in 1902. It continued as a place of worship, this time housing the First Church of Christ Scientist, which utilized the building until 1948. From that point until 1987, it functioned as a meeting hall for the Independent Order of Odd Fellows. It was in early 1988 that planning for the Freemason Abbey Restaurant began.

The renovation was undertaken with a strong sense of pride, enthusiasm, and dedication, as is generally the case with those who are working with historic structures, and especially the case with those converting a reverent locale into a structure intended for a very different use. The church's back building was completely refurbished to house a pristine, efficient kitchen capable of producing delicious, attractive meals one at a time but up to two hundred per hour! We can vouch that this part of the endeavor was an undeniable success.

In the mid-1990s, the eatery began selling whole lobsters as a special on Wednesday evenings. The number of customers coming specifically for lobster increased dramatically, so the chef began offering whole lobsters all week long. Freemason Abbey takes great pride in the quality of its lobsters, purchasing them directly from New England lobstermen and flying them overnight to the restaurant. It serves only offshore lobsters because of their superior taste and texture. And it specifies a size of over 1 pounds. Did you know that a 1 -pound lobster is over eight years old? If your lobster arrives with barnacles, consider yourself lucky, because it should be chock-full of meat. Although you may not want to dip it in butter, those of you watching your weight should feel good about ordering lobster, since it has less total fat, cholesterol, and calories than crab, shrimp, or chicken. Freemason Abbey and lobsters have become so synonymous that the restaurant serves over a thousand whole, fresh lobsters every month.

Those of you not quite so interested in lobster can select from several other seafood selections, including the Seafood Fantasia, a combination of shrimp, onions, peppers, cream, and Parmesan tossed with fettuccine and then topped with backfin crab. The range of beef selections includes Prime Rib, Filet Mignon, and Smoked Gouda and Tenderloin Penne. An entire section of the menu is dedicated to light entrées and salad choices. Feeling ever so "crabby" the day we visited, we strongly considered the Crab-Stuffed Mushrooms and the Chesapeake Crab Dip. Ultimately, Debbie had a crock of creamy She-Crab Soup, while Karen opted for the piquant Shrimp Salad Wrap. We also shared a serving of Brandy Bread Pudding that was the best in three states! Our mood was immediately improved, as only a delicious meal can do.

 ARTICHOKE DIP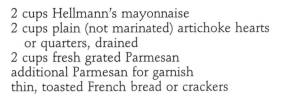

2 cups Hellmann's mayonnaise
2 cups plain (not marinated) artichoke hearts
   or quarters, drained
2 cups fresh grated Parmesan
additional Parmesan for garnish
thin, toasted French bread or crackers

Preheat oven to 425 degrees. Combine mayonnaise, artichokes, and 2 cups Parmesan in an electric mixer on low speed. Pour into a glass or ceramic baking dish and sprinkle with a thin coating of Parmesan. Bake uncovered for 25 to 30 minutes until cheese is browned on top. Serve with French bread or crackers. Serves 2 as an appetizer.

Note: Other brands of mayonnaise tend to separate when heated, resulting in an oily effect.

 SEAFOOD QUICHE

1 deep-dish pie shell
¼ pound baby shrimp, peeled
½ pound sea scallops
1¼ cups grated Swiss cheese
¾ cup half-and-half
1 tablespoon parsley flakes
pinch of salt
pinch of white pepper
pinch of nutmeg
4 large eggs

Preheat oven to 475 degrees. Bake pie shell on a baking sheet for about 10 minutes until lightly browned. Steam shrimp and scallops about 5 minutes until done. Chill seafood completely, then place in bottom of pie shell. Top with cheese. In a small saucepan, heat half-and-half, parsley, and spices until hot *but not boiling*. Beat eggs in a medium bowl. Whisk in a small amount of half-and-half mixture to temper eggs. Pour entire mixture into saucepan, whisking quickly to keep eggs from scrambling. Pour over shrimp and scallops in pie shell. Reduce oven to 350 degrees and bake for 30 to 40 minutes until set. Serves 6.

HOMESTEAD. 1766

Sam Snead's Tavern
The Homestead
Hot Springs, VA 24445
www.thehomestead.com
540-838-1766

My first reaction upon learning of this restaurant was to ask, "Why would a restaurant in Hot Springs, Virginia, be named after Sam Snead?" Since I have a father and a brother who are both avid golfers, I was well aware of who Sam Snead was and what he contributed to the game. However, I was oblivious to the fact that he grew up here and that he called the area home even during his adulthood. In many ways, The Homestead and Snead's success on the links are closely tied. As a boy, Sam was a caddy on The Homestead's Old Course. It was here that he began to learn the game. During his teens, he worked at The Homestead making hickory-shaft clubs. He also helped during the construction of The Cascades Golf Course just down the road. Upon becoming a professional golfer in 1934, Snead was hired as the first golf pro at The Cascades. Many a guest benefited from his prowess at the rate of just three dollars per lesson!

His influence was palpable as I sat in the tavern for dinner. Young golfers from far and wide filled the restaurant. All were there for the Southern Amateur Golf Championship. Their awe and admiration were clear as they pointed to the memorabilia. They were particularly interested in the display highlighting Snead's numerous holes in one. Many of the novices simply shook their heads in amazement at the sheer number. Others pointed out the difficult courses on which they'd occurred.

The atmosphere in the restaurant is definitely that of a pub. The dark green walls and pine woodwork give it the feel of a "nineteenth hole." A massive stone fireplace with pewter displayed on its mantel sits at one end of the eating area. A painting of Snead hangs above, as if presiding over the activity. I was seated near the bar at a simple wooden table. A server quickly brought out a basket of fresh rolls and a large glass of sweet tea. The Potato Skins seemed to be the most popular appetizer that evening, although there are several other appealing selections. Many of the entrées being served were beef, which was not surprising, since the menu features a twenty-two-ounce Porterhouse, a New York Strip, a Rib Eye, a Texas Cowboy Steak, and Filet Mignon. Several barbecue choices are offered as well. I opted for one of the more unusual items, Sam's Shrimp and Grits. The Cajun-seasoned shrimp nestled in a bed of creamy cheddar grits made a tasty combination.

This bustling eatery started out as the Bath County National Bank, built just after the turn of the twentieth century for fifteen thousand dollars. Of that amount, seven thousand were spent on the vault alone. The door weighed two thousand pounds but was balanced so that it could be closed easily with just one hand. The locks were set up on a timing mechanism to open at a specified time. The only other way to get into the vault was to blast it open! Today, the vault houses the restaurant's excellent wine selection. Believe it or not, I actually overlooked it on my way in, since there was so much memorabilia grabbing my attention. One trip is not enough to take it all in. Next time, I hope Karen will be along.

 FRENCH ONION SOUP

6 medium onions
1 tablespoon butter
2 quarts beef bouillon
½ cup dry white wine
8 slices day-old French bread
salt and freshly ground black pepper to taste
¾ cup Gruyère cheese
¾ cup grated Parmesan

Peel and trim onions, cut in half, and mince fine. Melt butter in a 5-quart saucepan over medium-high heat. Add onions and sauté until golden brown, stirring from time to time. Add bouillon and wine and bring to a boil. Adjust heat to maintain a gentle simmer. Cook for 30 minutes. While soup is cooking, preheat oven to 375 degrees. Arrange bread slices on a baking sheet and cook

in middle level of oven until golden brown. When soup has finished cooking, season with salt and pepper. Soup may be stored for later use, if desired.

Just before serving, preheat broiler. Grate cheeses. Gently heat soup if it has been stored. When soup is hot, ladle it into 8 individual ovenproof serving bowls. Float toasted bread slices on top. Divide cheese evenly among serving bowls. Place under broiler until cheese is melted and bubbly. Serve at once. Serves 8.

 OLD-FASHIONED SPICE CAKE

Cake

⁷/₈ cup flour
⅓ teaspoon baking powder
¼ teaspoon baking soda
¼ teaspoon cinnamon, ground
⅛ teaspoon ginger, ground
⅛ teaspoon cloves, ground
pinch of freshly ground nutmeg
pinch of salt
4 tablespoons butter
½ cup dark brown sugar
⅓ cup sugar
1 egg yolk
2 eggs
¼ cup plus 1 tablespoon buttermilk, divided
2⅔ tablespoons raisins, chopped
2½ teaspoons orange peel, chopped

Butter and flour two 10-inch cake pans. Set aside. Preheat oven to 350 degrees. Sift flour with baking powder, baking soda, cinnamon, ginger, cloves, nutmeg, and salt into a 1-quart bowl. Set aside. In a large mixing bowl, cream butter until light and fluffy. Add brown sugar and sugar. Beat until sugar is dissolved and mixture is fluffy. Scrape down sides of bowl with a spatula. Add egg yolk and eggs, mixing thoroughly. Scrape down bowl again. Add reserved flour mixture, blending well. Scrape down bowl and add 2 tablespoons of the buttermilk. Mix well and reserve. Add raisins and orange peel to mixture and blend. Add remaining buttermilk and mix to combine thoroughly. Divide batter evenly between the 2 prepared pans. Set pans onto lower middle and upper middle oven racks to bake for about 20 minutes until cake springs back when touched. When done, remove pans from oven and turn cakes out of pans onto wire racks to cool. While cakes are cooling, prepare frosting.

Frosting

11 tablespoons butter
3 cups powdered sugar
¼ cup sugar
⅓ cup milk
⅓ cup orange peel
1 cup raisins

In a large mixing bowl, cream butter until light and fluffy. Add powdered sugar and sugar gradually, mixing until well blended. Heat milk in a small saucepan until it feels warm to the touch. While milk is heating, mince orange peel and set aside. When milk is ready, add it little by little to butter and sugar while mixing on low speed. When frosting is perfectly smooth, add raisins and orange peel, blending thoroughly. Set aside until cake is completely cool.

When ready to frost cake, place 1 layer on a serving plate. Cover with half the frosting. Top with the second layer. Spread remaining frosting evenly over top and sides of cake. Refrigerate for at least 1 hour. Keep chilled until 30 minutes before serving. Serves 16.

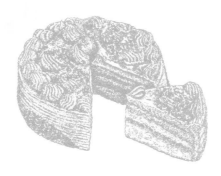

360 Main Street
Washington, VA 22747
540-987-3600

The drive between Luray and Warrenton took us along US 211 on a bright, sunny day. We weren't scheduled to stop in Sperryville, but the brick-red buildings with crisp white trim and contrasting black tin roofs were just too intriguing to pass by. What we discovered was more than just local business. It was a philosophy and a way of life.

Sunnyside Farms is housed in the main structure of a two-building complex. The structures, dating back to the 1800s, once functioned as a school for local children from kindergarten through seventh grade. The double-door entrance was reminiscent of where each of us went to school, so we felt quite at home as we stepped inside. As we expected, the long, wide hallway was lined with doorways. Though they no longer open into classrooms, each is a portal to a discovery all its own. The first door on the left takes visitors into a general store of sorts, where natural and organic foods are sold. Old milk cans and other farm paraphernalia are used as accents throughout the room. In the adjoining classroom, set up like a deli

replete with hanging meats, more tasty items are for sale. Down the steps, in the section that was added in 1939, the old gymnasium has been converted into a fabulous gift shop offering a wide variety of items for home decorating, all in keeping with Sunnyside's fresh, natural aura. The stage where many a school play took place is now the Sunnyside library, where visitors can browse among more than fourteen hundred titles.

Our favorite spot was the cheery white café just to the right of the front doors. Old chairs and farm implements, all white-washed, hang near the ceiling, adding a pristine quality to the room. The original chalkboard along one wall features a plethora of interesting sayings about healthy living and healthy eating. One of our favorites was, "The apple doesn't fall far from the tree when you grow and eat the apple locally," which embodied our personal philosophy of supporting local business. Another saying—"The convenience of fast food is somewhat offset by the inconvenience of a heart attack"—made us laugh out loud.

The café serves up such delicious treats that we had difficulty in deciding. When we arrived, the staff was taste-testing new ice-cream flavors, but we homed in on the baked goods. Chocolate Chip, Oatmeal Raisin, and Peanut Butter Cookies were all available. The scones are very popular, Cherry Scones being the choice on the day we visited. The gentleman in front of us enjoyed a wedge of Bok Choy and Onion Quiche. Ultimately, we chose a Harvest Bar, a Raspberry Bar, and some Sunnyside Farms Cider to enjoy as we drove. All were wonderful! If you're looking for a more substantial meal, the Sunnyside Grill is every bit as appealing, featuring free-range chicken and Kobe beef.

After a delightful chat with several staff members, we met briefly with J. B. Kidwell, the general merchandise manager, who emphasized what this operation is all about. Four adjectives describe Sunnyside Farms: fresh, natural, organic, and local. How many more does one need to describe great food?

ROASTED SALMON WITH APPLE CIDER MUSTARD GLAZE

2 cups apple cider
2 tablespoons Dijon mustard
4 6-ounce salmon fillets, skin on
salt and freshly cracked black pepper to taste

Preheat oven to 375 degrees. In a saucepan over medium heat, reduce cider until it measures about ¼ cup. Stir in mustard and set aside. Season salmon with salt and pepper. In an ovenproof sauté pan, sear skin side of salmon for 1 minute. Turn and put in oven for 8 minutes. Remove salmon and switch oven to broil. Spoon Apple Cider Mustard Glaze liberally over salmon. Return salmon to oven for 1 to 2 minutes until glaze starts to brown slightly. Remove from oven and serve. Serves 4.

 BRANCH AND BRAMBLE COBBLER

6 medium York or Enterprise apples
2 cups blackberries
½ cup plus ⅓ cup sugar, divided
1 cup all-purpose flour
1 teaspoon baking soda
¼ teaspoon salt
4 tablespoons butter
1 large egg
¼ cup buttermilk
whipped cream

Preheat oven to 350 degrees. Peel apples if desired, although it isn't necessary if they've been washed thoroughly. Remove seeds, core, and cut into wedges. Combine apples, blackberries, and ½ cup sugar and place in a 2-quart cast-iron, earthenware, or glass baking dish. In a small bowl, combine flour, baking soda, and salt. Cream butter and ⅓ cup sugar together. Beat in egg. Add half of dry ingredients and beat on low speed just until incorporated. Add buttermilk, beating until incorporated. Add remaining dry ingredients and beat just until batter is smooth. Drop spoonfuls of batter on top of fruit to cover it, leaving a ½-inch border around edge of dish. This allows room for expansion during cooking. Bake for 40 to 45 minutes until top is golden brown and fruit is tender when pierced with a skewer. Let cool at least 15 minutes before serving. Serve with whipped cream if desired. Serves 4 to 6.

102 Salem Avenue
Roanoke, VA 24011
540-342-3937

Billy's Ritz is situated at the corner of Salem Avenue and Market Street. Once the Ritz Hotel, this century-old building got its name from the old hotel and from another business that once operated a little farther up the street. When Billy Huddleston's bar went under, an enterprising businessman bought all his furniture and accouterments, moved them into the Ritz Hotel, and opened an upscale saloon. Stuck for a name, he went with tradition and called the saloon Billy's. When current owners John and Betsy Williams acquired the property in 1979, they decided to incorporate both of the previous names, and Billy's Ritz was born.

The main dining room is large and square. Its high tin-tile ceiling is painted a creamy brown. You'll see several beautiful old mirrors and here and there an occasional photograph of a jazz master such as Count Basie. I loved the two pedestal cherubs hold-ing aloft their circular lights just inside the main doors.

I sat at one of the long windows and watched the world go by while I checked out the menu. Debbie was dining elsewhere that evening, but I was very comfortable in the relaxed atmosphere by myself. The menu is fairly short, which I love because it makes choosing easier. In the end I opted for an extremely tasty Herb-Roasted Fillet of Salmon with Horseradish Mashed Potatoes and Asparagus. I was, however, sorely tempted by the Mixed Grill of lamb chops, quail, and rabbit sausage and the Spicy Sea-food Stew with shrimp, scallops, and crab. My efficient server, Chip, arrived at the table with hot bread and a small bowl of Mari-nated Olives and Artichoke Hearts. I took the opportunity to ask him about the intrigu-ing starter listed as Selected Cheeses. He in-formed me that I could choose three cheeses from a wide selection that included every-thing from Grafton Classic Reserve Ched-dar to Rosemary Jack to Brindamour, a Corsican sheep-milk cheese covered in herbs, juniper berries, and chile peppers. The cheeses are served with bread, grapes, and Peach Chutney—delicious!

After enjoying the salmon, I duly con-sulted Chip about the best way of allocat-ing my dessert calories. He extolled at length the virtues of the Molten Chocolate Cake. I was also interested in the most unusual Lemon Goat Cheese Cake with Blueberry Sauce—that is, until Tiramisu, my favorite dessert, was mentioned. It was heavenly, very moist and full of coffee flavor, a treat to be savored.

🐎 WALNUT CRÊPES 🐎

1 cup whole milk
1 cup all-purpose flour
3 large eggs
¼ cup chopped walnuts
2 tablespoons sugar
2 tablespoons unsalted butter, melted
1 teaspoon grated orange peel
¼ teaspoon salt
Sautéed Pears (recipe follows)
Crème Fraiche Ice Cream (recipe follows)

Place first 8 ingredients in a blender and process until smooth, scraping sides occasionally. Cover and chill batter in blender container for at least 2 hours. Reblend for 15 seconds. Heat a nonstick skillet over medium-high heat. Brush skillet with melted butter. Pour in ¼ cup batter, tilting skillet quickly to coat bottom evenly. Cook about 45 seconds until top of crêpe seems dry and bottom is golden. Turn crêpe over and cook about 30 seconds until brown spots appear on bottom. Transfer to a plate and repeat with remaining batter. Place plastic wrap or parchment paper between crêpes.

To assemble crêpes, preheat oven to 400 degrees. Brush a baking sheet with butter. Place a crêpe on sheet. Place 4 slices Sautéed Pears on ¼ of the crêpe. Fold crêpe in half over slices. Place 4 more pear slices on crêpe over first 4 and fold crêpe in half again, form-ing a triangle. Repeat with each crêpe. Place in oven and heat about 2 minutes until just warmed through. Remove from oven and place on plates. Drizzle with a little pear syrup and serve with Crème Fraiche Ice Cream. Serves 6 to 8.

🐎 SAUTÉED PEARS 🐎

¼ cup unsalted butter
½ cup light brown sugar
4 large D'Anjou pears, peeled and cored
4 teaspoons fresh lemon juice

Melt butter in a large nonstick skillet over medium-high heat. Add sugar and stir for 1 minute until sugar melts. Cut each pear in half, then cut each half lengthwise into 6 pieces. Add pear slices and lemon juice to skillet and cook. Turn slices frequently for 3 to 4 minutes until pears begin to release juice and a syrup forms in the skillet. Remove from heat and allow to cool. Yields 4 cups.

🐎 CRÈME FRAICHE ICE CREAM 🐎

2 cups crème fraiche
2 cups buttermilk
¼ cup fresh lemon juice
1¼ cups superfine sugar

Combine all ingredients in a blender. Blend until very smooth. Chill until cold, then freeze in an ice-cream maker. Place in a covered container in freezer. Yields 4 cups.

🐎 🐎 🐎 🐎 🐎 🐎

14900 Forest Road
Forest, VA 24551
www.cowsandcrabs.com
434-534-6077

The land on which this funky little restaurant stands was once part of the Radford farm, a homestead begun in the 1800s. The Radfords sold this parcel to raise some much-needed cash. A Mr. Porter purchased the plot and built a store that he called Porter's Place. It quickly became a gathering place for locals. Amid the area news and town gossip, canned goods were purchased, gasoline was dispensed, and short-order menu items were prepared.

Mr. Porter sold the store to Mr. Watson, a gentleman from New York, in 1948. For whatever reason—the different environment or something else entirely—Mr. Watson owned the business for only four years before turning it over to Jessie Reynolds in 1952. At that time, the name was officially changed to Reynolds Place, although locals simply referred to it as "Jessie's." He and his wife continued to run their filling station and restaurant until 1991. It then became Bear Creek Tavern after undergoing renovations to make it a full-scale restaurant rather than a short-order affair.

Today's owner, Benjamin McGehee, has deep ties to the area. His parents and grandparents owned local businesses. He has managed to create a fine-dining restaurant with a comfortable, rustic atmosphere, leaving the building erected by Mr. Porter remarkably unchanged. The walls of exposed wood accented by antique tools, nautical artifacts, and old photos provide a subtle backdrop for the chef's tasty concoctions. If you visit on a sunny weekend, be sure to sit awhile on the large deck out back for live music, good food, and a fabulous view of the Blue Ridge Mountains in all their glory.

When we visited Benjamin's on a cold, rainy day in October, we were glad to try something warm and hearty. Karen choose the mildly spiced Black Bean and Chicken Chili, which contained large chunks of chicken, black beans, kidney beans, and generous helpings of sour cream and shredded Jack cheese. Debbie opted for the Slow-Cooked Pulled Pork Barbecue Sandwich, which came with Coleslaw and French Fries. Both luncheon choices were extremely tasty. Thinking ourselves unable to eat another mouthful, we pushed back our plates and took a look at the dessert tray. We saw homemade Glazed Gingerbread Cake, Crème Brûlée, Pumpkin Pie, and Peanut Butter Pie, as well as our choice, a warm and scrumptious Deep-Dish Apple and Apricot Pie, served with Vanilla Ice Cream and Caramel Sauce.

Had we come for dinner, Karen would certainly have tried the New Zealand Green-Lip Mussels, sautéed in Hefewiezen Wheat Beer with cilantro, bacon, and Garlic Butter. Debbie's eye was caught by the Homemade Jumbo Lump Crab Cakes with Corn and Bell Pepper Succotash and Tarragon Cream Sauce. As might be expected from the restaurant's name, both the lunch and dinner menus include a large selection of cows, crabs, hoofs, and claws, all of which are delicious.

Although it's a little out of the way, Benjamin's (as the locals now call it) is well worth the trip. Where else can you see trees growing through the middle of the dining room and enjoy delicious fare, too?

🦞 BLACK BEAN AND CHICKEN CHILI 🦞

1 to 1½ pounds boneless, skinless chicken
  breasts, cooked and cut up
1¼-ounce packet chili seasoning
4 cups tomato sauce
3 14-ounce cans black beans
14-ounce can red kidney beans
1 teaspoon garlic powder
1 teaspoon chili powder

Combine all ingredients in a large crockpot. Cook on low for at least 4 hours to blend flavors. Serves 6 to 8.

🦞 SEAFOOD SCAMPI 🦞

2 tablespoons olive oil
6 tiger shrimp
8 sea scallops
2 teaspoons chopped garlic
2 teaspoons chopped shallots
¼ cup white wine
2½ cups angel hair pasta, cooked according to
  package directions
½ cup diced tomato
salt and pepper to taste
2 tablespoons butter
6 tablespoons shredded Parmesan
parsley for garnish
scallions for garnish

Heat oil in a medium sauté pan. Add shrimp and scallops. Cook until halfway done. Add garlic and shallots. Deglaze pan with white wine. Add pasta, tomatoes, and salt and pepper. Remove from heat and add butter, mixing until melted. Garnish with Parmesan and sprinkle with parsley and scallions. Serves 2.

hotel strasburg

213 South Holliday Street
Strasburg, VA 22657
www.svta.org/thehotel
540-465-9191

In today's world of mega-corporations, it's hard to conceive of one physician having his own private hospital. But in the 1890s, Dr. Mackall R. Bruin had just that. He did make house calls, riding on horseback through the rough terrain of the northern Shenandoah Valley. However, if his patients were able, they got their care at Dr. Bruin's hospital on the corner of Queen and Holliday Streets in Strasburg. His original shingle is displayed on the second floor of the hotel. Current guests occasionally confide, "I was born here."

When Dr. Bruin ran off with one of his nurses in 1915, he left his wife and family behind. To sustain herself and her children, Mrs. Bruin converted the hospital into an inn. The three-story white structure was open to travelers and long-term residents alike. During that era, it was typical for teachers to be female and unmarried, and

many sought lodging here. One such educator reminisced during a subsequent visit, "When I lived here during the 1940s, I paid thirty-five dollars a month, and that included two meals a day."

The ambiance here speaks to the hotel's past. The Victorian era, it seems, is alive and well. Today's lobby gives a hint of what it was like many years ago, when the hotel was the social hub of this community. The furnishings and accessories are an eclectic and interesting combination of the Queen Anne, Renaissance Revival, and Eastlake styles. Antimacassars still adorn the armchairs, giving the public spaces a homey touch. The Belgian sideboard valued at over fifteen thousand dollars is not to be missed.

The menu in the hotel's restaurant features traditional standbys and comfort foods alongside unusual items. The delicious Pot Pie is the restaurant's signature dish. The Gourmet Chicken Salad Wrap with apricots, walnuts, and raisins sounded tasty, as did the Roast Turkey Wrap with Cranberry-Pecan Relish. For a heartier midday appetite, the Steak Provençale, smothered with peppers, onions, tomatoes, mushrooms, and Gorgonzola, is a sure winner.

While Karen was elsewhere, I had the enviable assignment of having dinner here. The Crab-Stuffed Rainbow Trout is a menu favorite, and the Seafood Au Gratin was also popular the night I dined. I started with the Crab and Lobster Bisque, hoping to thaw a bit on a chilly evening. I followed that with the Blackened Tenderloin Bites, one of the many appetizer choices. Served with Couscous, Gorgonzola, and Horseradish Cream, they proved an interesting combination. You'll appreciate the Ginger Habanero Pumpkin Pie recipe on this page, contributed by chef Tim Perry.

Visitors flock to Hotel Strasburg not only for the food and accommodations but for the local attractions as well. When the town was founded in 1761, it was known as Stony Lick, a name that belies its easygoing atmosphere today. Prominent politicians and celebrities are among those who have made their way here. Whether they've come to enjoy Massanutten Mountain, the bends of the Shenandoah River, or just the slower pace, they've found the right place at Hotel Strasburg.

 GINGER HABANERO PUMPKIN PIE

Crust

1½ cups gingersnaps, crushed
6 tablespoons butter, softened
¼ cup sugar
¼ teaspoon cinnamon, ground
½ teaspoon fresh ginger, grated
1 teaspoon dried habenero peppers, crushed

Preheat oven to 350 degrees. Lightly grease a springform pan. In a medium bowl, combine all ingredients with a fork until moistened. Press mixture evenly over bottom and up sides of pan. Bake 10 to 15 minutes until crust is lightly browned and firm to the touch.

Filling

2 cups pumpkin pie filling
²⁄₃ cup brown sugar
½ teaspoon salt
2 teaspoons cinnamon, ground
½ teaspoon fresh ginger, grated
¾ cup milk
2 eggs, beaten
1 cup heavy cream
¼ cup brandy
6-ounce package dried cranberries
1 teaspoon dried habenero peppers, crushed

While crust is baking, combine pumpkin, brown sugar, salt, cinnamon, and ginger in a mixing bowl. Beat in milk, eggs, cream, and brandy until well combined. Remove crust from oven and reduce heat to 325 degrees. Line crust with a layer of cranberries. Sprinkle with habeneros. Pour filling over top and bake for about 1 hour until knife inserted in center comes out clean. Serve plain or with whipped cream flavored with freshly grated ginger. Yields 1 pie.

Warm Springs Inn

US 220 and VA 39
Warm Springs, VA 24484
540-839-5351

The red-and-white buildings that comprise Warm Springs Inn sit atop a knoll just across the road from the Jefferson Pools, today privately owned. These are the springs that brought notoriety to this area more than two hundred years ago. The warm mineral springs evolved as a spa destination as early as the mid-1750s. The pool is about 120 feet in circumference and holds forty thousand gallons of water. The octagonal structure that surrounds it is impressive in its design and its enormity—even more so when you realize it was constructed in 1761! The town boomed as news of the springs spread. Hotels, dining rooms, taverns, livery stables, and churches were built as visitors flocked to the spa. Thomas Jefferson was one of those travelers, seeking the healing waters for his rheumatism at age seventy-five. His visit lasted more than three weeks, during which he enjoyed the springs several times a day.

In 1790, the community of Warm Springs was chosen as the county seat of newly formed Bath County. By the early 1800s, a clerk's office, a brick courthouse, and a jail were constructed. Those community buildings were converted to an inn and restaurant some 150 years later by Mr. and Mrs. Edmund Routiers, who had immigrated to America some years earlier when Edmund became the pastry chef at The Homestead.

Edmund Routiers was a whiz with cocoa. Not only did he make delectable creations, he also used the cocoa to paint! Some of his works, including a painting of Winston Churchill and friends, once hung in the lobby. It became Dali-esque after the cocoa started to melt when the painting was placed too close to the fireplace. This story came from the granddaughter of Mr. and Mrs. Routiers in the 1980s, while the inn was still under the family's proprietorship.

The lobby of the inn once served as the local courthouse. Today, it is the high-ceilinged, spacious entrance hall. To the right is the wide staircase that many a well-known guest has climbed on their way to overnight accommodations. A cozy bar area is accessed through the doorway to the left. The dining room is visible straight ahead. The traditional feel of the décor is mirrored in the breakfast and dinner menus. For dinner, appetizers range from Onion Rings to Crabmeat-Stuffed Mushrooms to Escargot. The entrée selections offer something for everyone, choices of shrimp, duck, crab, beef, pasta, and pork all appearing on the lengthy menu. In these mountains, trout is always a sure bet, so the only decision for many guests is Pan-Fried Trout or Trout Almandine.

Tradition also abounds in the guest rooms, which are decorated with antiques, quilts, and braided rugs. As I got ready to leave, I looked out across the property. The shuffleboard courts and the horseshoe pit situated under a shade tree certainly completed the feel of yesteryear. It's a shame Karen wasn't with me for a bit of friendly competition.

 ## CHEESE OMELET

2 strips bacon
2 teaspoons butter
2 eggs
2 tablespoons milk
salt and pepper to taste
4 tablespoons sharp cheddar, shredded
1 teaspoon tomato, diced

Fry bacon in a skillet. Let cool, crumble, and set aside. Melt butter in an omelet pan. Mix eggs with milk and salt and pepper. Add to pan. Gently scramble eggs until they begin to set. Add cheese, bacon, and tomatoes to center of eggs. Fold in half. Serve on a warm plate. Serves 1.

 ## CROCKPOT APPLE BUTTER

12 to 14 cooking apples
2 cups apple juice
2½ cups sugar
1½ teaspoons cinnamon
½ teaspoon cloves

Wash, core, and quarter apples but do not peel them. Fill a lightly oiled crockpot with apples and apple juice. Cover and cook on low for 2 to 4 hours until apples are tender. Remove apple mixture and press through a sieve or food mill. Measure apple mixture and return to crockpot. Add 1 cup sugar per pint of apples. Add cinnamon and cloves. Cover and cook on high for 6 to 8 hours, stirring every 2 hours. Remove cover after 3 hours to allow mixture to cook down. Pour mixture into 5 or more newly sterilized, hot half-pint jars. Screw on caps over lids and place in boiling water for 10 minutes. Remove jars from water and tighten caps. Yields 5 or more half-pints.

LINDEN ROW INN

HISTORIC INN · DOWNTOWN RICHMOND

100 East Franklin Street
Richmond, VA 23219
www.lindenrowinn.com
804-783-7000

With good company like Janine Charbeneau of the Richmond Convention and Visitor's Bureau and Susan News, Linden Row's director of sales and catering, it would be impossible not to have an enjoyable evening. We were fortunate to have dinner with these ladies in Linden Row's dining room, once the stables for this lovely property. The kitchen was once the carriage house.

The land on which Linden Row sits was part of a hundred-acre tract owned by Thomas Rutherfoord, who made his fortune in tobacco, milling, and real estate. At the time of his ownership, this parcel was west of Richmond's city limits. When the state decided to build a penitentiary, Rutherfoord's property along Franklin Street was one of the potential sites. As an alternative, Rutherfoord volunteered twelve acres farther west. Today, it's hard to imagine how differently this area would have developed if it were home to the stark walls of a prison rather than the graceful facades of townhouses.

In 1811, Elizabeth Poe, an actress at the

Richmond Theater, became ill and died. She left as orphans her two young children. Mr. and Mrs. John Allan raised her son Edgar and gave him their last name as his middle name. Mr. Allan was a business partner with Charles Ellis, who bought the eastern end of Rutherfoord's property in 1816. Ellis used this land as his garden, known for its beautiful roses, jasmine, and linden trees, which he viewed from his home across the way on the corner of Second Street. Upon the Allans' return from a five-year trip to England, they resided with Charles Ellis. Edgar Allan Poe romped in the garden with the Ellis children. Local legend has it that this is the enchanted garden Poe mentions in his famous poem "To Helen."

Fleming James, another business partner of Ellis's, purchased the land in 1839. Eight years later, he built a row of five houses called Linden Square, after the linden trees Ellis had cultivated. In 1853, the western end of the block was purchased by Thomas Rutherfoord's sons, Samuel and Alexander. They built five more houses just like the ones Fleming James had erected a few years earlier. Those elegant houses now comprise Linden Row Inn.

As we nibbled on salads of spring greens, Susan relayed even more of the inn's history. Just before the Civil War, the two westernmost houses were occupied by the Southern Female Institute. Pupils saw Confederate president Jefferson Davis ride by on horseback. Another renowned girls' school was operated here by Virginia Pegram, the widow of General James Pegram, Mexican War hero. Then Virginia Randolph Ellett located her school here. Early pupils receiving their schooling from Miss Ellett were Irene and Nancy Langhorne. Irene later became Irene Gibson, the famous "Gibson girl," and Nancy became Lady Nancy Astor, the first female member of the British Parliament.

The menu at Linden Row Inn is equally fascinating. Choosing our entrées was difficult, but ultimately an order of Crab Cakes (for which Linden Row is well known), two orders of Bluefish with Scallops, and a selection of Spicy Thai Shrimp arrived to the tasty satisfaction of everyone. As dinner wound to a close, we discussed with thankfulness the efforts of Mary Wingfield Scott, the local architectural historian who saved the surviving eight houses from being razed in 1950. Every historic building needs such a guardian angel.

VIRGINIA GENTLEMAN BOURBON PECAN PIE

½ cup plus 1 teaspoon brown sugar, divided
8-inch pie shell, baked
2 ounces bittersweet chocolate
1 cup pecans, toasted
¼ cup heavy cream
1 teaspoon gelatin
2 tablespoons butter, softened
1 egg yolk
4 tablespoons Virginia Gentleman bourbon
½ cup sour cream

2 egg whites
1 teaspoon powdered sugar
Cream Custard (recipe below)

Sprinkle 1 teaspoon of the brown sugar over pie shell. Set aside. Melt chocolate, then mix it with pecans. Set aside to cool. In a medium saucepan, warm cream and gelatin. In a medium mixing bowl, combine butter, remaining brown sugar, egg yolk, and bourbon. Add it to the mixture in the saucepan and simmer over low heat, stirring. Cool over ice until mixture is almost set. Fold in sour cream and pecan mixture. In a small bowl, whip egg whites with powdered sugar until stiff. Fold into custard mixture. Fill shell and chill. Serve with Cream Custard. Yields 1 pie.

CREAM CUSTARD

4 tablespoons water
½ cup sugar
½ cup corn syrup
¼ cup cream
2 tablespoons unsalted butter
1 tablespoon Virginia Gentleman bourbon

Combine first 5 ingredients in a medium saucepan over medium heat. Bring to a boil, stirring constantly for 2 to 3 minutes. Add bourbon. Reduce slightly and serve. Yields about 1 cup.

109 South St. Asaph Street
Old Town Alexandria
Alexandria, VA 22314
703-683-1776

To use one of Karen's expressions, Portner's is "chockablock" full of antiques. A Tiffany stained-glass lamp created in the likeness of a butterfly is displayed in the front window of the restaurant. It's just one of the many beautiful and interesting pieces that antique lovers will find here. The ceiling from New York's Commodore Hotel graces one of the dining rooms. On the third floor in an area decorated in the Gothic Revival style of the 1870s, guests will find the ceiling and two walls from the Philadelphia estate of department-store magnate John Wanamaker. Wanamaker is credited with establishing the country's first department store in 1876.

Not only can guests view an array of interesting artifacts, they can also experience a wide variety of atmospheres within this one eatery. If you like ambiance that's light and airy, then the greenhouse effect of the atrium is for you. On warm summer evenings, patio dining is available. And the dining room called Creighton's Emporium has

a turn-of-the-twentieth-century apothecary as its focal point. Four floors of dining rooms, each with its own personality, are sure to tweak the interest of just about everyone.

The restaurant is named for local businessman Robert Portner, a German immigrant who opened a brewery in Alexandria during the Civil War. Portner was so successful that he was able to expand his operation over four blocks on either side of Pendleton Street between North St. Asaph and North Washington Streets. Although much of the brewery has been destroyed, Portner's legacy as the last man to brew beer in Alexandria lives on.

Portner's was once the home of Columbia Fire Company No. 4. No doubt, the firefighters were involved in many exciting events through the years. One of the most comical came in 1883, when local residents assisted the town council in chasing away hogs so the company's new steam engine could proudly make its way down the street.

The portions here are large. Even the dinner salads deliver a full meal. The menu includes a variety of choices. As with the décor, there's something for everyone. Fajitas, Quesadillas, Wings, and a variety of burgers are available alongside such choices as Grilled Salmon, Sirloin, and Meat Loaf. The wait staff is very knowledgeable and friendly, so if you can't quite decide, ask for a recommendation.

We arrived for a late-Sunday-evening meal after traveling all day. Seated downstairs in Creighton's Emporium, we perused the menu and immediately agreed that one visit would not be enough to completely experience the décor and the culinary offerings here. Karen enjoyed the Beer-Battered Halibut with Tartar Sauce and Waffle Fries, while Debbie munched her way through the tasty Blue Cheese and Pear Salad in Balsamic Vinaigrette. With so much to offer visit after visit, Portner's is a new experience every time.

QUESADILLAS

4 10-inch stone-ground flour tortillas
1 cup grated Monterey Jack cheese
1 cup grated colby cheese
2 ripe avocados
4½-ounce can whole chile peppers
1 cup Salsa Cilantro (recipe follows)
2 teaspoons crushed red peppers
3 tablespoons vegetable oil
¼ cup sour cream

Sprinkle tortillas evenly with both cheeses. Thinly slice avocados and place slices over cheeses. Halve chile peppers and place over avocados. Spread salsa over peppers, reserving about a tablespoon for garnish. Sprinkle with red peppers. Pour oil into a 12-inch sauté pan. Cook tortillas 1 at a time over moderate heat until cheeses begin to melt and tortillas are lightly browned. Remove from pan, fold in half, and place in a casserole dish. This can be kept in a 140-degree oven for up to 45 minutes. Before serving, spoon sour cream and reserved salsa over tortillas. Serves 4.

 SALSA CILANTRO

6 tomatoes
2 to 3 jalapeños, cored
2 medium finley diced red onions
1 teaspoon cumin
1 bunch fresh cilantro, stemmed
1½ teaspoons sugar
¾ teaspoon salt

Coarsely chop tomatoes and jalapeños and set aside. In a food processor, process remaining ingredients until mixture resembles relish. Add to tomatoes and peppers. Store in a tightly covered container in the refrigerator. Keeps for several days. Yields about 2 cups.

Silver Thatch Inn

3001 Hollymead Drive
Charlottesville, VA 22911
434-978-4686

Hessian soldiers captured at the Battle of Saratoga by General Horatio Gage and his troops were marched south to Charlottesville, Virginia. Here, on the grounds of a former Indian settlement, they built a two-story log cabin to serve as their jail. It's been said that the ghost of one of the Hessians snatches pillows to playfully haunt overnight visitors. However, the attractive, romantic ambiance of the guest rooms of today's Silver Thatch Inn will quickly make guests forget about such rumors.

The central part of the inn was built in 1812. It was subsequently utilized as a boys' school. In the second half of the 1800s, when the property changed hands several times, it served as a tobacco plantation and as a melon farm. By 1937, it was owned by B. F. D. Runk, dean of the University of Virginia. He added the final wing of the structure with the help of the architect responsible for the renovation and reconstruction of Colonial Williamsburg. Photos prior to Runk's tenure show the positive effect this had on the dwelling.

The year 1983 saw the home pass into the hands of a young couple who had visions of creating a full-service inn. They added a cottage and restaurant and opened the property as the Hollymead Inn. Known as the Silver Thatch Inn today, it operates under the expert guidance of Jim and Terri Petrovits.

Many guests of the inn come to get away, using it as an opportunity to focus attention on spouses or traveling companions. To that end, there are no televisions or telephones in the guest rooms. Rather than being the communal experience other inns offer, breakfast is served at private tables. Later in the day, just a few steps from their rooms, guests can enjoy a divine dinner. The dining rooms are open to the general public as well.

On a chilly November evening, we were seated in a quiet dining room with white-washed walls trimmed in forest green. A picture of a magnolia, the true flower of the South, hung above the mantel. Windsor chairs crafted of dark wood contrasted nicely with the tables covered in white linen, lending an air of subdued elegance. In the adjacent dining room, farm implements and baskets hung from the ceiling, creating a slightly more casual atmosphere.

The Lobster Potato Cakes and Smoked Trout- and Whipped Chèvre-Filled Crêpes are just two examples of the mouth-watering starters. Entrée selections like Pan-Seared Duck Breast with Citrus-Glazed Fennel, Warm Cornbread Pudding, and Cranberry Coulis promise a night to remember. Whether you're inclined toward overnight accommodations or a memorable dinner, the only bad choice here is choosing to stay away!

SPAGHETTI SQUASH

1 large spaghetti squash
3 to 4 tablespoons butter
12 fresh mushrooms, sliced thin
2 medium zucchini, sliced thin
2 medium tomatoes, seeded and diced
salt and pepper to taste
1 cup shredded Parmesan
dollop of unsalted butter

Cook squash in a 5-quart Dutch oven or a large pot for 1½ hours, maintaining no more than a medium boil. Add water as needed. In a sauté skillet, melt butter and stir in mushrooms, zucchini, and tomatoes. Stir continuously until vegetables are tender. Set aside. Remove squash from pot and allow to cool slightly. Preheat oven to 350 degrees. Cut squash in half. Scoop out squash and place in a lightly greased casserole. Add vegetables, salt and pepper, and Parmesan, mixing until combined. Heat in oven until warmed through. Top with unsalted butter. Serves 4 to 6.

 MUSHROOMS ALBEMARLE

12 very large mushroom caps
1 pound pork sausage
1 green pepper, diced
½ red pepper, diced
½ medium red onion, diced
1½ teaspoons minced fresh garlic
¼ cup grated Parmesan
½ cup grated fontina cheese

Preheat oven to 400 degrees. Cook mushrooms in a large skillet until barely tender. Heat a large sauté pan on high and crumble sausage into pan a little at a time. Stir until sausage loses its pink color. Add vegetables and garlic and sauté until barely tender. Place mushrooms in a lightly greased, shallow casserole dish. Top with sausage and vegetables. Top with cheeses. Bake for 15 minutes. Serves 6 to 8.

 MINT SAUCE

½ cup sugar
¼ cup white wine vinegar
¼ cup water
10-ounce jar mint jelly
1 cup fresh mint leaves, chopped

In a small saucepan, combine sugar, vinegar, and water over medium heat. Add jelly and stir to incorporate. When jelly dissolves, add mint leaves. Do not let sauce cool, as it will harden. Serve over lamb. Yields about 2 cups.

CHAPTER 5

A Stroll Down Main Street

Log House 1776 Restaurant

We take issue with the statement, "If you walk along the main street on an August afternoon there is nothing whatsoever to do," written by Carson McCullers in *The Ballad of the Sad Café*. Perhaps she wasn't as fortunate as we have been in enjoying restaurants situated along quite interesting Main Streets. We're confident that once you visit one or two of these eateries, you'll agree. Wherever McCullers was, it certainly wasn't Main Street, Virginia!

LOG HOUSE 1776 RESTAURANT

520 East Main Street
Wytheville, VA 24382
276-228-4139

Sitting along the main thoroughfare in Wytheville is the Log House 1776 Restaurant. It seems that along about 1776, a young man decided to work for a large landowner and was granted permission to build a two-room tenant house on this site. During construction, the young man felt the stirrings of patriotism and went to fight for colonial freedom in the Revolutionary War. Little else is known about the young man other than that his name was Will. Because of this lack of information, some presume he may not have returned from battle to occupy the house he'd built.

A log addition was constructed in 1804. The remainder of the structure was erected in 1898. During the early 1800s, it was home to apprentices working for the Rich Brothers furniture factory. After mastering cabinetmaking, the apprentices moved on, starting many other furniture factories in the South. Rich Brothers produced a wide variety of products, including the well-known Wythe County pie safe, distinguished by its urn-and-tulip design on the tin inserts.

During the Civil War, the house was owned by Joseph Chadwell. Also living on the property in a smaller log cabin was Benjamin Steptoe, a freed slave, and his wife, who served as a nanny for the Chadwell children. Steptoe and Chadwell left together to fight for the Confederacy. When Chadwell was killed, Mrs. Steptoe and the newly widowed Mrs. Chadwell took a wagon, retrieved the body, and brought it back to Wytheville to be buried locally. Descendants of the Steptoes still live in the area.

Inside the log house today are two intimate dining rooms holding an eclectic mixture of five or six tables each. Both rooms have fireplaces with gas logs. I chose to sit facing one of them at a small table set for two. Each table was adorned with some type of antique fabric, whether quilted, tatted, or brocaded.

Nursing a cold, and dining alone since Karen was back in Pittsburgh, I opted for comfort food. On another occasion, I might have chosen the Fried Catfish, one of the several pasta dishes, or the Chicken Verde Pecan. I selected the Confederate Beef Stew, made from a recipe of the era and served with Coleslaw and Green Beans. A welcome treat was the warm bread just out of the oven, served on a pewter plate. The service was swift and attentive, and I was quickly too sated to attempt the delicious dessert offerings.

I visited on the brink of spring, a trifle early to enjoy the landscaping. The gardens on the property were established in memory of Abby Chadwell and Nancy Steptoe, who gardened together. It's been said that Nancy brought all the Chadwell children to the garden at seven o'clock each morning for thirty minutes of silence. By looking at the flowers and listening to the singing and chirping of the birds, Mrs. Chadwell and Mrs. Steptoe hoped to instill a love of and appreciation for nature. So, if the weather permits, savor the opportunity to indulge in the beauty of the garden and the depth of its history.

 CHICKEN MARENGO

4 6-ounce chicken breasts
20-ounce can plum tomatoes, drained
1½ cloves garlic, crushed
1½ tablespoons olive oil
2½ tablespoons tomato paste
¾ teaspoon sugar
¾ teaspoon parsley flakes
¾ teaspoon Italian seasoning
¾ teaspoon black pepper

1½ cups fresh mushrooms, sliced
2 tablespoons dry white wine
¼ cup green olives, sliced

Preheat oven to 350 degrees. Place chicken in a greased baking pan and cover with aluminum foil. Bake for about 20 minutes until center is no longer pink.

While chicken is baking, slice tomatoes into thirds and place in a medium saucepan. Add garlic, olive oil, tomato paste, sugar, parsley, Italian seasoning, and pepper. Simmer for 10 minutes. Remove from heat. Add mushrooms and wine, stirring well to combine. Remove chicken from oven and place on 4 plates. Spoon sauce over top and garnish with olives. Serves 4.

Note: This dish is said to have been a favorite of Thomas Jefferson. The chicken may be prepared by baking, broiling, or grilling, depending on your preference.

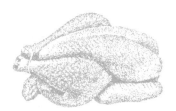

SINCE 1752

THE
SMITHFIELD INN

112 Main Street
Smithfield, VA 23430
757-357-1752

The pale yellow house with the shady porch lined with rocking chairs is known today as The Smithfield Inn. It was built in 1752 by Henry Woodely and is one of several eighteenth-century buildings still standing proudly in town. Old documents describe the original brick house as "upwards of 50 feet in length, with four rooms below and three above and a good cellar." In 1756, the property was sold to William Rand. Three years later, he applied for a tavern license. In 1792, the inn changed hands again, this time going to Mallory Todd, who rented it to various occupants. The vestry of Christ Episcopal Church took ownership in the mid-1850s and was responsible for significant repairs in 1875. The Goodsons, Gards, and Briggses called the place home in the early 1900s.

It remained relatively unchanged until proprietorship went to Mr. and Mrs. Daniel Sykes in 1922. The Sykeses renovated the kitchen and the dining-room wing, which allowed them to provide the home-cooked meals, leisurely formality, and refined service for which they became renowned. Duncan Hines wrote about the place, and it was featured in the *Mobil Travel Guide*—quite a distinction for its time! By the time Mrs. Sykes retired in 1968, the Sykes Inn had been a favorite dining destination of local residents for more than forty years.

After several interim owners, Joe Luter III and Smithfield Foods purchased the inn. Luter has ties to the Sykes family, and the inn has ties to the town of Smithfield, so it was a logical venture. Under the expert guidance of Janice Scott, The Smithfield Inn of today re-creates the luxury and gentility of the Old South in both the dining room and the guest suites. Elegant wall coverings provide a backdrop, while rich draperies and gilded frames add an exclamation point. Our favorite feature is the floral settees that provide seating at each table.

We arrived for a late lunch and were joined by Janice and Gretchen Heal, the marketing director for the inn. We each ordered something different, so it was fun to see the variety when lunch was served. The Grilled Salmon and Berry Salad was light and wonderfully refreshing. The Crab Salad, made with shrimp, lump crabmeat, avocado, cucumber, plum tomatoes, and baby lettuce, was served in a Red Chile Tortilla Bowl and topped with Lime-Horseradish Dressing. The Chunky Chicken Salad was a delicious combination of chicken, dried cherries, celery, toasted pecans, and Sour Cream Mayonnaise. Served on the side were two Smithfield Ham Biscuits, for which the inn is famous. Yum! A ramekin of Peanut Soup also arrived for us to taste. Wonderfully creamy, it was a delight to the taste buds. Then came the desserts. Janice insisted that we sample, so we did our level best to do each one justice. The Bread Pudding in Bourbon Sauce was excellent, as was the Apple Dumpling. Janice explained that she'd tried to move the Sweet Potato Pecan Pie to just the fall menu, but too many diners had requested it, so it's a year-round item. The caramelized glaze on the Crème Brûlée had just the right crunch, and the Lemon Chess Pie was so good we asked for the recipe.

For years, guests have been arriving at this inn. Some have come by sailing ship, others by stagecoach. Still more have come by steamboat, railroad, or car. But all have come for the same things—fine food and generous hospitality. We encourage you to treat yourself.

 CORN CUSTARD

2 teaspoons cornstarch
½ cup sugar
2 large eggs
12-ounce can evaporated milk
16-ounce can cream-style corn
¼ cup butter, melted

Preheat oven to 400 degrees. Combine first 3 ingredients in a large bowl. Add milk and corn. Mix well. Pour into a buttered 8-by-8-inch or 6-by-9-inch baking dish. Pour butter over top. Bake for about 50 minutes until custard has set but still jiggles or until a straw inserted in center comes out clean. Serves 6 to 8.

 GRILLED SALMON AND BERRY SALAD

4 cups mixed salad greens
2 cups iceberg lettuce
½ cup strawberries, quartered
½ cup blackberries
½ cup raspberries
2 tablespoons almond slivers, toasted
½ cup Raspberry Dressing
4 5-ounce salmon fillets, grilled

In a large bowl, combine greens and lettuce. Divide evenly among 4 serving plates or shallow bowls. Top each with ¼ of the fruits. Sprinkle with almonds, then drizzle with a Raspberry Dressing. Top each salad with a salmon fillet. Serve immediately. Serves 4.

circa 1888

The Joshua Wilton House
Inn and Restaurant

412 South Main Street
Harrisonburg, VA 22801
www.joshuawilton.com
540-434-4464

The Joshua Wilton House was built in 1888 by a gentleman of the same name. From Waterloo in the province of Ontario in Canada, he moved to Harrisonburg just after the Civil War. Here, he purchased significant acreage, became president of the First Virginia Bank, and was quite successful with his foundry and his hardware store, reaping the benefits of Reconstruction. Wilton quickly rose to prominence in the community. He was also instrumental in bringing electricity to the area.

Since Wilton was in the hardware business, it's not surprising that the construction quality of the home was top-notch. Both the interior and exterior walls are sixteen inches—or three bricks—thick. Craftsmen from all over the country were brought in to complete the hand-carved mantels and faux-marble fireplaces. The result was a showplace in which the Wiltons resided for forty years.

After the Wilton years, the house belonged to the Shenk family, who also had a forty-year tenure. After the children all left home and Mr. Shenk passed away, Mrs. Shenk briefly took in boarders. Some years later, the structure ceased being a family dwelling and took on the role of a frat house. Tau Kappa Epsilon bought the house in 1968 and retained the property over the next ten years. It's hard to imagine the elegant structure of today hosting Harrisonburg's version of the movie *Animal House*.

The Macher family subsequently purchased the home and converted it into apartments, which were rented primarily to college students. It's not surprising, then, that many visitors to The Joshua Wilton House today reminisce about either living here during their college days or at the very least having been to a party or two.

When Craig and Roberta Moore began renovations after buying the property in 1986, they were amazed at the number of valuable items that remained, after so many owners and so many college students. The original mantels and the leaded glass trimming the main entrance were both unharmed. The parquet floors, heavy oak doors, and gingerbread trim are original as well. After years of zoning battles and lots and lots of restoration, the doors of the inn finally opened in May 1988 on the hundredth anniversary of the house. The first guests were descendants of Joshua Wilton.

The restaurant is on the first floor of the home and the guest rooms upstairs. The menu changes slightly each day and is altered completely several times a year to take advantage of seasonal foods. Entrée choices such as Thai-Style Grilled New York Strip Steak and Moroccan Chicken Tagine present unique flavor combinations. The Grilled Shrimp, served over rice noodles with Poached Asian Pears and Hawaiian Pesto, was a gastronomic treat. Equally unusual was the Chorizo Sausage-Stuffed Quail, served over Cinnamon-Scented Risotto.

We arrived for a late dinner after a very busy day. The understated elegance of the dining rooms encouraged us to unwind. We did just that, dining on Corn and Crab Chowder, a Spinach Salad tossed with ruby red grapefruit, red onion, and avocado, and an entrée of Wild Rockfish. It's obvious why reviews describe The Joshua Wilton House as "serving the most exquisite food in town."

VENISON MEDALLIONS WITH SWEET POTATO PURÉE

3 pounds sweet potatoes
2 tablespoons olive oil, divided
1 venison leg, deboned and
   trimmed to medallions
salt and pepper to taste
2 tablespoons butter
2 tablespoons brown sugar
Maple Balsamic Sauce (recipe follows)

Preheat oven to 350 degrees. Oil sweet potatoes with 1 tablespoon of the olive oil. Place in oven and roast until tender. While potatoes are cooking, season medallions with salt and pepper. Heat remaining oil in a skillet. Pan-sear medallions in hot oil, browning on all sides until medium-rare. Set aside and keep warm. In a large mixing bowl, whip potatoes, butter, and sugar. Keep warm. To serve, arrange medallions around a generous dollop of sweet potatoes and top with Maple Balsamic Sauce. Serves 6.

Maple Balsamic Sauce

1 cup balsamic vinegar
1 cup maple syrup
3 slices bacon, cooked and chopped
1 tablespoon minced shallots
1 cup veal stock
1 cup Pinot Noir

Combine vinegar and syrup in a medium saucepan. Bring to a simmer over medium heat. Reduce by half. Add bacon and shallots. Continue to reduce. Add stock and wine and reduce again by half. Strain and reserve. Yields about 1½ cups.

7783 Main Street
Middletown, VA 22645
www.waysideofva.com
540-869-1797

If the oft-told story of George Washington cutting down the cherry tree is truly fiction, then the Wayside Inn can be credited with perpetuating the popular myth. A majority of the inn's dining rooms pay homage to our first president with portraits, prints, and other memorabilia, including a ring containing a lock of Washington's hair. Whimsically displayed in the dining room is the very stump that little Georgie is purported to have chopped.

The inn opened in 1797 as Wilkenson's Tavern to provide bed and board for travelers along the Black Bear Trail. In the early 1800s, it became a stagecoach stop and a relay station. Because of the rough terrain and uncertainties along the Valley Pike (now US 11), schedules fluctuated greatly. The inn employed a young boy to scan the horizon from a nearby hill for approaching stagecoaches. When he spotted one, he ran back to alert the cook. Fires were quickly rekindled so famished passengers didn't have to wait for their repast.

Although the first service to travelers started here in the late 1700s, a portion of the inn dates back to 1742. It was built from bricks made in the 1600s and then brought over as ballast for sailing vessels. The ceilings in that section of the structure are low, presumably because the average person's height was less than it is today. Plank tables and the original brick fireplace complete the ambiance of a centuries-old tavern.

During the Civil War, the inn was a haven for soldiers on both sides. Many sought refuge here during the strife. Although one soldier was shot in the back as he crossed the threshold, the inn was largely spared the ravages that the conflict brought to so many other buildings. That is perhaps even more surprising since Stonewall Jackson's famous Valley Campaign of 1862 passed within a few miles of the inn. Later in the war, the Battle of Cedar Creek also took place nearby. It commenced on October 19, 1864, when Confederate troops under General Jubal Early surprised the Eighth and Ninth Federal Corps. Initially, the engagement was a rout for the Confederates, but General Philip Sheridan arrived from Winchester to rally his men. By afternoon, he launched a decisive counterattack, regained the battlefield, and effectively broke the back of the Confederate army in the Shenandoah Valley. Public sentiment surrounding this victory and Sheridan's successes in Georgia helped Lincoln win reelection at a critical juncture.

After the conflict ended, Jacob Larrick bought the inn and changed the name to

Larrick's Hotel. It was sold in the early 1900s to Samuel Rhodes, who christened it the Wayside Inn. In the 1960s, a Washington financier and antique collector took the helm, filling the inn with myriad pieces of Americana. A devastating fire in 1985 almost closed the inn for good. Fortunately for travelers venturing down that same valley road today, they can still stop in for home-style dishes such as Spoon Bread, Peanut Soup, and Chicken Pot Pie and also partake of such offerings as Roasted Vegetable and Penne Pasta, Steak Jameson, and Prime Rib. When they do, they'll experience what's billed as America's longest continuously operating inn.

 SPOON BREAD

1 quart milk
3 tablespoons butter
3 tablespoons sugar
3 eggs, separated
1¼ cups cornmeal

Preheat oven to 400 degrees. Bring milk to a boil with butter and sugar in a large saucepan. In a small bowl, whip egg whites until stiff. Add cornmeal to milk and cook for 3 minutes, stirring constantly until quite stiff. Beat egg yolks until pale yellow. Remove cornmeal mixture from heat and stir in egg yolks. Allow to cool. Fold in egg whites and bake in a shallow casserole dish for 20 to 30 minutes until lightly browned. Serves 10.

PEANUT SOUP

1 stalk celery, diced fine
1 medium carrot, diced fine
1 small onion, diced fine
3½ cups chicken stock
1 cup creamy peanut butter
13-ounce can evaporated milk
dash of sugar

In a large saucepan, sauté celery, carrots, and onions until tender. Add stock and bring to a boil. Reduce heat. Gradually add peanut butter, stirring constantly. Mixture may stiffen at first but will become smooth. Add evaporated milk and sugar. Heat through but do not boil. Strain and discard vegetables. Serves 6.

The WILLSON-WALKER HOUSE Restaurant

30 North Main Street
Lexington, VA 24450
www.willsonwalker.com
540-463-3020

As is the case with many historic homes, the Willson-Walker House is named for two of the more significant families that occupied the structure.

William Willson was a local merchant and postmaster and the treasurer of Washington College. He commissioned this home to be built in 1820. The property consisted of the main house, an icehouse, a smokehouse, a stable, a carriage house, two other outbuildings, and a large garden. This was documented by an advertisement in the *Lexington Gazette* on June 29, 1838, announcing that the homestead was for sale. The ad did not achieve results. Willson's wife, Sally, ultimately sold the property at auction ten years after her husband's death. James Paxton, Lexington's first mayor, was the top bidder at three thousand dollars.

A year later, Main and Washington Streets in Lexington were lowered by six to eight feet in an effort to diminish the traffic problems resulting from the steep grades on both thoroughfares. The exterior of the home had to be modified to accommodate those changes. The portico had to be set on a high foundation, and the front door was moved to the side of the house.

After the Paxtons' tenure, the home belonged to a succession of families well known in the area. Hugh Lyle Wilson, Calvin McCorkle, and Alexander Glasgow all set up residence at some point prior to 1911.

When Harry Walker bought the house that year, he converted it to a meat market and grocery store. To suit his purposes, the doors and windows were altered, and the porch and first floor were lowered to street level. Walker also had the front door moved back to the Main Street side of the house. Today, it's hard to imagine the elegant interior being used as a butcher shop!

In 1983, Josephine Griswold purchased the building and restored its pre-1911 facade. The result is a lovely red-brick structure with an inviting two-story porch trimmed with a white railing and supported by four grand Doric columns. The interior was transformed into two high-ceilinged dining rooms with burgundy walls, each with a faux-marble mantel surmounting its fireplace. The lighting is subdued, mirrored wall sconces creating an intimate atmosphere.

The menu is as appealing as the surroundings. The Potato-Crusted Trout, featured in an issue of *Blue Ridge Country* magazine, is a popular choice. The Salmon and Crab Crustada certainly caught my eye, as did the Reuben Quesadilla. Even the House

Salad has a special twist, topped with caramelized walnuts and served with a choice of interesting salad dressings such as Honey Raspberry or Champagne Vinaigrette. For dinner, the Pear Florentine Salad, the BBQ Shrimp Kabobs with Grilled Pineapple Salsa, and the Grilled Vegetable and Chicken Strudel all sounded scrumptious. The guests at the next table, who were celebrating their wedding anniversary, found the Crab and Lobster Soup so wonderful that I asked my server to bring me a sample. It was really good! Since Debbie was dining elsewhere, I saved half of the fabulous Maple Pecan Cheesecake Pie for her to taste. After all, good food is meant to be shared with friends.

 POTATO-CRUSTED TROUT

½ cup clarified butter
2 Idaho potatoes
2 8-ounce trout, deboned
generous pinch of salt
¼ cup butter
1 teaspoon lemon juice
1 teaspoon chopped chives
2 lemon wheels or wedges for garnish

Heat clarified butter in a nonstick sauté pan over high heat. While pan is getting hot, grate potatoes and squeeze out all water. Sprinkle trout with salt, then press grated potatoes on the flesh. When pan has just started to smoke, place trout potato side down in hot butter. After about 2 minutes, potatoes will be brown and crispy. Carefully remove butter and flip trout. Continue cooking an additional 2 minutes. In a small bowl, combine ¼ cup butter, lemon juice, and chives. To serve, top each trout with half of butter mixture and garnish with lemon. Serves 2.

The Highland Inn
Main Street
Monterey, VA 24465
540-468-2143

Even though Karen wasn't along to help me enjoy it, the drive north on US 220 was fabulous! It was a sunny summer day when I made the sojourn. The mountains and the lush greenery of George Washington National Forest were spectacular. Add to that a rushing mountain stream and pale pink mountain laurel in full bloom, and the scenery can't get much better. My destination that morning was the hamlet of Monterey, which sits just seven miles south of the West Virginia border. Originally, the town was called Highland, but the name was changed when Zachary Taylor was elected president of the United States. Monterey was chosen in recognition of General Taylor's military victory at the Battle of Monterey, Mexico.

This area is known as "Virginia's Switzerland" because of its beautiful mountainous terrain. In the early 1900s, it was a popular destination for wealthy citizens looking to escape the summer heat of lowland cities.

Sitting along Monterey's Main Street, spanning much of a city block, is The Highland Inn. Built in 1904 and dubbed "the Pride of the Mountains," this landmark hotel graciously served its clientele for seventy-five years under the name Hotel Monterey. The original owner was local businessman Silas Crummett, who paid just six thousand dollars for the three-story structure. One of the best architectural features of the hotel has always been its elaborate Eastlake-style two-level porch. It's easy to imagine guests such as Henry Ford, Harvey Firestone, and John Philip Sousa seated in rocking chairs and relaxing in a cool breeze on this very porch. German general Erwin Rommel is said to have been an extended guest while in the United States studying the battle tactics of Stonewall Jackson.

Following Silas Crummett's tenure, the hotel passed to the Patterson family. During the Pattersons' time, it functioned as a lively social center for the community. The Carwells were the next to take possession. Their years were marred by a tragic fire in 1919, the poisoning death of Mrs. Carwell, and the disappearance and subsequent death of Mr. Carwell. Eventually, the Showalters took control. Mrs. Showalter, known as a gracious and competent hostess, has been credited with the foresight and perseverance that allowed the structure to survive to the present.

Today, the inn is in the capable hands of Gregg and Deborah Morse. Its clean white exterior trimmed with green shutters sends visitors back more than a few decades. Inside, the Victorian feel of the lobby continues the illusion that guests are caught up in a lovely time warp. Meals are served in either the Monterey Dining Room or the more casual Black Sheep Tavern. A buffet on Sundays and one night a week allows diners to sample a wide variety of regional American cuisine. On other evenings and at Saturday lunch, guests can order from the menu, perhaps selecting the popular Rainbow Trout, the Maple Mustard Pork Tenderloin, or the Pecan-Crusted Chicken with Ginger Mayonnaise. And for dessert, the delicious Maple Pecan Pie is too good to pass up.

 PECAN-CRUSTED CHICKEN WITH GINGER MAYONNAISE

1 egg
2 tablespoons milk
2 6-ounce boneless, skinless chicken breasts
¼ cup flour
½ cup finely chopped pecans
2 tablespoons mayonnaise
2 teaspoons ginger

Preheat oven to 350 degrees. In a small bowl, mix egg and milk, beating until well combined to form an egg wash. Dredge chicken in flour, then put through egg wash. Press chicken into chopped pecans so it is coated on both sides. Place chicken in a lightly greased baking dish. Bake for 20 to 25 minutes until done. While chicken is cooking, combine mayonnaise and ginger. When chicken is done, top each breast with a tablespoon of Ginger Mayonnaise before serving. Serves 2.

 MAPLE PECAN PIE

1 cup pecan halves
½ cup maple syrup
½ cup light Karo syrup
3 eggs
1 cup light brown sugar
1 tablespoon cornstarch
9-inch deep-dish piecrust, unbaked

Preheat oven to 350 degrees. In a large bowl, combine first 6 ingredients. Pour into piecrust. Bake for about 1 hour until center is firm. Cool to room temperature before cutting. Yields 1 pie.

 COLD OVEN POUND CAKE

1 cup shortening
⅓ cup butter
3 cups sugar
5 eggs
3 cups all-purpose flour
1 cup evaporated milk
2 teaspoons vanilla

Cream together shortening, butter, and sugar. Beat in eggs 1 at a time. Add flour, milk, and vanilla. Place in a greased and floured 10-inch tube pan. Place in a cold oven. Turn oven on to 350 degrees. Bake for 1¼ to 1½ hours until a toothpick inserted in center comes out clean. Serves 12 to 16.

Toliver House Restaurant

209 North Main Street
Gordonsville, VA 22942
540-832-3485

This great old house, built in 1874, retains its original charm. Overlooking Main Street, the two-story building has watched the world go by for more than a century. It offers three dining rooms and the Nathaniel Gordon Room, an intimate drinking establishment next to the kitchen. The light, airy dining rooms have wooden floors, lace curtains, and linen-clad tables. The more down-to-earth bar area has wooden tables and chairs and a jukebox in the corner. The bar is small but well stocked. It's clear that this room is favored by locals and out-of-town visitors alike. In the summer, guests can laze around outside on the old-fashioned front porch while waiting for their meals.

The walls of this establishment are covered with myriad photos, most of which were taken locally. We both noted how little many of Gordonsville's buildings have changed over the years. Toliver House is one of them. Constructed as a home, it has served the area well as a general store, a nursing home, apartments, and now a res-

taurant. Today, it's very much a local hot spot, offering live entertainment on weekends by groups such as the Irish favorite Rye Grass Rollers. Even the jukebox is much in demand. On balmy nights, visitors pull back the tables and chairs and dance in a convivial atmosphere redolent of the past.

Mike DeCanio, the current owner, was a teacher who somehow fell into the business of running a restaurant. He prides himself on the fact that the soups, sauces, and dressings are all homemade. Mike chatted with us on the day we visited, in between trips to the tiny kitchen to ensure that meals were prepared perfectly and promptly. The cuisine is unashamedly American, starting with appetizers such as Crab Cakes, Smoked Salmon, and Mushroom Caps Bourguignon. We were both tempted by the Brunswick Stew, Mike's own concoction of chicken, tomatoes, lima beans, and corn, and the homemade Onion Soup, which had just a hint of Madeira and melted Gruyère cheese.

Each entrée on the dinner menu has an interesting name. Mike's signature dish is the Taliaferro, which consists of large broiled shrimp served with lobster, butter, and sherry. Karen would have chosen the Winchester Pork Loin Cutlets Milanese in Tomato Cream Caper Sauce, while Debbie was more interested in the Blue Ridge, an herb-crusted breast of chicken in a pool of Roasted Garlic Sauce.

Since we were visiting at lunchtime, we both opted for one of the special house sandwiches. Debbie loved the Smoked Pork Barbecue and Karen the New Orleans Peacemaker, which consisted of fried oysters on a toasted sub roll with lettuce, tomato, and Creole-Style Tartar Sauce. Each sandwich arrived with a Breaded Deep-Fried Pickle Spear—delicious!

If you want to visit Toliver House, be sure to make reservations, especially if you are visiting at lunchtime, since Mike does not always open for lunch. But whenever you come, you're sure to have a scrumptious meal. And if you like to dance, put a quarter in the jukebox.

CELERY SEED DRESSING

½ teaspoon salt
1 cup chopped red onion
1 cup sugar
1 teaspoon Dijon mustard
¾ cup red wine vinegar
2 cups vegetable oil
2 tablespoons celery seed

Place salt, onions, sugar, and mustard in a food processor and blend thoroughly. With processor running, add vinegar until well blended. With processor running, add oil very slowly in a fine stream. Allow to completely blend for 2 minutes. Add celery seed and pulse momentarily to blend. Yields 3 cups.

CHICKEN BREASTS IN TOMATO CREAM CAPER SAUCE

2 tablespoons butter
½ tablespoon chopped garlic
¼ teaspoon red pepper flakes
2 cups tomatoes, drained and puréed
½ cup heavy cream
1 teaspoon thyme
2 tablespoons parsley
3 tablespoons capers, drained
½ cup flour
2 eggs
1 cup fresh breadcrumbs
¼ cup Romano cheese, grated fine
4 chicken breasts
2 tablespoons olive oil

In a large sauté pan, melt butter over medium heat and sauté garlic and red pepper flakes for about 3 minutes. Add tomatoes and sauté for an additional 3 minutes. Add cream, thyme, and parsley and reduce for about 10 minutes until mixture reaches desired consistency. Stir in capers and set aside.

Place flour in a small, flat dish. In another small, flat dish, beat eggs. In a third flat dish, combine breadcrumbs and cheese. Dip chicken in flour, then eggs, then breadcrumb mixture.

Preheat oven to 350 degrees. In a large ovenproof sauté pan, heat oil over medium heat. Sauté chicken for about 3 minutes on each side until golden brown. Place pan in oven for 15 minutes. Serve chicken with sauce. Serves 4.

The Mimslyn Inn

401 West Main Street
Luray, VA 22835
www.mimslyninn.com
540-743-5105

Henry Brooks Mims and his lovely wife, Elizabeth, were experienced innkeepers. In the late 1800s and early 1900s, they owned and operated the old Lawrence Hotel on the corner of Main and Court Streets and the Mansion Inn on Main Street in Luray. They were a close-knit family who determined from the start to bring their two sons, Ralph and John, into the business. Unfortunately, Henry Mims died rather earlier than expected. But this did not deter Elizabeth and her two sons from purchasing the old Borst Mansion on the west side of Luray as the site for a brand-new hotel. The old mansion, a hospital during the Civil War, was moved to Court Street, and the Mims family brought in a coal-fired steam shovel all the way from Richmond to begin excavation for their new hotel.

Thus, The Mimslyn Inn was born. The Mimses envisioned a grand Colonial-style structure reminiscent of the Old South. They succeeded beautifully in the large, imposing brick building with enormous white columns, set back from the road on fourteen acres of lawns and formal gardens. The Mims Material Company provided the wherewithal for construction. And in keeping with the family tradition, many products from Virginia were used. The bricks were made in Glasgow, Virginia. The slate for the roof was quarried in Buckingham, Virginia. The bathroom tile was from Roanoke. The window frames were made on site by a local blacksmith. J. R. Mims designed the winding staircase and closely supervised its construction.

Eventually, the inn was opened for an afternoon housewarming party. The *Luray Page News and Courier* carried the word that "over 700 guests enjoyed dining and dancing as they looked in wonder at the Mimslyn's modern facilities." The Mims family continued to own and operate the inn until 1974. Current owners Mr. and Mrs. Wayne Alexander of Chester purchased the inn in 1984.

The main dining room, just a few short steps up from the impressive lobby with its large fireplace and winding staircase, remains the same as ever. The large fan windows on two sides and the high ceiling gave the room a bright and sunny feel on the morning I visited. The windows allow guests to enjoy a panoramic view of the surrounding mountains and the valley below. I was sorry Debbie wasn't along to enjoy the scenery. One can imagine the weddings and family functions that have taken place in the grand dining room over the years. I was intrigued to notice the framed pink-and-green floral plate, a single piece from the service especially commissioned for The Mimslyn Inn in 1940.

The dining room is extremely popular with the local populace and visitors alike. The à la carte dinner menu is short and simple but very appealing. I probably would have opted for the Stuffed Mushrooms with Crab Imperial, followed by the Apple Sausage-Stuffed Porkchops or the Beef Tenderloin Tips in Bordelaise Sauce.

The buffet-style lunch is an incredible value for the money. On the day I visited, the two entrées were Manicotti and Chicken Marsala. The accompaniments included Parsley Buttered Potatoes, Peas and Carrots, and Roasted Yellow Squash with Tomatoes, all of which I enjoyed. The selection of homemade desserts included Strawberry Pie, Lemon Chiffon Pie, Pecan Pie, Chocolate Mousse Pie, and Cinnamon Apple Bread Pudding. Thanks to offerings like these, a meal at The Mimslyn Inn is sure to be satisfying.

 CRAB IMPERIAL

1 egg
1 egg yolk
¼ teaspoon Worcestershire sauce
3 drops Tabasco
½ cup mayonnaise
½ teaspoon brown mustard
1 teaspoon Old Bay seasoning
⅛ teaspoon salt
1 pound lump crabmeat
½ tablespoon green pepper, diced fine
½ tablespoon red pepper, diced fine
1 cup breadcrumbs

Preheat oven to 350 degrees. In a medium bowl, combine egg, egg yolk, Worcestershire, Tabasco, mayonnaise, and mustard. Add Old Bay and salt and mix well. In another bowl, combine crabmeat, green peppers, red peppers, and breadcrumbs. Fold egg mixture into crab mixture. Place in a 9-by-9-inch ovenproof casserole dish and bake for 20 minutes. Serves 4 as an appetizer.

OYSTERS CASINO

15 strips bacon
3 cups butter
1 large green pepper, chopped fine
5 ounces mushrooms, chopped fine
4 ounces shallots, chopped fine
¼ cup pimentos, chopped fine
30 oysters on the half shell

Preheat oven to 475 degrees. In a medium sauté pan, half-cook bacon on both sides. Remove from heat, drain, and cut each slice into 4 pieces. Set aside. In another medium sauté pan, melt butter. Sauté peppers, mushrooms, shallots, and pimentos until soft. Drain vegetables and divide among oysters. Top each oyster with 2 pieces of bacon. Place prepared oysters on a large baking sheet and bake for 15 minutes. Serve immediately. Serves 12 as an appetizer.

The
MARTHA WASHINGTON INN
A Camberley Hotel

150 West Main Street
Abingdon, VA 24210
www.marthawashingtoninn.com
540-623-3161

The Martha Washington Inn was built in 1832 for just under fifteen thousand dollars as a private residence for General Francis Preston and his wife, Sara. Preston was a lawyer, a member of the state senate of Virginia, and a brigadier general in the War of 1812. His wife was the niece of well-known statesman Patrick Henry. Unfortunately, General Preston did not enjoy his lovely home for long, passing away in 1835. Fortunately, the couple was blessed with fifteen children. The first son, William, rose to prominence as the governor of South Carolina, while daughter Susanna once served as the first lady of Virginia while her husband, James McDowell, was governor. Daughter Sarah was also a first lady. Other children and grandchildren went on to marry into many prominent families of the day.

Today, the home is the epitome of genteel Southern hospitality. The elegant brick structure with a third-story mansard roof sits proudly along Abingdon's Main Street. The original living room of the home now functions as the lobby of the inn. The grand stairway and the parlors are much as they were during the nineteenth century. The rare, elaborate Dutch Baroque grandfather clock was shipped from England by one of the Prestons' daughters. Over nine feet tall, it sits in the east parlor.

In 1858, the Preston family sold the property, making way for the home's transformation into a women's college. In honor of the first lady of our nation, the upscale school was named Martha Washington College. The Civil War had a profound effect on the institution, as its students became nurses and its campus became a training ground for the Washington Mounted Rifles. During the war, there were frequent skirmishes in and around Abingdon. The wounded soldiers of both sides were cared for here at "the Martha," as locals affectionately dubbed it. It was during that time that many legends and ghost stories about the property began to circulate.

Although Martha Washington College survived the Civil War, the Depression, typhoid fever, and declining enrollment took their toll, forcing the school to close in 1932. For a while, the facility was used to house actors and actresses appearing across the street at the Barter Theater, the longest-running professional resident theater in America. Notables such as Patricia Neal, Ned Beatty, and Ernest Borgnine are a few of the prominent performers who worked here early in their careers.

In 1935, the lovely mansion took on the role it has today, that of an inn providing luxury to its guests. Eleanor Roosevelt, Harry Truman, Lady Bird Johnson, Jimmy Carter, and Elizabeth Taylor have all been guests here.

Breakfast in the Martha's dining room is certainly a great way to start the day. Karen enjoyed an unusual Spicy Crawfish and Scrambled Egg Taco, while Debbie savored the Sweet Potato Pancakes. The luncheon and dinner menus provide tastes of traditional Southern fare while catering to today's eclectic appetites. *Tradition* is an appropriate word for everything The Martha Washington Inn embodies. You'll be wise to visit and start a tradition of your own.

TROUT SOUTHERN TRADITION WITH CRABMEAT STUFFING

1 tablespoon clarified butter
¼ cup chopped celery
⅓ cup sliced green onions
¼ cup chopped bell pepper
½ teaspoon minced garlic
1 teaspoon fresh chopped thyme
1 teaspoon fresh tarragon
⅓ cup grated white cheddar
6 ounces lump crabmeat
salt and pepper to taste
4 rainbow trout, deboned and butterflied
½ cup yellow cornmeal
¼ cup peanut oil
2 cups sliced mushrooms
¼ cup bourbon
¼ cup Southern Comfort
2 cups heavy cream
2 teaspoons white-wine Worcestershire sauce
2 tablespoons cold butter

Heat clarified butter in a sauté pan. Add celery, onions, bell peppers, garlic, thyme, and tarragon. Sauté for about 5 minutes until celery is just softened. Remove from heat. When cooled to room temperature, add cheese and crabmeat. Mix well. Add salt and pepper. Divide stuffing among trout and fill each fish. Press together firmly. Preheat oven to 325 degrees. Dredge trout in cornmeal. Heat oil in a large skillet. Place trout in skillet and lightly brown for about 2 minutes per side. Remove from pan and place on an ovenproof platter. Bake for 12 to 15 minutes. While baking, drain all but 1 teaspoon of oil from skillet. Add mushrooms and sauté for 3 minutes. Carefully add bourbon and Southern Comfort. *This will flame if you're not careful.* Cook until reduced to ¼ cup. Add cream and Worcestershire. Reduce until well thickened. Remove from heat. Add cold butter in small pieces, shaking pan to incorporate. To serve, place each trout on a plate and spoon sauce over top. Serves 4.

Hilda Crockett's Chesapeake House

Main Street
Tangier Island, VA 23410
757-891-2331

A visit to Hilda Crockett's Chesapeake House can be summed up in one statement: It's an experience. To begin with, access to Tangier Island is by passenger ferry. There are no cars on the island because the roads are too narrow. Ferries leave from Reedville and Onancock at midmorning and return at midafternoon, which leaves plenty of time to partake of the restaurant's all-you-can-eat feast. The fixed-price meals include Clam Fritters, Baked Virginia Ham, Potato Salad, Coleslaw, Pickled Beets, Applesauce, Green Beans, Corn Pudding, Chesapeake Bay Crab Cakes, Rolls, and Pound Cake.

The menu has remained the same through several generations. Hilda Crockett, a descendant of one of the English families who settled the island, started the restaurant with only a dime to her name. She borrowed the money to purchase the white frame house and then prepared meals to help make the mortgage payments. At first, her primary customers were hunters and traveling sales-men—or drummers, as they were called then. Her home-cooked meals quickly became legendary. Before long, people were standing in line to dine at the Chesapeake House. Her daughter, Bette B, operated the restaurant from 1974 until October 2002, using the same successful recipes that brought her mother success. Today, Denny and Glenna Crockett have taken the helm, but that's about all that's changed.

Breakfast is served for overnight guests on the island and for those with alternate transportation. Like lunch and dinner, it's all you can eat for one fixed price. Scrambled Eggs, Bacon, Virginia Ham, Chesapeake-Style Fried Potatoes, Fried Bread, and other items are available to start your day. As one advertisement for the restaurant reads, "If you leave hungry, it will be your fault, not ours." We certainly did not leave hungry, enjoying every bite of everything that was offered. As expected, we had to wait a bit, but the pace of life on the island is so serene that it's impossible to be impatient.

At times, little appears to have changed since Captain John Smith, on an exploratory mission for England, purchased Tangier in 1608 for the price of two overcoats. At that time, the island consisted of six ridges rising above the marsh. Only three of those are inhabited today, with Main Ridge being the center of town.

According to local lore, it was in 1686 that John Crockett and his eight sons became the first to settle here, but nothing has been found to verify this. The first Crockett on record may have been Joseph, who bought 475 acres of land in 1778. Other histories declare William Crockett the island's first settler. He had only a prayer book to read until 1775, when a merchant-ship captain gave him a Bible. That gift caused such a stir that many families came for nightly Bible readings.

In 1800, the census showed the population of Tangier to be seventy-nine, most of whom were Crocketts or descendants of Crocketts. Today, not much has changed with the Crockett lineage or their way of life. A local pamphlet explains, "Our quaint ways may be misunderstood as slow, but time is abundant here and we wish it not away."

CLAM FRITTERS

2 cups clams
1 teaspoon pepper
1 cup pancake flour
½ teaspoon salt
1 egg, beaten
½ cup milk
oil for frying

Put clams through a meat grinder, then place them in a medium bowl. Add pepper, flour, salt, egg, and enough milk to make a stiff batter. Drop by small spoonfuls into hot oil and fry until golden brown. Drain on paper towels. Serves 6.

CORN PUDDING

½ cup to 1 cup sugar
3 tablespoons cornstarch
2 eggs, beaten
16-ounce can white cream-style corn
5⅓-ounce can evaporated milk
2 tablespoons butter

Preheat oven to 350 degrees. In a large mixing bowl, combine sugar and cornstarch, sweetening the mixture to your personal taste. Add eggs and mix until blended. Pour in corn and milk and mix thoroughly. Grease a 1½-quart ovenproof casserole and pour in corn mixture. Dot with cubes of butter and bake for about 1 hour. Serves 4 to 6.

POUND CAKE

1½ cups butter
3 cups sugar
6 eggs
2 tablespoons lemon extract
1 tablespoon vanilla extract
3 cups flour
1 teaspoon baking powder
1 cup milk

Preheat oven to 350 degrees. Prepare a Bundt pan by greasing it with shortening and dusting it with flour. In a large bowl, cream butter and sugar until light and fluffy. Beat in eggs 2 at a time. Continue beating while adding extracts. Sift flour and baking powder together. Reduce speed on mixer. Beginning and ending with flour, add flour mixture alternately with milk. Bake for about 1 hour until a toothpick inserted in center comes out clean. Do not overbake. Serves 16.

Candelora's
at the Purcellville Inn

36855 West Main Street
Purcellville, VA 20132
540-338-2075

The Purcellville Inn, beautifully restored to its former glory, now houses an elegant restaurant on the first floor and a cozy tavern in the basement. Surrounded by trees and overlooking the local golf course, it is a lovely setting. The dining room is painted a pale yellow that is echoed in the elegant swags and jabots hanging at each window. Brass candlestick sconces ring the walls, marble sculptures complete the European décor, and the polished wooden floors, fresh flowers, and candles add an air of romance. In the winter, guests are seated close to the fireplaces. In the summer, the large outdoor patio is the dining area of choice. It's an ideal place to linger over a glass of excellent wine and an appetizer.

We arrived on a cold spring day for lunch at the tavern. The atmosphere was friendly and the wait staff efficient. The tavern is small but comfortable. The yellow stucco walls and stone fireplace are cheerful, as were the patrons at the small wooden bar. There were only six or seven small tables for lunch, but we had been told that the food was worth the wait.

Chef and owner Frederick Petrello is very proud to offer a selection of the most delicious homemade Italian dishes. He enjoys creating the many old favorites served here, as well as the innovative and interesting new items on the menu. The Lamb Sausage Provençale (served with Mushroom-Tomato Demi Sauce), the Shrimp Adriana (featuring fresh shrimp sautéed with sun-dried tomatoes and artichoke hearts and served with Rose-Cream Sauce), and the Veal Saltimbocca (in which the veal medallions are sautéed with sage, prosciutto, and garlic) all sounded absolutely delicious.

Of course, the menu has a large number of pasta selections, such as Fusilli Petrello and Sausage Alfredo. For the more conservative patrons, the traditional Pasta Primavera or the Cannelloni of the Day will definitely hit the spot!

We had some difficulty deciding what to sample but ended up trying Uncle Joe's Portabello Boule Sandwich, served with roasted red peppers and Goat Cheese Spread. We simply had to taste one of the pasta dishes and so consulted the other diners about our choice. The Ravioli Pomodoro was the hands-down favorite. Lunch was great, and we were full to the brim. But when you visit, do make sure to leave room for dessert. According to the locals, both the Cannoli and the homemade Spumoni are can't-miss items.

The next time we're in town, we've already decided to sample the Sunday brunch menu. It includes Pane Romano—thick slices of bread marinated in eggs and cinnamon and served grilled with fresh berries, syrup, and powdered sugar. It's a real treat to savor. As chef Petrello would say, *bouno appetito*!

SAUSAGE AND ZITI PEPERONATA

1 pound ziti
¼ cup plus 1 teaspoon extravirgin olive oil, divided
1 pound sweet fennel sausage
¼ cup water
1 tablespoon chopped garlic
1 cup green julienned bell pepper
½ teaspoon basil
½ teaspoon oregano
16-ounce can tomatoes, crushed
salt and pepper to taste
4 slices mozzarella

Preheat oven to 350 degrees. Cook ziti according to package directions until al dente. Drain. When cool, toss pasta with 1 teaspoon of the olive oil to prevent sticking. Set aside. Place sausage and water in a small ovenproof container and bake for about 20 minutes until completely cooked. Remove from oven and drain. When cool, slice sausage and set aside.

In an ovenproof skillet, heat remaining olive oil and garlic. Be careful not to burn garlic. Add bell peppers, basil, and oregano and sauté until translucent. Add tomatoes and sausage. Season to taste. Allow to simmer for 10 minutes. Add cooled pasta to skillet and toss to combine. Top skillet with mozzarella and place in oven for about 5 minutes until cheese is golden brown. Serve immediately. Serves 2.

SHRIMP AND BOWTIE PASTA POMODORO

1 pound bowtie pasta
¼ cup plus 1 teaspoon extravirgin olive oil, divided
1 tablespoon chopped garlic
1 tablespoon chopped scallions
1 pound fresh pink medium shrimp, cleaned and deveined
6 large tomatoes, cored and chopped
¼ cup fresh basil, julienned
¼ cup fish stock
¼ cup butter
salt and pepper to taste
Parmesan for garnish
2 sprigs fresh basil for garnish

Cook pasta according to package directions until al dente. Drain. When cool, toss pasta with 1 teaspoon of the olive oil to prevent sticking. Set aside. In a large, deep skillet, heat remaining oil, garlic, and scallions. When garlic and scallions are brown, add shrimp, tomatoes, and basil and bring to a simmer. Allow to cook for 10 minutes. Add fish stock and butter and season to taste. Remove from heat. Add pasta and toss well. Plate pasta and garnish with Parmesan and fresh basil. Serves 2.

CHAPTER 6
There's a Tavern in the Town

Rice's Hotel / Hughlett's Tavern

"There is nothing which has yet been contrived by man by which so much happiness is produced as by a good tavern or inn." So said the prolific writer Samuel Johnson in March 1776. The essence of Johnson's comment is reflected in the establishments in this chapter. Some of these taverns have a more modern ambiance than in their early days, while others have retained their rustic charm. All serve up the enjoyment of good company combined with great food. Enjoy!

The
TAVERN

222 East Main Street
Abingdon, VA 24210
276-628-5795

The range of entrées here is quite varied. The Trout is given some zip with Jalapeño Cilantro Sauce. The Filet Mignon is stuffed with spinach, shrimp, bacon, ricotta, and cream cheese. The Scallops are finished with Basil Cream Sauce before being topped with cheddar and Parmesan. The Carbonara Florentine is offered in four variations. Since this is a "scratch kitchen" where each entrée is made fresh upon being ordered, it makes the variety all the more impressive. Each entrée is served with a salad featuring one of The Tavern's homemade dressings. If the rest are as good as the Garlic Parmesan, they're all winners.

The restaurant is housed in a building that is the oldest in Abingdon and one of the oldest west of the Blue Ridge. Built in 1779, it was used as a tavern and inn for stagecoach travelers. Guests here have included such notables as orator Henry Clay; Louis Philippe, king of France; President Andrew Jackson; and Charles L'Enfant, the designer of Washington, D.C.

As is the case with many such taverns, a post office was once located here. Situated in the east wing, it was the first post office on the western slope of the Blue Ridge. The original mail slot can still be seen today.

Over the past two hundred years, The Tavern has also served as a bank, a bakery, a general store, a cabinet shop, a barbershop, a private home, and an antique shop. During the Civil War, it functioned as a hospital for wounded soldiers. The Harris family, the proprietors at that time, continued at the helm for another hundred years! In 1965, they sold the property to Mary Dudley Porterfield, whose husband was the founder of Abingdon's well-known Barter Theater. During the Depression, theatergoers could obtain a performance ticket with the donation of food.

Emmitt F. Yeary, a local attorney, purchased The Tavern in 1984 and restored it to its original prominence. Almost ten years later, Max Hermann came to The Tavern after a twenty-year stint in the United States Air Force. Some of the German items on the menu reflect Hermann's heritage.

As I sat with Max in the lovely courtyard, I asked him why he'd made the transition from military man to tavern owner. He explained that he bought the building because it reminded him of those in Europe. It was only after six months of extensive research into the location's previous businesses that he embarked on his restaurant venture. If the crowd on the Monday night that I dined was a fair indication, then Max's conclusions were right on the mark.

While I enjoyed my sampler, I observed

the other diners around me. The Tavern has a relaxed, unhurried atmosphere, and the other guests seated in the courtyard were taking advantage of it, deep in conversation with their companions. Inside, tables in the low-ceilinged dining rooms were full. Balcony seating was popular, and space around the casual bar just inside the front door was at a premium. Max told me that his Jambalaya always gets rave reviews. After one bite, I agreed. I saved enough for Karen to sample when our paths rejoined. As I savored my Blackened Yellowfin Snapper and my Lamb Chops with Fresh Mint Sauce, I quickly comprehended Max's successful formula—fabulous food in a relaxed atmosphere. What more does one need?

GARLIC PARMESAN DRESSING

5 cloves garlic
½ jalapeño pepper, seeded
5 egg whites
2 cups olive oil
¾ cup sugar
1 tablespoon dried basil leaves
4 cupsgrated Parmesan
1½ cups white vinegar
pinch of salt
pinch of pepper

Purée garlic and jalapeño in a food processor. Set aside. Place egg whites in a medium bowl. Slowly add olive oil to emulsify. Add remaining ingredients, then stir in puréed mixture. Blend until creamy. Store in refrigerator. Yields about 8 cups.

 FIVE-GRAIN BREAD

1½ cups honey, divided
4½ cups hot water, divided
4 tablespoons dry yeast
3½ cups warm water
½ cup olive oil
2 eggs
3 cups whole-wheat flour
½ cup cornmeal
½ cup sunflower seeds
1½ tablespoons poppy seeds
1½ cups oats
½ cup brown sugar
8 cups hi-gluten flour
egg wash
additional oats for garnish
additional poppy seeds for garnish

Preheat oven to 350 degrees. Combine ½ cup of the honey, 1 cup of the hot water, and yeast in a medium bowl. Let sit until foamy. In a large mixing bowl, combine remaining ingredients through brown sugar. Add yeast mixture just to blend. Add hi-gluten flour 1 cup at a time until dough pulls from sides of bowl. Flour a board and knead dough for at least 5 minutes. Transfer to a large bowl and let rise for 90 minutes, then transfer to 2 bread pans and let rise for 45 minutes. Brush with egg wash and sprinkle with oats and poppy seeds. Bake at 350 degrees for 35 minutes. Yields 2 loaves.

659 Zachary Taylor Highway
Flint Hill, VA 22627
www.griffintavern.com
540-675-3227

Jim and Debbie Donehey purchased land in Flint Hill in February 1997 after falling in love with the area. They moved permanently to Flint Hill several years later. As the wait staff tells it, the only difficulty with the move was that they couldn't find a good burger or a cold draft beer for lunch. Debbie had always dreamed of owning a restaurant, and Jim wanted an English-style pub. So when the Bradford House came on the market, it seemed like an opportunity too good to miss.

Back in 1837, the property was part of 231 acres sold to Alfred Dearing. Dearing divided and sold the land to Thomas Settle and ten unnamed gentlemen in September 1868. Settle eventually built a Victorian-style house on his parcel. The Bradford family purchased the property in 1967, after which the home was known as the Bradford House. Micah and Vandy Solomon later bought the property and ran a CD duplication business from the house. The Doneheys bought the Bradford House in 2001 and spent almost

nine months renovating it.

This beautiful building now houses two dining rooms, a pub with an area to play darts, and a deck for outside dining. It is the wonderful culmination of Jim and Debbie's dream. Jim is an avid collector of griffins, mythological creatures with the body of a lion and the head and wings of an eagle. So finding a new name for the building was easy. Visitors will also discover the Griffin Tavern Pantry Shop on the right-hand side of the spacious wraparound front deck. This great little store is located in what was once the house's office or library. It sells wraps, hoagies, salads, desserts, breads, and a wide selection of British imported goods. Though Debbie wasn't with me that day, I had an easy time describing the merchandise to her, since I bought one of almost everything the shop sells.

The charming dining rooms have high ceilings, wooden floors, and stone fireplaces. I sat in the bar and checked out the menu, which includes many items that will please English visitors, like Bangers and Mash, Shepherd's Pie, and Fish and Chips. And for the non-Anglophiles among us, there are delicious selections such as the Five-Napkin Cheeseburger, the Garden Salad with Ginger-Soy Dressing, and the highly recommended Griffin Wings with Blue Cheese Dressing.

Legend has it that griffins had such sharp vision and keen hearing that they could discover where buried treasure lay. This Griffin is certainly a treasure in its own right here at Flint Hill!

 ZUCCHINI BREAD

3 eggs
1¾ cups sugar
½ cup orange juice
½ cup canola oil
2½ cups zucchini, grated coarse
3 teaspoons vanilla extract
2½ cups all-purpose flour
½ teaspoon baking powder
2 teaspoons baking soda
1 teaspoon salt
3 teaspoons cinnamon
½ cup nuts, chopped

Preheat oven to 325 degrees. Beat eggs in a medium bowl. Add sugar, orange juice, oil, zucchini, and vanilla. Mix well. In another bowl, sift together flour, baking powder, baking soda, salt, and cinnamon. Add nuts and mix to combine. Stir dry mixture into wet mixture until combined. Pour into 2 well-oiled loaf pans. Bake for 60 to 75 minutes, turning pans every 20 minutes, until toothpick inserted in center comes out clean. Slice and serve. Yields 2 loaves.

 FISH AND CHIPS

4 baking potatoes
canola oil for frying
1½ cups light beer
2 cups self-rising flour
1½ teaspoons kosher salt, divided
1 teaspoon paprika
4 3-ounce pieces fresh cod, haddock, or scrod

Cut potatoes into finger-sized pieces. Heat oil to 350 degrees and cook potatoes for 3 minutes. Remove potatoes and set aside. In a flat dish, combine beer, flour, 1 teaspoon of the salt, and paprika to make batter. Put potatoes back in heated oil and cook for a further 5 minutes until golden brown. Remove from oil and set on paper towels to drain. Sprinkle with remaining salt.

Dip fish in batter, shake off excess, and fry in oil for 3 to 4 minutes, turning often. Remove from oil and drain on paper towels. Plate Fish and Chips and serve immediately. Serves 2.

Note: The Griffin Tavern serves Fish and Chips the English way, with malt vinegar.

683 Thomas Jefferson Parkway
Charlottesville, VA 22902
434-977-1234

Exiled from Scotland for his religious beliefs, John Michie purchased a thousand acres from Major John Henry, the father of well-known orator Patrick Henry. When the Michie Tavern was opened by Michie's son, William, in 1784, it quickly became the social center of the community, providing food, drink, lodging, and entertainment. The beverages served here were produced primarily by E. C. Booze, hence our current colloquialism. Only travelers were allowed inside the inn. Stagecoach drivers were forced to stay outside. To accommodate the drivers' refreshment needs, a bar was constructed on the front porch. And we thought the drive-through window was a modern invention.

Remarkably, ownership remained in the Michie family until the early 1900s. In 1927, the tavern was sold and moved seventeen miles to its present location, a mere half-mile from Thomas Jefferson's beloved Monticello. Within a year of the move, the tavern reopened as a museum and restaurant. Guests may tour the tavern and several other historic buildings on the property, including the Meadow Run Grist Mill and the General Store.

The tavern is a prime example of the Colonial Revival period. The dining room, or "ordinary," is on the first floor. On the second floor is the Assembly Room, which at various times served as a ballroom, a schoolroom, a place of worship, and space for extra accommodations when the inn was beyond capacity. It's been reported that the sounds of a party from long, long ago can still be heard emanating from the upper rooms. Visitors may be invited to dance the Virginia reel, as the people who gave birth to those spirits once did. They may also sip an eighteenth-century tavern punch or have the opportunity to write with a quill pen.

Our experience didn't extend quite that deeply into the 1700s. We were, however, summoned to dine by the clanging of a dinner bell. Upon entering the ordinary, guests are immediately transported back in time as they step into a low-ceilinged log room. The several dining rooms have large fireplaces and mantels strewn with pewter. The menu is a prix fixe buffet consisting of Colonial Fried Chicken, Black-Eyed Peas, Beets, Green Bean Salad, Coleslaw, Stewed Tomatoes, Potato Salad, Biscuits, Cornbread, and Cobbler in the summer. During the cold months, Green Beans, Mashed Potatoes and Gravy, and Garden Vegetable Soup are substituted for some of the items. There is no need to heap your plate here. After you're seated on one of the benches at the long plank tables, servers in period costumes are available to refill your plate. As moist and good as the Colonial Fried Chicken is, you may ask not just for seconds but for thirds as well! Save room for the Cobbler, though. It's delicious.

 COLONIAL FRIED CHICKEN

1 cup self-rising flour
¾ teaspoon oregano
2 teaspoons garlic salt
2 tablespoons seasoning salt
1 teaspoon pepper
2- to 3-pound fryer, cut up
3 cups shortening

Combine flour and seasonings. Roll chicken in flour mixture. Melt shortening in a Dutch oven or other heavy, deep pan. Fry chicken pieces in shortening at 350 degrees for 12 to 15 minutes on each side until tender. Serves 6.

 GARDEN SQUASH CAKE

1 pound butternut squash, peeled and diced
1 cup molasses
1 cup sugar
½ cup butter, melted
3 cups flour
4 teaspoons baking powder
¼ teaspoon baking soda
½ cup milk
1½ teaspoons vanilla extract, divided
¾ cup confectioners' sugar
2 teaspoons water

Boil squash until tender. Drain thoroughly and mash. Combine molasses, sugar, and butter with 1 cup squash. Beat until smooth and creamy. Sift together flour, baking powder, and baking soda. Stir into creamed mixture. Blend in milk and 1 teaspoon of the vanilla. Pour mix into a large, greased loaf pan. Bake at 300 degrees for 45 minutes until done. Remove from pan and cool on a rack.

When cake has cooled, combine confectioners' sugar, water, and remaining vanilla to make glaze. Glaze cake and serve. Serves 8.

 COLONIAL SYLLABUB

1 quart whipping cream
¾ cup sugar
¾ cup lemon juice
1 cup sherry
½ cup brandy
nutmeg for garnish

Whip cream until peaks form. Add sugar and mix until it dissolves. When cream is stiff, add lemon juice, sherry, and brandy. Whip for about 2 minutes longer. Spoon into parfait glasses and refrigerate for 3 to 4 days. Mixture will separate after a couple of days, with cream on top and liquid at bottom of glass. Garnish with nutmeg before serving. Serves 6 to 8.

301 Mill Street
Occoquan, VA 22125
www.occoquaninn.com
703-491-1888

Prior to the establishment of Occoquan, the falls of the Occoquan River hinted at the industrial potential of this town. In 1736, the Virginia General Assembly authorized construction of a public warehouse on the lower side of the river. John Ballendine and his brother-in-law, Charles Ewell, bought the warehouse site in 1755 and began building a town. Ballendine constructed not only a warehouse but also forges, gristmills, bake houses, sawmills, storehouses, and homes. His own home, a gray stone mansion known as Rockledge, was built in 1758. It still stands on a hill above Occoquan, overlooking what Ballendine began so many years ago. The broken walls of cotton mills and iron foundries are still here, too, to remind residents and visitors of Occoquan's early days.

Not surprisingly, this area played a part in the Civil War. Early in the conflict, General Wade Hampton was responsible for the Confederate defenses south of Bull Run. His range stretched from the town of Dumfries to Bacon Race Church, now known as Hoadly. He commanded Confederate batter-

ies on the hill behind Rockledge and at strategic points along the Potomac River, including Firestone, Cockpit Point, and the town of Potomac, later known as Quantico. Trenches stretched for a mile and half from Occoquan to Colchester. General Hampton's headquarters were located at the corner of Union and Commerce Streets in what was then the Hammill Hotel.

The Occoquan Inn was built in 1810, long before the war. This has been the site of an inn or tavern since the days when colonists and Indians peacefully coexisted here. The inevitable changes that came with the growing population sent the Indians farther west. Legend has it that just one of the tribe remained behind. That particular Dogue Indian is said to have taken a fancy to the innkeeper's wife. One night, as he descended the wooden steps after visiting her, he was discovered by the angry, jealous husband and shot on the spot. Years later, the image of this last remaining Indian was identified in the smoke from the fireplace. His spirit has also been spotted in the large mirror of the second-story ladies' room. This tall man with long black hair and a dignified face is even said to visit the restaurant from time to time.

Lunch is served in the Virginia Grill, which offers choices such as Confederate Chili and traditional Virginia Peanut Soup. Since it was a nippy day when I visited, that was my choice, along with the Spinach and Mushroom Salad. For more hearty appetites, sandwiches such as the Chicken Ranchero or the Deli Stack should fit the bill. The dinner menu offers traditional entrées with a Virginia flair. Beef Jefferson, Steak Mount Vernon, and Veal Occoquan all sound creative and delicious.

As has been the case throughout our three books, I did not experience the presence of any spirit here. Karen and I have tried from state to state but haven't yet managed to actually meet one of them. However, I certainly didn't let that dampen my enjoyment of my noonday meal.

VIRGINIA PEANUT SOUP

¼ cup olive oil
½ pound carrots, chopped rough
½ pound yellow onions, chopped rough
½ pound celery stalks, cut rough
¼ cup concentrated chicken base
12 cups water
1 pound fresh chicken carcass
¼ cup fresh tarragon leaves
1½ cups clarified butter
½ to ¾ cup flour
¾ pound creamy peanut butter
¾ tablespoon Kitchen Bouquet
2 cups heavy cream
salt and pepper to taste
crushed peanuts for garnish

Preheat oven to 350 degrees. Glaze a medium baking sheet with olive oil. Spread vegetables evenly over pan. Bake for 1 hour, turning vegetables occasionally. Combine chicken base with water. Add vegetables, chicken carcass, and tarragon. Simmer for 2 hours. Strain mixture thoroughly and refrigerate. After simmering, you should have about 8 cups usable stock. When stock has completely cooled, skim off fat. Melt butter in a medium saucepan. Whisk in ½ cup flour to make a roux, using a little more if necessary. Simmer on very low heat for 30 minutes until roux becomes a dusty brown. Transfer stock to a heavy-bottomed stockpot and begin heating. When stock is just below a boil, add peanut butter, stirring to blend. Add roux, stirring constantly so it doesn't settle on bottom of pan and burn. Stir in Kitchen Bouquet, then cream. Season with salt and pepper. Simmer on low heat for another 10 minutes. Remove from stove and run through strainer again. May be stored in refrigerator for later use or served immediately. Garnish with crushed peanuts. Serves 8.

Rice's Hotel/Hughlett's Tavern
73 Monument Place
Heathsville, VA 22473
804-580-7900

This old tavern stands on a land grant given to John Hughlett in 1663. When he died, the property was willed to his son, John Hughlett II. More than 130 years after the original grant, yet another John Hughlett made a request in his will. He asked that "the rents of the ordinary be put to the use of schooling and raising my grandson, John Hughlett." The tavern was sold to Griffin Foushee in 1824. Records show that a substantial tax increase was levied in 1832, and again in 1833, probably indicating that the tavern underwent significant expansion. Foushee functioned as a landlord, eventually renting the property to yet another Hughlett, Thomas.

Shortly after the Civil War, John Rice took ownership and changed the name from Hughlett's Tavern to Rice's Hotel. It operated as such until the early 1930s. Under Rice's guidance, the hotel was a fashionable spot to dine and stay. It became a favorite with the drummers, or traveling salesmen, who passed this way. A photograph taken at that

time shows the hotel looking very much as it does today.

We met Peggy Fleming, president of the Rice's Hotel/Hughlett's Tavern Foundation, one summer afternoon for a personal tour. The foundation oversees the property from upkeep to strategic planning. It was formed in 1992, two years after Cecelia Fallin Rice gave the landmark to the Northumberland Historic Society. Another dedicated group, the Tavern Rangers, meets every Thursday morning. The Rangers grew from the first volunteers who cleared weeds and overgrowth in 1992. Today, they identify, preserve, recycle, and maintain materials, sort out artifacts and archaeological finds, and do anything else needed for the building and grounds. One of their recent projects is the two-story porch that runs the length of the building.

Stepping across the threshold, guests are immediately transported back in time. The original wooden beams are visible in the entry, reminding guests that this was an inn for the common people. As the tavern's literature states, "There is no record of anyone famous having ever eaten or slept here!"

Juxtaposed against this simplicity is the creativity of the menu. The Caesar Salad is enlivened with Parmesan crisps and sliced strawberries. The Spinach Salad is topped with spicy candied walnuts, goat cheese, and Lemon-Balsamic Vinaigrette. Entrées such as Roasted Duck Pot Pie and Pepper-Seared Prawns with Tomato-Ginger Chutney certainly caught our attention.

Hughlett's was built as a courthouse tavern. As such, it was important to the community. At that time, court was in session fairly infrequently, so court days brought many people to town to socialize or conduct business. It was a time for lively camaraderie, and the tavern was the center of activity. Under the able guidance of the foundation, the spirited history of Rice's Hotel/Hughlett's Tavern lives on.

 BOUILLABAISSE

2 tomatoes
2 tablespoons olive oil
1 bulb fennel with stem, chopped
4 cloves garlic, smashed
zest of 1 orange
1 onion, diced
2 ribs celery, diced
1 carrot, diced
2 apples, diced
5 pounds lobster shells, gills removed
1 pound shrimp shells
3 sprigs thyme
2 stars anise
1 teaspoon saffron
4 quarts cold water
¼ cup fish sauce
4 tablespoons butter
24 mussels
12 shrimp
12 scallops
4 baby bok choy, cores removed
Basil Pesto Mashed Potatoes (see next recipe)

Preheat oven to 450 degrees. Toss tomatoes with oil and sear them in a smoking hot sauté pan until they blister and turn black, then transfer them to a roasting pan with fennel stems, garlic, orange zest, onions, celery, carrots, and apples. Add lobster and shrimp shells on top of vegetables and roast for 25 to 30 minutes until lobster shells are bright red and dry. In a stockpot, combine shells and rest of vegetables with thyme, anise, saffron, and water. Bring to a boil, then reduce to a simmer. Allow to simmer for 2 hours. Strain stock and discard shells. Place stock in a saucepan and boil until reduced by ⅓. Add fish sauce, butter, mussels, shrimp, and scallops and simmer for 3 minutes. Add bok choy and simmer for 30 seconds. Place Basil Pesto Mashed Potatoes in individual bowls with bok choy and seafood, followed by broth. Serves 8.

 BASIL PESTO MASHED POTATOES

8 cloves garlic
1 cup olive oil
16 red bliss potatoes, whole, skin on
2 cloves garlic, minced
1 cup heavy cream
3 tablespoons unsalted butter
salt and pepper to taste
1 cup fresh basil leaves, packed
¾ cup grated Parmesan
1 ounce Macadamia nuts

Put whole garlic cloves and oil in a small saucepan. Bring to a low simmer for 15 minutes until tender. Reserve oil. Place potatoes in a pot with enough water to cover them.

Bring to a boil, then reduce to a simmer for 20 minutes until fork tender. Strain. Add minced garlic, cream, and butter. Mash until well combined. Season with salt and pepper. In a food processor, combine basil, Parmesan, Macadamia nuts, whole garlic cloves, and 1/3 cup of the reserved oil. Blend for 15 seconds. Add to potatoes. Serves 8.

BITTERSWEET CHOCOLATE MARQUIS TORTE

1¼ pounds bittersweet chocolate, divided
1¾ cups unsalted butter, divided
¾ cup plus 2 teaspoons sugar, divided
14 large eggs at room temperature

Preheat oven to 400 degrees. Line a baking sheet with a half-sheet of parchment paper. Chop ½ pound of the chocolate and 1 cup of the butter into small pieces. Place in a mixing bowl with ¾ cup of the sugar. Place bowl on a double boiler. Remove bowl when most of the sugar has dissolved and chocolate has melted. Using a wire whisk, incorporate 6 of the eggs 1 at a time. The mixture should resemble brownies. Pour mixture onto parchment paper. Place remaining half-sheet of parchment paper on top of cake mixture to prevent it from drying out. Bake for 8 to 12 minutes. When done, paper should pull slightly away from cake, which should be springy to the touch. Let cool. Place in the refrigerator for 30 minutes. Cut one 9-inch round piece from cake and place on the bottom of a springform pan. Chop remaining chocolate and butter into small pieces and place in a mixing bowl. Place on a double boiler and allow to melt completely. Remove and cool to 85 degrees. Separate remaining eggs and place yolks in a mixer. Add 1 teaspoon sugar. Mix on high until it reaches ribbon stage. Fold whipped yolks into melted chocolate. In a mixing bowl, whip egg whites and remaining 1 teaspoon sugar to form soft peaks. Fold egg whites into chocolate mixture. Pour into springform pan and tap to remove air bubbles. Refrigerate for 3 to 4 hours before serving. Serves 8.

The Tavern of Port Royal

304 Main Street
Port Royal, VA 22535
www.thetavernofportroyal.com
804-742-5333

John Roy was born around 1683. During his early adulthood, he was employed by John Buckner as a tobacco inspector in a warehouse. This was a much-desired position, since its appointment implied political connections. Tobacco was of significant economic importance, and inspectors were paid well. Around 1716, John Roy grew interested in purchasing the warehouse from Buckner. When the general assembly increased taxes and raiders broke into the warehouse, damaging the scales and setting fire to the building, Buckner was all too ready to sell. Under Roy's guidance, the business prospered.

Port Royal was established as a business center. Local-government services were a long time in coming to the town. For example, a jail was not built until a hundred years after the town's founding. Economic success continued, however, as ships of considerable tonnage were able to make their way down the Rappahannock River to the port. The community was so successful that at one point it almost became the state capi-

tal. How history might have been different!

At the advent of the twenty-first century, Historic Port Royal, Inc., was founded by a group of local citizens who wanted to preserve local buildings of historic note. Lisa Burch and her mother, Joyce Carter, purchased The Tavern at Port Royal because of the very same desire. Lisa was a history major in college and ran a major catering operation in the D.C. area, and Joyce owned a local catering company, so the undertaking seemed like a perfect fit.

The day we visited, the front dining room was full. We were seated in the back dining room next to the fireplace. It was a welcome location on a brisk winter day. The décor here is mauve and rose. The tables and windows are draped effusively with burgundy and white toile. Because of the weather, Debbie opted for the savory homemade Chili, served in a bread bowl. Karen chose the Brunswick Stew, accompanied by Sweet Onion Hush Puppies. The portion sizes were quite ample and the flavors truly enjoyable. Both of us would have been quite happy with the "Sides for Lunch" choice, in which guests choose three side dishes from a list that includes Rice Pilaf, Coleslaw, Mashed Potatoes, and Maple-Whipped Sweet Potatoes. The Barbecue and the Fried Chicken caught our attention as well.

For dinner, the restaurant is well known for its Crab Cakes. Several other seafood selections are on the menu, such as Flounder Stuffed with Crabmeat and Sautéed Red

Snapper. The Prime Rib is a popular beef entrée. Lisa and her mother buy all their ingredients locally—unless they've grown them in the garden at the back of this 1850s home, that is.

The structure began its existence as the home of the Catletts, an influential family in town. Through the years, it passed through many owners. In 1977, the building was converted to The Tavern of Port Royal. According to one of our sources, it is the only large home remaining intact along Main Street. Under the watchful eye of its current owners, this part of historic Port Royal is in good hands.

 ASPARAGUS SAUTÉ

¼ to ½ cup Riesling or other white wine
2 tablespoons butter
1 teaspoon garlic powder
1 teaspoon shredded Parmesan or Romano
1 teaspoon salt
1 teaspoon black pepper, ground coarse
1 bunch asparagus

Place first 6 ingredients in a sauté pan over medium-high heat. Rinse asparagus and remove woody ends. When mixture in pan is warm, add asparagus. Sauté for 8 to 12 minutes. Serve immediately. Serves 4 to 6.

SUMMER CRAB SALAD

1 pound lump crabmeat
pinch of salt
pinch of pepper
pinch of sugar
¼ cup chopped mixed green, red, and yellow
  bell peppers
¾ cup mayonnaise
3 or 4 lettuce leaves
3 or 4 lemon slices for garnish
12 cherry tomatoes for garnish

Mix crabmeat with salt, pepper, sugar, and bell peppers. Gently fold in mayonnaise, trying not to break crabmeat. Refrigerate immediately. Serve on leaf lettuce. Garnish with lemon slices and cherry tomatoes. Serves 3 to 4.

Half Way House
PETERSBURG TURNPIKE, RICHMOND, VIRGINIA
Established 1760

10301 Jefferson Davis Highway
Richmond, VA 23237
804-275-1760

The Half Way House derives its name from its location halfway between Petersburg and Richmond. Built in 1760 on a land grant from George II, it served as a stagecoach stop and ordinary. The Hatcher family owned the property almost continuously from the time of the land grant until it was purchased by Richmond resident W. Brydon Tennant, who saw the historical value of the structure and wanted to make sure it was maintained. It began to function again as a restaurant when Fred and Dorothy Benders opened their operation here in 1942. Rick and Sue Young took over from the Benders family in 1982.

George Washington slept here, as did Robert E. Lee and Ulysses S. Grant. Thomas Jefferson, Patrick Henry, and Jefferson Davis were also guests. It is believed that Benedict Arnold used the tavern as he made raids up the James River toward Richmond in 1781. It is also said that poet James Whitcomb Riley, inspired during the night, scribbled some new verse on the wall of his accommodations. Research has shown that the well at the south end of the house was in use during a visit by Charles Dickens in 1842. Perhaps the most interesting story of all involves the Marquis de Lafayette, who stayed here in 1780 while his army camped nearby. In Hopewell, a woman by the name of Susanne Boling happened to be at the Mitchell House, where British general Charles Cornwallis was staying. After overhearing Cornwallis planning an attack on Lafayette's flank, she rowed across the Appomattox River and journeyed the twelve or so miles to the Half Way House to warn Lafayette, thus thwarting Cornwallis's plan.

The Half Way House retains much of its old ambiance. Guests will note the brick walls, the original fireplace, and the slightly askew windows. A variety of Delft-inspired plates line the walls, which are also decorated with copper cookware. Pottery pitchers and occasional pieces of antique furniture add to the historic décor.

To enter the dining room, visitors traverse the original brick steps, now smooth from the centuries of famous (and infamous) individuals who have come through the doors. The menu consists of appetizers such as Fried Artichoke Hearts, Smoked Salmon, and Onion Soup Gratinée. Debbie chose to order a salad and the appetizer du jour, Mini Crab Cakes. Karen opted for the specialty of the house, a petite Filet Mignon with Fried Shrimp. Since this was our final appointment after a week's research, we decided to close with delicious homemade desserts. Karen's Chocolate Raspberry Torte was outstanding, and Debbie voiced the same opinion of her Virginia Peanut Butter Pie.

The furniture here is indicative of the periods throughout which the Half Way House has served weary travelers. Two corner cabinets in what was once the ladies' parlor (now a private dining room) date back to the original inn. We stood and stared, realizing we were looking at the very same articles gazed upon by the influential individuals discussed above. Glad we had a modern vehicle with comfortable seats and air conditioning, we left the Half Way House steeped in history and sated by a wonderful meal.

BAKED STUFFED POTATOES

6 large baking potatoes
8-ounce container sour cream
6 tablespoons butter
¼ cup dried chives, chopped
salt and white pepper to taste
8-ounce package Monterey Jack and cheddar mix, shredded

Preheat oven to 400 degrees. Bake potatoes for about an hour until tender. Cut potatoes in half lengthwise and scoop out skins into a large bowl. Add remaining ingredients except cheese. Mix thoroughly. Spoon potato mixture back into skins, mounding slightly. At this point, potatoes can be wrapped and refrigerated for 1 to 2 days, if desired. When ready to use, reheat potatoes at 325 degrees for about 15 minutes until warmed through. Top with cheese. Melt cheese under broiler or in oven. Serve hot. Serves 12.

BROCCOLI CASSEROLE

1½ pounds broccoli
½ teaspoon salt
¼ cup butter
¼ cup flour
1 cup milk
¾ cup chicken stock
1 teaspoon lemon juice
1 to 2 tablespoons dry sherry
salt and pepper to taste
½ cup shredded cheddar
¼ cup slivered almonds, toasted

Preheat oven to 375 degrees. Cut broccoli into spears. In a large saucepan, bring 1 inch water to a boil. Add broccoli and salt. Cook, covered, for 8 to 12 minutes. Drain broccoli and transfer to a 2-quart baking dish. Melt butter over medium heat. Blend in flour, milk, and stock. Cook until thick and bubbly, stirring frequently. Add lemon juice, sherry, and salt and pepper to taste. Pour sauce over broccoli in baking dish. Sprinkle with cheddar and almonds. Bake uncovered for 15 to 20 minutes until bubbly. Serves 4 to 6.

Buckhorn Inn circa 1811

US 250
Churchville, VA 24421
540-337-8660

Situated in a clearing in the lush greenery of George Washington National Forest, the Buckhorn Inn has provided creature comforts for weary travelers since 1811. We certainly fit that description the day we visited, stopping by unannounced after an off-the-beaten-path journey that was significantly longer than expected. The innkeepers, Kevin and Kim Daly, greeted us warmly and made us feel right at home. Other guests were enjoying the early-evening breeze as they lounged on the wide wraparound porch.

We were seated in the dining room to the left of the lobby. Its rustic décor includes plank walls and floors. Antiques are displayed on the hearth, while a collection of crocks is arranged on a shelf encircling the room. The other dining room is very different in its feel. Floral wallpaper adorns the walls, and the woodwork is painted a lively green. According to Kevin, this room is a favorite with overnight guests for their breakfast, as it is enlivened at that time of day by the cheery morning sun.

Both dining rooms are part of the original eight-room inn. As the well-to-do began traveling from their homes in the east to the well-known springs farther west, the inn became a favorite stopping point. At that time, it was known as the Dudley House, named for its original proprietor. In 1854, Elinor Jackson, the first wife of Stonewall Jackson, wrote to her sister-in-law, Laura, about their stay here before traveling to the Warm Springs area.

Many stories have been told about the tavern's ghost. According to legend, it is the spirit of a guest murdered after a night of gambling, whether because he couldn't pay his debt or because he raked in too much of someone else's money.

During the Civil War, the inn was a hospital, seeing to the needs of the sick and wounded from the nearby Battle of McDowell. After the war, it again became a center of social activity. During the late 1800s and early 1900s, the inn was well known for its dances and music. As we examined the memorabilia along the front hall, we came across an invitation to just such an event.

With the arrival of our food, we settled into the dining room again. Karen enjoyed her Filet Mignon, which was topped with blue cheese and walnuts. Debbie was quite satisfied with her delicious Stuffed Shrimp, filled with lump crabmeat and Gruyère cheese. The varied menu offers excellent veal, poultry, and beef selections. The desserts are homemade by Kim. We opted to share a piece of her Carrot Cake. It was moist and full of chunky bits of nut. Best of all, it was slathered in White Chocolate Cream Cheese Frosting.

To no one's surprise, not a morsel was left! To walk off a few calories, we accompanied Kevin upstairs to take a peek at the guest rooms. Thanks to their great food and comfortable, roomy accommodations, the Dalys have succeeded in continuing a longstanding tradition of hospitality.

MARINATED CARROTS

5 cups peeled and sliced carrots
1 medium onion
1 small green pepper
10½-ounce can tomato soup
½ cup salad oil
1 cup sugar
¾ cup cider vinegar
1 teaspoon prepared mustard
1 teaspoon Worcestershire sauce
1 teaspoon salt
½ teaspoon pepper

Place carrots in a pot of water and bring to a boil. Reduce heat to medium and cook until tender. Drain and cool. Cut onion and green pepper into round slices and mix with cooled carrots. Combine remaining ingredients in a container with a lid. Shake well. Pour over vegetables. Cover and marinate in refrigerator for at least 12 hours. Drain before serving. This dish keeps for up to 2 weeks in refrigerator. Serves 8 to 10.

PEANUT BUTTER PIE

½ cup creamy peanut butter
¾ cup confectioners' sugar
9-inch piecrust, baked
⅓ cup flour
½ cup sugar
⅛ teaspoon salt
2 cups milk
2 egg yolks, beaten slightly
2 teaspoons margarine, melted
1 teaspoon vanilla
prepared whipped topping

In a medium bowl, mix peanut butter and confectioners' sugar until crumbly. Place on bottom of crust, reserving 2 tablespoons. Combine flour, sugar, salt, milk, and egg yolks in a medium saucepan. Place over high heat until mixture comes to a rolling boil. Stir until thickened. Remove from heat and add margarine and vanilla. Pour over peanut-butter mixture. Let cool. Spread with prepared topping and sprinkle with leftover peanut-butter mixture. Refrigerate. Yields 1 pie.

The Inn at Montross

21 Polk Street
Montross, VA 22520
www.innatmontross.com
804-493-0573

Way back in 1683, the justices of Westmoreland County gave permission to John Minor to keep an ordinary at this location, with the firm understanding that he was not to sell or dispense "wine, spirits, cider, or other strong liquor during the term of the session" of the county court. By 1730, ownership had come into the hands of the Spence family, who operated it as Spence's Tavern. Sometime during the 1790s, the original building was destroyed, most likely by fire, and a new building was constructed on the existing foundation.

A 1997 renovation uncovered much of the heart-pine floor from the 1790s rebuilding. Today, this long-ago ordinary is anything but, offering an excellent dining experience on the first floor and guests rooms above. The ambiance is as soothing as the watercolor paintings of local buildings that hang on the walls. The simplicity of the polished wooden tables and floors is enhanced by the antique kitchen implements hanging on the walls.

Traveling without Debbie on this occa-sion, I enjoyed a Saturday-evening dinner at the inn. Obviously a popular place with visitors and locals alike, it was hosting many young people from Colonial Beach High School on what happened to be prom night! I wondered about the Caribbean music playing in the background. It turned out that the prom had a Caribbean theme. I chatted back and forth with the young people as they arrived in pairs to enjoy dinner before going on to the dance.

Checking out the menu, I almost succumbed to greed and ordered an appetizer. One of my favorites, Escargot, was on the menu, as were Bruschetta, Colossal Wings, and Black Bean Chili. Always a fan of rockfish, I eventually selected as my entrée the Crab Imperial-Stuffed Rockfish with Sautéed Vegetables and Wild Rice. This was preceded by a delicious salad with a homemade Honey-Mustard Dressing that packed quite a kick. The fairly extensive entrée list includes a wide selection of burgers and steaks. The Rack of Lamb with Mint Coulis sounded good, as did the Chicken Pompadour. The side dishes included Wild Rice Pilaf, Baked Potatoes, Steak Fries, and Creamy Mediterranean Pasta Salad. Guests are well advised to save room for dessert here. The four selections on the night of my visit were Cinnamon Cheesecake, Lemon Pound Cake with Raspberry Ice Cream, Peanut Butter Cheesecake, and Double Chocolate Fudge Cake.

In addition to its Friday- and Saturday-night dinner seatings, the inn is a popular destination for special holiday meals. The monthly wine dinners are also well attended.

The Inn at Montross is located in the Northern Neck region of Virginia, so named because of its location on the northern peninsula created by the Potomac and Rappahannock Rivers. I encourage you to make the inn one of your destinations when you find yourself in this "neck" of the woods.

NORTHERN NECK ASPARAGUS SOUP

4 tablespoons butter
1 pound asparagus, chopped
1 medium potato, chopped coarse
¼ cup coarsley chopped yellow onion
⅓ cup coarsely chopped celery
1 clove garlic, crushed
1 sprig fresh thyme

1 bay leaf
2 tablespoons flour
2 tablespoons sherry
4 cups low-sodium chicken broth
½ cup heavy cream
salt, pepper, and cayenne to taste

Melt butter in a large stockpot. Add asparagus, potatoes, onions, celery, garlic, thyme, and bay leaf. Sauté, stirring occasionally, for 10 to 15 minutes. Separate tips from rest of asparagus and set aside. Add flour. Stir constantly until incorporated, being careful not to burn. Add sherry to deglaze pan. Be sure to scrape ingredients from bottom of pan. Add chicken broth and simmer for 45 minutes. Remove pan from heat and pour contents into a blender. Purée until smooth. Return soup to pan over low heat. Add cream. Season with salt, pepper, and cayenne. Garnish with asparagus tips and serve immediately. Serves 4.

CHAPTER 7
Homeward Bound

The Babcock House

Thoughts of home usually involve a fondness and longing for a
familiar space. Although the families that once lived and loved
in the restaurants in this chapter have long since moved on, the doors
are now open for today's families to create memories of their own
while enjoying a meal in the comfort of home.

The Manor House at Poplar Springs
9245 Rogues Road
Casanova, VA 20139
www.poplarspringsinn.com
540-788-4600

The Manahoac Indians once roamed the land on which Poplar Springs is located. As far back as 1608, Captain John Smith identified the Manahoacs as part of the larger Sioux Nation. Rogues Road was originally an old Indian trail and a major territorial boundary. Indian spear points are often dug up here. Unfortunately, by the eighteenth century, the Indians were long gone, and the land was part of a ten-thousand-acre tract stretching from Midland to Casanova. Robert "King" Carter left some of the land to his grandson Charles Carter, who in turn sold about two thousand acres including three farms to Colonel Robert Randolph. Randolph, who served in the Revolutionary War, divided the land among his three sons, but it was his daughter's child who eventually built the fieldstone manor house here. After a tour of Europe, Robert Randolph Hicks and his new wife, Rose Beatrice

Sutton, chose to style their house after the sixteenth- and seventeenth-century homes they had seen abroad.

The land here is very stony. Union soldiers who camped in the area during the Civil War built several chimneys with the stone. Locals from the village of Casanova were drafted to help pick stone from the fields for use in building the manor house. In fact, there is a gentleman who still occasionally dines here who remembers working in the fields and picking up fieldstones as a small child.

Sitting in the main dining room, we were totally overwhelmed by the thirty-foot-high stone walls, the dramatic beams, and the fabulous tapestry hanging over the huge fireplace. Equally impressive are the balconies, the arched windows, and the double French doors that open onto a flagstone terrace offering marvelous views of the rolling lawns beyond. The old library has been turned into a bar where one can sip an apéritif and peruse the menu, or imbibe an after-dinner cognac before turning in for the night.

Wherever guests choose to sit, the meal is sure to be memorable. Debbie opted for the Local Apple Roquefort Salad with Apple Cider Glacé, followed by Coriander-Crusted Rockfish with Sautéed Turnip Greens, Poached Fingerling Potatoes, and Citrus Beurre Blanc. Karen began with the Poached Lobster Salad. For her entrée, she chose the Strip Loin of Bison with Green Peppercorn Butter, Sauté of Oyster Mushrooms, and

Crispy Potato Cake. Our side dishes included Herbed Potato Soufflé and Creamed Brussels Sprouts with Pine Nuts and Smoked Bacon. We can honestly say that each item was more delectable than the last. That judgment includes the intermezzo, Plum Port Sorbet, in which sweet and tart tastes were mixed to perfection!

We chatted with chef Howard Foer and some of the staff while sipping coffee and trying to decide which of the desserts to select. It's very clear that the staff members love what they do. The service is impeccable, friendly, and informative. Howard tries very hard to use local produce and herbs. The Manor House hosts many special events throughout the year, but it's still possible for locals and hotel guests to dine most of the time. We completed our wonderful meal by sharing a Champagne and Meringue Vacherin with Caramel Balsamic Strawberries and a White Chocolate Chestnut Bavarian with Hazelnut Dacquoise—a sumptuous ending to a never-to-be-forgotten meal!

SUMMER PEACH SOUP

12 ripe peaches, peeled and chopped rough
3 tablespoons peach schnapps
3 tablespoons Cointreau
1½ cups orange juice
²/₃ cup water
¹/₃ cup sugar
½ tablespoon finely chopped fresh ginger
¼ teaspoon cinnamon

¼ teaspoon nutmeg
pinch of salt

Place peaches, schnapps, and Cointreau in a large sauté pan over high heat and burn off alcohol. Add orange juice, water, and sugar and bring to a boil. Reduce heat and simmer. Add ginger, cinnamon, and nutmeg, stirring to combine. Simmer for a further 30 minutes, stirring as necessary. Remove from heat and pass mixture through a medium sieve. Add salt. Chill well before serving. Serves 6 to 8.

SAGE WITH CHEDDAR BREAD PUDDING

2 cups heavy cream
6 eggs
½ loaf brioche, cubed
1 cup shredded sharp cheddar
1 cup fresh sage, minced
2 tablespoons salt
½ tablespoon pepper

Preheat oven to 350 degrees. In a medium bowl, whisk together cream and eggs. Set aside. In a large bowl, combine brioche, cheese, sage, salt, and pepper. Pour egg mixture over bread and fold together to combine. Pour mixture into an ovenproof casserole dish and bake for 15 to 20 minutes. Serves 8 as a side dish.

The Summit
RESTAURANT

95 College Street
Christiansburg, VA 24073
540-382-7218

Salmon Victoria in Warm Dried Cherry and Caramelized Onion Vinaigrette—yum! Chicken Taj Mahal in Curry Sauce with Cashew, Raisin, and Onion Relish—again yum! Grilled Eggplant layered with portabello mushrooms, served in a sauce made from fresh and sun-dried tomatoes—a definite yum for vegetarian palates. These delectable entrée choices are typical of what guests enjoy at The Summit Restaurant, owned and operated by Robin and Abdul Sharaki.

From the time of its construction in 1888, this Victorian home has been one of Christiansburg's finest. It was originally occupied by the Kyle Montague family. Within five years of taking up residence, Mr. Montague fell on hard times and traded homes with his brother-in-law, James S. Childress. According to Floyd "Sonny" Childress, who lived in the house until he was fifteen, his uncle Kyle proposed swapping back a few years later, when he was financially stable again. This infuriated the

elder Mr. Childress, and the brothers-in-law never spoke again. In 1931, during the Depression, it was Mr. Childress who found himself in financial difficulties. Though he sold the home, the family retained residence, renting it from the new owner, W. A. Calhoun, for fifty dollars per month.

The year 1941 saw the beginning of a time when the property was used for a variety of purposes. For a while, it served as an apartment building. Later, it housed the Christiansburg Parks and Recreation Department. It was in 1999 when the Sharakis purchased it and began returning it to its previous elegance. It was quite an undertaking, involving nine months of work and the removal of forty tons of debris!

Each of the three dining rooms has a unique fireplace. The ceilings soar to eleven feet. Lace curtains adorn the windows. Walls and woodwork painted cream and tan and accented with gold add to the elegance. The wall mural in the Magnolia Room employs the decoupage technique and typifies the Victorian era. It was here that I enjoyed dinner with my daughter, Dori, and her friend Victoria Roberts. Each of our entrées was accompanied by the soup du jour. We were fortunate that, on that Friday evening, the selection was Egyptian Lentil Soup. Completely different from what I expected, this smooth concoction was a tremendous hit with all of us. The flavor was similar to that of chili, but that's where the resemblance ended. There were no beans, no ground meat, and no tomatoes—just a smooth, creamy base utilizing potatoes and carrots and a secret combination of other ingredients. We could have made a meal on the soup alone. Instead, we sampled a Crab Cake with Cream Sauce and enjoyed entrées of Free-Range Chicken and Sesame-Coated Salmon.

When Karen and I began our research on Virginia's historic restaurants, we came across a blurb about The Summit Restaurant in a statewide travel guide. In trying to learn more, we discovered an interesting tidbit—The Summit has been nationally recognized for having one of the best bathrooms in America! A unique honor, it's just a hint of the good things this restaurant has to offer.

 AFRICAN BEAN SOUP

2 cups kidney beans
¼ cup butter
2 to 3 medium onions, chopped
2 red bell peppers, chopped
½ cup chopped mushrooms
2 cups hot water
14-ounce can coconut milk
2 15-ounce cans whole tomatoes
4 tablespoons tomato purée
2 large heads broccoli, cut into florets
curry powder, pepper, and vegetable salt to taste
grated coconut for garnish

Soak kidney beans in water overnight. Drain and rinse. Place beans in a large pot. In a large sauté pan, melt butter over medium heat and sauté onions, peppers, and mushrooms. Set aside. Add water, cream of coconut, tomatoes, tomato purée, and broccoli to beans. Simmer for about 20 minutes. Add curry, pepper, and vegetable salt. Stir in sautéed vegetables. Spoon into serving bowls and garnish with coconut. Serve with warm bread. Serves 4.

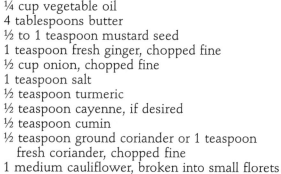 POTATO CAULIFLOWER CURRY

¼ cup vegetable oil
4 tablespoons butter
½ to 1 teaspoon mustard seed
1 teaspoon fresh ginger, chopped fine
½ cup onion, chopped fine
1 teaspoon salt
½ teaspoon turmeric
½ teaspoon cayenne, if desired
½ teaspoon cumin
½ teaspoon ground coriander or 1 teaspoon fresh coriander, chopped fine
1 medium cauliflower, broken into small florets
4 small or 2 large potatoes, diced into ¾-inch cubes
1 tomato, chopped fine

Preheat oven to 325 degrees. Heat oil and butter over moderate heat until butter is melted. Add mustard seed, ginger, onions, and salt. Stir for 3 to 4 minutes. Add remaining spices and continue stirring for 3 minutes. Add cauliflower, potatoes, and tomato. Continue stirring for 5 minutes. Transfer to a baking dish and bake for 40 minutes. Serves 6.

Stone House Tea Room

106 Loudoun Street SW
Leesburg, VA 20175
www.norrishouse.com
703-779-2933

Not long after Carol and Roger Healey took ownership of the Norris House Inn, a film crew knocked on their door, looking for a period fireplace. The one at the inn wasn't appropriate for a variety of reasons, but the one next door at the Stone House Tea Room was perfect. Director Gabriel Garcia and his crew set up their equipment and filmed a scene of *Timeless*, a documentary that retells a Revolutionary War story little known in the United States but widely taught in many Spanish-speaking countries. The colonists were underfunded and underarmed in the face of the British military. The Spanish monarch dispatched two frigates to aid them. The frigates arrived in America after a stop in Cuba. During the layover in Havana, it was decreed that the citizens relinquish their gold in an effort to raise capital for the war effort against Britain. In the course of an afternoon, over a million dollars in gold was collected. The pivotal scene filmed at the Stone House is of the Span-ish emissary notifying the colonists that this funding will be forthcoming. Additional vignettes for the movie were filmed in the gardens of the two properties.

The gardens play an important role for the inn and the tearoom. Horticulturist Jackie Ellis uses what is seasonally available to provide lovely arrangements for both places. On the day we visited, magnolia leaves and pine cones were artfully showcased. During the summer, a profusion of fresh flowers can be seen during the Stone House Tea Room's thematic teas. Some of the topics that have been covered at these teas are "Valentine's Day Posies and Tussy Mussies," "Silk and Dried Flower Arrangements," and "Wreath Making." Not all of the Saturday-afternoon teas are organized around a theme or an educational program, but the Healeys and their daughter, Natasha Grotke, who operates the tearoom, have found that these are among the most popular.

Built around 1750, the Stone House Tea Room has from time to time been called "George Washington's House," based on information that he once stayed here. In honor of that supposed event, a bedroom on the second floor of this quaint stone cottage has been dubbed the "General's Retreat." More substantial proof exists that statesman Henry Clay came here. During Clay's bid for the presidency, his campaign trail led him through Leesburg. He visited this stone house and signed the wall of the icehouse before leaving. During the demolition of the latter structure, a keen pair of eyes spotted his handwriting. It has been preserved and is now displayed on the wall of the tearoom.

As we sat and sipped tea with the Healeys, the yellow walls trimmed in crisp white provided a sunny backdrop on an unbelievably frigid day. Blue and white window treatments accompanied by blue, white, and yellow table linens complete the cheery décor. We enjoyed Honeydew and Cantaloupe with Orange-Lime Yogurt Sauce, Smoked Salmon with Caper Cream Cheese Finger Sandwiches, Smoked Chicken and Walnut Spread, and Egg Salad, all deliciously served on Blue Willowware. Calories don't count when you're feasting on Macaroon Bars, Ginger and Chocolate Cookies, Lemon Bars, and Carrot Cupcakes. And what would a proper English tea be without Cream Scones and Devonshire Clotted Cream? In our experience, the Stone House is the perfect place to enjoy an afternoon tea.

CREAM SCONES

2 cups all-purpose flour
2 teaspoons sugar
1 teaspoon salt
1 tablespoon baking powder
1 to 1½ cups heavy cream

Preheat oven to 425 degrees. In a large bowl, sift together dry ingredients. Starting with 1 cup cream, gradually add enough cream to form a soft dough. Knead lightly on a floured board, handling dough gently to retain the air needed for the scones to rise. Roll out to ½- to ¾-inch thickness. Cut into 2-inch rounds with a cookie cutter and arrange on an ungreased baking sheet, leaving space around each round. Bake for 10 to 12 minutes until light golden brown. Do not overcook. These scones are best served the same day. Serve with Devonshire Clotted Cream and preserves. Yields 7 or 8 scones.

SMOKED CHICKEN AND WALNUT SPREAD

2 whole smoked chicken breasts (1 teaspoon Liquid Smoke may be added to cooked chicken breasts if smoked chicken is unavailable)
¼ cup chopped walnuts
¼ teaspoon chopped fresh thyme
1/8 teaspoon chopped garlic
½ cup mayonnaise
salt and pepper to taste
cocktail bread, pumpernickel, or other bread
30 walnut halves

Purée all ingredients except bread and walnut halves in a food processor. Spread mixture liberally on bread and serve open-faced topped with walnut halves. Serve immediately. Yields 30 finger sandwiches.

The Babcock House

106 Oakleigh Avenue
Appomattox, VA 24522
www.babcockhouse.com
434-352-7532

The historic town of Appomattox is most noted as the location where General Robert E. Lee surrendered to General Ulysses S. Grant near the end of the Civil War. It's also the location of The Babcock House, built in 1884. The original owner of the home was Samuel Patterson Coleman, Jr., who later ceded possession of the house to Dr. Julian Abbitt, his wife, and their children.

Just twenty-four years after its construction, the five-room house was sold at auction to H. C. Babcock for the sum of $1,815. The Babcocks added rooms so that the structure could be used as a boardinghouse as well as a family home. It was here that Dr. Havilah Babcock grew up. For many years, he was chairman of the University of South Carolina's English Department. He was once quoted as saying, "School teaching occasionally interfered with hunting and fishing, but never too seriously." It's not surprising then, to discover that Dr. Babcock gained a national reputation as the author of magazine articles in *Field & Stream, Sports Afield, Life, Outdoors*, and *Hunting and Fishing*. In addition, he wrote books such as *Tales of Quails 'n Such, I Don't Want to Shoot an Elephant*, and *The Education of Pretty Boy*.

Annie Laurie Scruggs Babcock was the last of the family to live in this home. A lovely guest room on the second floor has been named in remembrance of her. Although Sheila and Jerry Palamar now own the home, the Babcock family is still close by. Annie Laurie's daughter lives right next door.

As we were touring the inn, Sheila Palamar told us that, long before she and Jerry were really serious about becoming innkeepers, she had a long list of possible names for such a property. When they bought this inn, none of those names was appropriate somehow. It just seemed right to officially call the property what everyone in town called it anyway—The Babcock House.

The Palamars have been collecting antiques for quite some time. These pieces add a lovely ambiance to the inn. Our favorite was the melodeon, purchased by Jerry when he was just fourteen. Since he didn't have a driver's license, he had to lug it home in his wagon. He refinished it himself, and it now stands in the inn's parlor. The pictures of previous members of the Palamar family also caught our eye as we toured.

Though breakfast is served only to overnight guests, lunch is available to the general public during the week. Items such as the Appomattox Station Club Sandwich, the General Lee Sandwich, and the McLean Sandwich (made of Tarragon Chicken Salad with grapes and walnuts) are named after things of significance to the area. Karen had the day's special, a Chicken Quesadilla, prepared just the way she likes it. Debbie, never one to pass up barbecue, chose the Pork Barbecue Sandwich. Topped with Coleslaw, it was deliciously filling.

The elegant candlelight dinners served here are by reservation only but are well worth a little advanced planning. *Arrington's Inn Traveler* magazine has designated The Babcock House as one of the best places in the United States and Canada for evening cuisine. Entrées such as Roast Pork Tenderloin in Raspberry Sauce, Creole Sautéed Shrimp, Baked Pecan Catfish, and Beef Fillet with Tangy Mushroom Sauce appeal to the wide-ranging palates of today's diners while paying homage to The Babcock House's proud Southern heritage.

SPICE-CRUSTED PORK TENDERLOIN

2 tablespoons ground cumin
2 tablespoons ground coriander
1 teaspoon salt
¼ teaspoon black pepper
1½-pound pork tenderloin
3 tablespoons olive oil
Chorizo Sausage Gravy (see next recipe)

Preheat oven to 400 degrees. Mix cumin, coriander, salt, and pepper in a bowl. Cut tenderloin into 4 equal portions. Dredge each piece in the spices. Heat oil in a heavy iron skillet over medium-high heat. Add pork and brown on all sides. Transfer skillet to oven and roast pork for about 10 minutes until a meat thermometer registers 160 degrees. Transfer to cutting board and let stand 5 minutes. Slice pork into ½-inch-thick medallions and divide among 4 plates. Pour warm Chorizo Sausage Gravy over pork and serve. Serves 4.

Chorizo Sausage Gravy

3 tablespoons butter
3 tablespoons flour
½ cup minced red bell pepper
¼ cup minced onion
1½ cups chicken broth
½ cup chorizo sausage, diced
¼ teaspoon cayenne

Melt butter in a heavy saucepan over medium heat. Add flour and cook about 20 minutes until golden brown, stirring frequently. Add bell peppers and onions. Sauté for 3 minutes. Gradually whisk in broth. Add sausage and cayenne. Increase heat and simmer for 5 minutes, stirring often. This gravy can be made ahead and reheated prior to serving. Yields 2 cups.

56 Rodes Farm Drive
Nellysford, VA 22958
www.mark-addy.com
434-361-1101

After checking in, I quickly changed my clothes so that I could take a walk and enjoy a beautiful day in idyllic surroundings. Crickets jumped and chirped in the meadows flanking the inn's long drive, as happy as I to enjoy a bit of spring. The Mark Addy is located just beyond the perimeter of the Wintergreen Ski Resort and not too far from Skyline Drive. Nestled amid the beautiful Blue Ridge Mountains, this stately, soft yellow mansion atop a verdant knoll was built in bits and pieces beginning in the 1800s, expanding as wealth and family size grew. Travelers flock to the inn during the fall, when the surrounding hills are ablaze with color, but I'll attest that the other guests during my stay were enjoying their springtime visit, relaxing in wicker chairs and rockers on numerous porches and balconies. Chef Gail Hobbs-Page's cooking school is also a great reason to check in, regardless of the time of year.

The main dining room is located just to the left of the home's two-story entryway.

A collection of blue and white plates lines the creamy white tone-on-tone walls. Accented by dark wood, highly polished pieces of silver, and crisp white table linens, the room has an elegantly casual feel. Just off the large dining room is a sun porch with a resplendent view of the mountains and the sunset. Along one wall of the porch is a mural featuring the birds that are prevalent here.

Soups such as Pumpkin Bisque with Cardamon Crème Fraiche and Roasted Red Pepper Soup with Pancetta Bacon are just a hint of the bounty served by chef Hobbs-Page. Among the appetizers are Hazelnut-Crusted Chèvre on Organic Spinach, Smoked Scottish Trout on Watercress, and Crab Enchiladas with Spicy Poblano Cream. Choices like Tapenade-Crusted Grouper, Pork Tenderloin with Pineapple Rum Salsa, and Rosemary Shrimp over Linguine with Garlic Cream make it nearly impossible to decide on an entrée. I began with the chèvre-and-spinach combination, which was wonderful. The pickled beet slices that accompanied this duo created a lovely flavor palate. My salmon entrée was served on a bed of Citrus Risotto and was surrounded by sautéed shiitake mushrooms and yellow squash. Too full for dessert, I wished that Karen had been along to help me enjoy the Poached Pears with Hazelnut Cream, topped with Chocolate Ganache. That delicacy will have to wait for another visit.

 CORNMEAL-CRUSTED GOAT CHEESE

1 pound chèvre, chilled
1 cup flour
2 eggs, beaten
½ cup cornmeal
pinch of salt
pinch of pepper
pinch of cumin
2 tablespoons olive oil

Preheat oven to 375 degrees. Cut chèvre into ½-inch disks. Put flour in 1 bowl and eggs in a second bowl. Mix cornmeal, salt, pepper, and cumin in a third bowl to make coating mixture. Dip chevre disks first in flour, then in egg mixture, and finally in coating mixture. Keep 1 hand "dry" and the other hand "wet." This will make things a lot less messy. Heat olive oil over medium heat in a large sauté pan. Sauté coated chevre on both sides in oil, then place in oven for about 3 minutes. Remove and allow to sit for a couple of minutes before serving. Serves 4 as an appetizer.

LAVENDER SHORTBREAD

2 cups all-purpose flour
¾ teaspoon salt
½ teaspoon baking powder
1 tablespoon fresh lavender, chopped
¾ cup unsalted butter, softened
2 tablespoons mild honey

½ cup confectioners' sugar
1 tablespoon sugar

Preheat oven to 325 degrees. Whisk together flour, salt, baking powder, and lavender in a bowl. Combine butter, honey, and confectioners' sugar in a large bowl using an electric mixer at low speed. Add flour mixture, combining until dough resembles coarse meal with some pea-sized butter lumps. Gather dough into a ball and transfer to a lightly floured surface. Knead dough about 8 times until it just comes together. Halve dough and form each half into a 5-inch disk. Roll out 1 disk between 2 sheets of parchment paper into a 9-inch round. Keep remaining dough at room temperature. Remove top sheet of parchment and transfer dough on bottom sheet of parchment onto a baking sheet. Score dough into 8 wedges by pricking dotted lines with a fork. Mark edges decoratively. Sprinkle dough with ½ tablespoon of the sugar. Bake shortbread in middle of oven for 20 to 25 minutes until golden brown. Slide shortbread on parchment to a rack and cool for 5 minutes. Transfer with a metal spatula to a cutting board and cut along score marks with a large, heavy knife. Repeat with other disk. Yields 16 wedges.

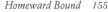

Rodes Farm Inn

826 Rodes Farm Drive
Nellysford, VA 22958
434-361-1400

The Yum-Yum Shop at Rodes Farm Inn sits at the end of Rodes Farm Drive, on the last five acres that remain of what was once the expansive Rodes Farm. Since 2001, when Virginia "Gina" Wood and her husband bought the property, they've had several opportunities to sell it, but none of the prospective buyers wanted to keep the five acres and the accompanying buildings intact. So the Woods have refused to sell.

The house served as the Kleinberg School for Girls until the early 1900s. It later became the center of a sixteen-hundred-acre farm where the Rodes family raised sheep and tended peach and apple orchards. In the 1960s, the farm was purchased by Wintergreen Properties, which converted the house into a restaurant by 1973 and operated it sporadically until 1998. Those previous restaurant endeavors never quite met with the success of Gina's undertaking.

It took the Woods a full year of renovations before they opened Rodes Farm Inn as a full-service dinner restaurant. The restaurant became so successful that Gina needed to reassess her priorities. Feeling that she was missing too much family time, she switched the restaurant's hours to breakfast and lunch. Dinner is still served, but in takeout containers to be enjoyed at home.

Today, the two front rooms of this classic 1800s two-over-two brick farmhouse function as the restaurant. To the left of the main hallway is the Yum-Yum Shop, whose offerings are appealingly displayed in a case. On the day of my visit, the entrée selections included Barbecued Meat Loaf, Marinated Salmon, Roast Chicken, and Lasagna. Sides such as Rodes Farm Apples, Green Beans, and Mashed Potatoes were also available. Much of the case was filled with wonderful-looking desserts like Key Lime Pie, Strawberry Cake, Chocolate Tortes, Strawberry Pie, and Glazed Pound Cake.

Neighbors meander over to have a cup of coffee and a midmorning snack. Others stop in to pick up dinner. If you can't get here by four-thirty, don't worry. Your selections will be packaged and left for you in a rocking chair on the front porch. Regular customers have worked out a system of payment for these "special deliveries" that is as folksy as the place itself.

To the left of the front hall are five tables for four, nestled in a dining room with creamy walls, a simple fireplace, and barnyard red trim. You'll notice the roosters in the draperies, in pictures on the walls, on the hearth, and atop the corner cupboard. Gina and I began chatting here, but she quickly suggested that we move to the wide front porch. Shetland ponies munched in the paddock nearby as Gina explained their next project—turning the Rodes Barn, where community barn dances were once held, into a permanent home for the local community theater. We rocked and talked as I enjoyed my snack of Hummingbird Cake and Sweet Tea. Karen had to be elsewhere that day, but the serenity of the pastoral setting left memories I later shared with her.

 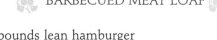

BARBECUED MEAT LOAF

2 pounds lean hamburger
1 cup oatmeal
1 cup finely chopped onion
½ cup lemon juice
2 eggs
salt and pepper to taste
Barbecue Sauce (recipe follows)

Preheat oven to 350 degrees. Lightly grease a baking sheet. Combine first 6 ingredients in a bowl. Shape meat into 8 individual oblong loaves and place on baking sheet. Bake for about 15 minutes until meat is firm. Spoon Barbecue Sauce over loaves until completely covered, using all sauce. Place back in oven and bake an additional 30 minutes. Serves 8.

BARBECUE SAUCE

1 cup light brown sugar
1½ cups ketchup
3 tablespoons yellow mustard
½ teaspoon ground cloves
½ teaspoon ground allspice

In a small bowl, combine all ingredients until brown sugar is dissolved and mixture is smooth. Yields about 1½ cups.

SWEET POTATO CASSEROLE

3 1-pound cans sweet potatoes
2 eggs
½ cup light cream
6 tablespoons butter, melted
1 cup sugar
juice of 1 lemon or ½ orange
1 cup light brown sugar
1 cup pecans, chopped
1 tablespoon cinnamon

Preheat oven to 375 degrees. Drain sweet potatoes. Place potatoes into a large bowl and mash well. Add eggs, cream, butter, sugar, and juice and mix well. Pour into a well-greased 13-by-9-inch casserole dish. In a small bowl, combine brown sugar, pecans, and cinnamon. Sprinkle evenly over top of potatoes. Bake for 30 to 35 minutes. Serves 8 to 10.

DANTE RISTORANTE

1148 Walker Road
Great Falls, VA 22066
www.danteristorante.com
703-759-3131

The Leigh House was built in the 1880s. In 1910, a north addition was constructed. Carpenter Frank Timsey was hired to do the job, earning two dollars per day for his efforts. Timsey lived in the attic for the year that it took him to complete the project. The structure contained many interesting architectural features, including dormers, gables with cut-through barge boards and fish-scale shingles, diamond-shaped windows, bay windows, and unique wooden trim. It was large enough that it had to be heated by three fireplaces, three coal stoves, and the kitchen range.

The home contained two rooms set aside for the offices of Dr. Alfred Leigh, Jr. Leigh graduated from the Medical College of Virginia in 1880 and immediately began his medical practice in Fairfax County. As was customary during that era, he made house calls, crossing the county in his horse and buggy until 1916, when he bought his first car. For patients too ill to remain at home, the Leigh House became the area's only "lying-in" hospital. In addition to doctoring, Leigh dabbled in farming on his twenty-four

and a half acres. The eighteen dollars per acre that he spent on the land is unfathomable in the modern world. After thirty-eight years of providing medical care to the community, Leigh passed away in 1918.

Today, the home is in the capable hands of Elio Domestici and Giuseppe DiBenigno. The fascinating history and the unique architecture captivated them as they looked for a location from which to operate their restaurant. Before they opened Dante Ristorante, they undertook ten months of renovations, including getting rid of four feet of mud from the basement. Giuseppe chuckled as he told us that every corner of the house has its own renovation story. Their efforts resulted in the beautiful hardwood floors, separate parlors, and classic Southern veranda that guests enjoy today.

Upon being seated, we gazed about the lovely pale green dining room, enjoying the brass sconces and botanical prints. As might be expected, the cuisine here is northern Italian. A fabulous Peasant Bread and an addictive Focaccia were quickly brought to the table and just as quickly disappeared. We could have made a meal on those alone. Appetizers such as Calamari Fritti and Carpaccio are quite popular. The Ossobuco and the Veal Scaloppine entrées came highly recommended by several sources. Karen opted for the Ravioli Stuffed with Pheasant, Mortadella, and Porcini. Debbie selected Ravioli in Tomato Cream Stuffed with Veal and Spinach. As one informant declared about Dante Ristorante, "Dessert is not to be ignored!" Debbie had the wonderful Profiteroles, while Karen settled on her perennial favorite, Tiramisu. We agreed that the tastiness of the meal, the serenity of the atmosphere, and the perfection of the service all combine to make Dante Ristorante a delightful experience.

 SEAFOOD LINGUINE

salt to taste
32 mussels
32 clams
12 shrimp
8 large sea scallops
24 calamari
3 tablespoons extravirgin olive oil
4 cloves garlic, chopped
fresh, crushed Italian parsley to taste
3 plum tomatoes, diced
½ teaspoon red pepper flakes
pepper to taste
1 pound linguine

In a large, covered pot, bring salted water to a boil. Rinse seafood, checking mussels and clams carefully for sand. Remove interior sacs and cartilage from calamari and discard. Slice calamari into thin rings. Remove shells from shrimp and devein. In a large, heavy skillet at medium temperature, heat olive oil and add garlic. Sauté until golden. Add calamari, clams, and parsley to skillet and cook for 2 minutes, stirring lightly. Add scallops, mussels, shrimp, and tomatoes. Add red pepper flakes and salt and pepper. Lower heat and simmer until clams and mussels open. Discard any unopened clams or mussels. Remove from heat and set aside. Add linguine to boiling water. Cook according to package directions until al dente. Drain pasta and place in serving bowls. Pour seafood mixture over top and serve immediately. Serves 4.

 TIRAMISU

1 cup espresso
3 tablespoons cognac
4 tablespoons sugar, divided
1 box ladyfingers (about 40 to the box)
3 eggs
3 tablespoons heavy whipping cream
8 ounces mascarpone cheese
bittersweet cocoa powder

In a medium bowl, combine espresso, cognac, and 2 tablespoons of the sugar until smooth. Dip ladyfingers in mixture until slightly moist. Arrange half of ladyfingers so they lie flat in a small, square baking dish. Separate eggs and whip yolks with remaining sugar until smooth. In a separate bowl, beat whipping cream with a wire whisk until firm. Blend mascarpone with egg-yolk mixture. Fold whipped cream into mascarpone mixture. Set aside. In a separate bowl, whip egg whites until stiff. Gently fold egg whites into mascarpone mixture. Spread half the mixture over soaked ladyfingers. Create a second layer of ladyfingers. Cover with remaining sauce. Refrigerate at least 3 hours. Sprinkle with cocoa powder just before serving. Slice into squares. Serves 6.

carrot Tree
at the
cole digges house

411 Main Street
Yorktown, VA 23690
757-246-9559

We arrived in Yorktown one summer morning having completely forgotten its Old World charm in the years since we last visited. As we walked around the small town of tiny white and red-brick houses with white picket fences and mature trees, it was easy to spot the Carrot Tree's flag waving in the gentle breeze outside the Cole Digges House. The outside of the house is lovely, thanks to the fading whitewash on the brick walls, the sea-foam shutters, and the three dormer windows protruding from the wood-shingle rooftop.

Yorktown began in 1691 when the Act for Ports was passed to establish fifteen town sites along the tidal area. On July 24 of that year, Benjamin Read's fifty-acre plot was selected for the York County port town. The land was divided into eighty-five half-acre lots. In 1703, Thomas Pate, a local ferryman, became the first to build a house here. At that time, an owner was required to build a house on his land within one year of purchase or the parcel reverted to the town. Thomas had a wife, Elizabeth, but she left

him, so the house went to his faithful housekeeper, Joan Lawson, when he died. Unfortunately for Joan, Elizabeth showed up at the funeral and had to be bribed with twenty dollars to ensure that Joan got the house. Eventually, the property passed to Cole Digges, who had the first house demolished and a far grander one erected in 1714. Digges was the grandson of William Cole, the secretary of the Virginia colony. The house is reputed to be the oldest in Yorktown.

The restaurant is located in the old library and parlor of the home. Both rooms have dark wood-paneled walls and random-width plank floors. The assorted rugs and the green gingham curtains at the windows make the rooms cozy and warm. Pewter sconces and pictures of historic buildings in Yorktown and Williamsburg line the walls. Every table has a glass cover that displays an extensive collection of vintage postcards. If you look carefully, you can even find old postcards of the Cole Digges House when it was named the Pate House, before the National Park Service established that the Pate House had been demolished by Cole Digges to clear a site for the present structure.

We sat with Glenn Helseth, the owner of the Carrot Tree, as he discussed his love for this historic building and his passion for food cooked from scratch. Visitors will really enjoy the meals served here. Everything from the bread and cookies to the soups and salads is made from scratch. Debbie and I sampled a large selection as we talked. We were very impressed by the home-baked cookies. The Peanut Butter, Chocolate Chip and Oatmeal Raisin varieties were all delicious. The Banana Walnut Bread was light and fluffy, and the Carrot Cake sandwiched together with cream cheese was moist and flavorful. Our favorite, however, was the Ham Biscuits— homemade buttermilk biscuits with sweet Virginia ham and the house dressing. They were scrumptious. Glenn's wife, Debi, does most of the cooking, getting up at an extraordinary hour in the morning to ensure that every morsel brought to the tables has been created fresh that day.

Glenn reminded us that, in colonial times, the pineapple was the sign for hospitality. And he suggested that, in our time, the carrot will come to be the sign for excellent food. So when you see the carrot flag waving in the breeze, drop in for a cookie. We're sure you'll agree with his suggestion.

 CRAB DIP

½ cup butter
1 bunch green onions, chopped
½ cup chopped parsley
2 tablespoons flour
2 cups heavy cream
1 tablespoon sherry
½ teaspoon salt
1 teaspoon Worcestershire sauce
¼ teaspoon cayenne
1 teaspoon hot sauce
½ pound grated Swiss cheese
2 tablespoons grated Parmesan
1 pound crabmeat
bread or crackers

In a heavy saucepan, melt butter over medium heat. Add green onions and parsley. Sauté about 8 minutes until soft. Stir in flour and cook for 3 to 4 minutes. Stir in cream slowly to thicken mixture. Add sherry, salt, Worcestershire, cayenne, and hot sauce. Turn heat to low and continue stirring until thick. Add both cheeses and incorporate until smooth. Fold in crabmeat. Pour into 3 or 4 small serving dishes and serve immediately with bread or crackers. Yields 3 cups.

 PECAN BARS

1¾ cups flour
¾ cup plus 3 tablespoons brown sugar, divided
¾ cup butter
3 eggs
3 tablespoons butter, melted
¾ cup dark or light corn syrup
pinch of salt
½ teaspoon maple flavoring
1½ cups pecans, chopped

Preheat oven to 350 degrees. In a medium bowl, combine flour and 3 tablespoons of the brown sugar. Cut in ¾ cup butter until mixture resembles peas. Press into a 13-by-9-inch baking pan. Bake for 15 minutes. Remove from oven and set aside to cool. In another bowl, combine remaining brown sugar, eggs, melted butter, corn syrup, salt, and maple flavoring. Stir well. Add pecans and pour mixture over cooled crust. Bake for 25 minutes. Yields 12 bars.

KESWICK HALL
AT MONTICELLO

701 Club Drive
Keswick, VA 22947
www.keswick.com
434-979-3440

We visited Keswick Hall on a cold November morning, our breath steaming in the air as we walked the few steps from the parking lot to the main entrance. Formerly known as the Villa Crawford, this elegant Tuscan villa was built close to the turn of the twentieth century. The entrance hall—decked out in pink, cream, and gold—had a roaring fire in its immense fireplace. This was echoed by the outdoor fireplace immediately behind it on the huge balcony overlooking the golf course. We were duly impressed by the flagstone floors, the beautiful rugs, the opulent columns, the Palladian arches, and the antique furnishings.

Owned and operated by Orient Express Hotels since 1999, this building was once the property of Sir Bernard Ashley. He created the feel of an English country hotel by using English fabrics. Most of those fabrics have been replaced, but visitors can still recognize the Ashley touch here and there.

Debbie and I sat in the breakfast parlor and talked to Michael Pownall, the general manager. He explained to us that he was attempting to turn this unique hotel into a place that sells the Virginia lifestyle on all levels, from the rooms and amenities to the food served. To this end, chef John Brand has created a menu using as much local produce, meats, and grains as possible. Although Keswick Hall will always house guests from around the world, Michael has hopes of attracting the locals to visit more often than just on special occasions.

The main dining room is called Fossett's in honor of Edith Fossett, a slave in the household of Thomas Jefferson. In 1802, Edith and fellow slave Fanny traveled to Washington to learn the art of French cooking from Honoré Julien, Jefferson's chef. They also learned to prepare desserts under the direction Etienne Lemaire. It was a difficult time for Edith, already married and pregnant at age fifteen. She must have been made of stern stuff indeed to acquire the necessary skills to make Lemaire comment that she would give Jefferson much satisfaction with her cooking.

The menu selections here include Aromatic Steamed Lemon Sole with Spaghetti Squash, Wilted Pea Greens, and Savoy Cabbage Casserole, as well as Virginia Pork Tenderloin with Fontina Polenta, Warm Spinach, and Porcini Mushroom Jus. Both of the entrées of local duck sounded wonderful—Pumpkin Seed-Crusted Breast of Duck and Spiced Duck Leg Confit with Brown Butter Spaetzle and Oven-Dried Strawberry Sauce. The extensive wine list features top vintages from quality producers. And don't forget to leave room for dessert. The choice will be difficult, as every one is homemade and creatively presented.

Located just outside the main gate is the Keswick Hunt Club, founded in 1896 and still active. In the off-season, the hunting dogs need to be exercised. The hounds are walked over the Keswick Hall grounds every day, much to the delight of the guests at the hotel. Staff members are always on hand to encourage visitors to join the dogs and their entourage on their daily constitutional. What a delightful Virginia custom, one of many to be enjoyed at Keswick Hall.

FIRE-ROASTED BEEF TENDERLOIN WITH MOREL MUSHROOM BREAD PUDDING

1 small onion, julienned
1 tablespoon vegetable oil
1 tablespoon minced garlic
½ pound crimini or button mushrooms, sliced
½ pound fresh morel mushrooms, washed
2 sprigs thyme
¼ cup white wine
1 small loaf bread, diced and oven-dried
½ cup chopped parsley
1 tablespoon Dijon mustard
¾ cup heavy cream
¾ cup milk
6 eggs
½ teaspoon nutmeg
3 ounces goat cheese
salt and pepper to taste

½ cup soy sauce
½ cup maple syrup
8 8-ounce beef tenderloin fillets

Preheat oven to 300 degrees. In a medium sauté pan, caramelize onions with oil. Add garlic and mushrooms. Sweat. Add thyme, then deglaze pan with wine. Place contents of pan in a large mixing bowl and add bread and parsley. Stir to combine. In a separate bowl, whisk together mustard, cream, milk, eggs, and nutmeg. Pour wet mixture over bread mixture and stir well to combine. Gently fold in cheese and season with salt and pepper. Place mixture in a well-greased 9-by-13-inch baking pan lined with parchment paper. Cover top of pudding with parchment paper to prevent burning. Bake for 1 hour. Remove from oven and slice into 8 pieces.

In a large, flat dish, combine soy sauce and maple syrup. Place fillets in mixture for 10 minutes on each side. Remove fillets from marinade and chill. Grill meat over an open flame to desired doneness. Plate each fillet with a serving of bread pudding. Serves 8.

THE HOMESTEAD. 1766

Cascades Club Restaurant at The Homestead
Hot Springs, VA 24445
www.thehomestead.com
540-839-1766

As I sat on the second-story screened porch in the pleasant breeze cooling the summer air, I listened to The Homestead's historian as facts, lore, and stories rolled off his tongue. They came as easily to him as the ABCs do to the rest of us.

It seems that Jacob Rubino, a wealthy New York stockbroker, vacationed at The Homestead. He so enjoyed the experience and was so enamored with the area that he decided to build a summer home here. He purchased seventeen hundred acres in the burg of Healing Springs. Sparing no expense, he hired an architectural firm from New York City to design his mansion. The creamy white brick came from Kentucky. The limestone was shipped from Indiana. All materials had to be hauled by mule-drawn wagons for miles along a dirt road and up the mountain just to reach the construction site.

The result was a lovely Italianate structure with a red tile roof. It was completed in the late 1890s. The Homestead acquired the property in 1923 and subsequently con-

verted it into the restaurant and pro shop for the Cascades Golf Course, which was built on Jacob Rubino's ample landholdings. Today's dining room is situated in what was once the living room, while the original dining room now serves as the bar area. The décor includes green and gold colors and tables and chairs of dark wood. The serving areas are marble-topped. In addition to the main dining room, two porches provide relaxing, enjoyable outdoor dining and boast vistas across the golf course to the mountains beyond.

The menu the day I dined was atypical. A lunch buffet was being served to accommodate the many young golfers there to participate in the Southern Amateur Golf Championship. I chose to create a vegetable platter from the buffet line, enjoying Baby Carrots, Green Beans, Roasted Red Potatoes, and Vegetable Lasagna in Creamy Alfredo Sauce. The regular menu features soups, salads, and sandwiches ranging from the ever-popular Barbecue to the indulgent Jumbo Lump Crabmeat Melt. My waitress told me that the Cobb Salad, made with shrimp and crabmeat, was one of the most popular luncheon choices. Karen later said that it would have been her choice if she'd been along.

The hospitality here has continued since the days of Jacob Rubino. He was a man known for his lavish parties. One of the sites of those parties was an indoor pool fed by the local springs. It was located in the area where the pro shop is today. Not only did

Rubino use those springs for pleasure, he also capitalized on them for business purposes. He had a spring-fed pond where he harvested watercress, which he sent to market in New York. He also bottled the spring water, shipped it to the city, and marketed it for medicinal purposes. Rubino certainly made the most out of his experiences in the area. Thanks to the championship golf, wonderful food, impeccable service, and beautiful ambiance, it's a sure bet that you will, too.

❦ STRING BEANS COUNTRY-STYLE ❦

2 tablespoons salt, divided
2 pounds fresh string beans
2 or 3 slices bacon
1 medium onion
1 tablespoon flour
3 cups water
1 cube chicken bouillon
¼ teaspoon beef stock concentrate
freshly ground white pepper to taste
freshly ground black pepper to taste

Fill a large saucepan with water. Add 1 tablespoon of the salt, cover, and bring to a boil. Snap beans at both ends and pull off any strings. Do not cut. Rinse beans in a colander under running water. When water comes to a boil, add beans all at once. Return water to a boil as quickly as possible. Once it comes to a boil, adjust heat to maintain a rapid simmer. Cook beans for 8 to 10 minutes until tender but still crisp. Remove pan from heat and put it under cold running water to stop the cooking process. Remove beans when tepid and drain in a colander. Set aside.

Cut bacon into matchstick-sized strips and set aside. Peel onion and chop fine. Set aside. Place a large saucepan over medium heat. Add bacon and cook, stirring with a spatula, until fat has been rendered. Stir in onions and sauté for about 1 minute. Add flour and blend thoroughly. Add water, mixing with a wire whisk. Add bouillon cube, beef stock, remaining salt, white pepper, and black pepper. Bring mixture to a simmer, stirring with the whisk. Simmer for 2 minutes, stirring occasionally. Raise heat to medium-high and add beans all at once. Return to a simmer and continue cooking for 4 to 6 minutes, stirring from time to time. Serve immediately. Serves 6 to 8.

MILK CHOCOLATE CHEESECAKE

butter for pan
13 tablespoons butter, divided
2 cups graham cracker crumbs
30 ounces milk chocolate
4 8-ounce packages cream cheese
½ cup powdered sugar
6 eggs
1 cup sour cream
¼ cup coffee liqueur
¼ cup mint liqueur

Butter a springform pan. Melt 5 tablespoons of the butter in a small saucepan. Put graham crackers crumbs in a 1-quart mixing bowl and stir in melted butter. Press crumb mixture onto bottom of springform pan, smoothing it out to an even thickness. Preheat oven to 350 degrees. Break chocolate into pieces and put them into the top half of a double boiler. Set over simmering water to melt chocolate. When chocolate is melted, remove from heat and reserve. Melt remaining butter in a small saucepan. In a large bowl, combine cream cheese and powdered sugar using an electric mixer. Continue mixing at medium speed until sugar is dissolved. Add eggs 1 at a time, mixing well after each addition and scraping sides and bottom of bowl with a rubber spatula. Mixture must be very smooth and free of lumps. When done, set aside. Stirring with a wire whisk, combine sour cream and liqueurs in a small bowl. Add melted butter, mixing thoroughly and scraping down bowl with spatula. Pour in melted chocolate and mix until very smooth. When mixture is free of lumps, combine it with cream cheese, using an electric mixer. Beat at medium speed until light and perfectly smooth. Pour into prepared pan and place on middle level of oven. Bake for 45 minutes to 1 hour. The top should have a light caramel color when done. Let cool in pan on a wire rack. Remove from pan and place on a serving plate. Chill for several hours before serving. Serves 12 to 16.

Two-Nineteen Restaurant

219 King Street
Old Town Alexandria
Alexandria, VA 22314
703-549-1141

According to *Gourmet* magazine, "Two-Nineteen serves some of the best Creole food to be found anywhere in the country." After I checked out the menu, I was extremely tempted by the Southern-Fried Calamari, the Louisiana Red Snapper Chowder, and the Cajun She-Crab Soup. Guests at the surrounding tables assured me that the Crawfish Etouffée, the Shrimp Clemenceau, and the Maryland Fried Oyster Sandwich were equally delicious. But in the end, I opted for the Seafood Gumbo, as it is one of my favorite dishes. I was not disappointed. Since one of the recipes I was given was for Red Beans, Sausage, and Rice, I also tried that dish. It was spicy and mouthwateringly good. I was sorry Debbie wasn't there to enjoy it with me.

The building was constructed in 1890 for local businessman Lewis MacKenzie. An extremely prosperous man, he wanted a comfortable and stylish house of the times.

The Victorian-style house had an ornate red-brick exterior and was reputed to be one of the most elegant homes in town. Rumor has it that the last private tenant, Edna M. Royster, found the house so comfortable that when she passed away, her ghost refused to move out!

During the 1960s and 1970s, Old Town Alexandria was in dire need of new investors, as many buildings had fallen into disrepair. In 1972, Clifford T. Cline bought the house intending to re-create the Victorian elegance of the past in a new restaurant. He invested an enormous amount of money in the interior of the house, as evidenced by the fine millwork in the chair rails, cornices, and mahogany bars. The antique furnishings were purchased as far away as London, where the matching marble fireplace mantels and many of the Victorian oil paintings were found. The mirrors were made by one of the few remaining craftsmen using a technique created at the turn of the twentieth century. Care was taken to ensure the authenticity of each and every detail in the house. It took over six years to complete the renovations, but the end result was well worth the wait. The Hungarian crystal chandeliers are lovely, as are the plush velvet chairs.

Besides the excellent cuisine, what makes the experience at Two-Nineteen so special is that you can choose from a variety of settings in which to eat your meal. Guests can enjoy the elegance of one of the three formal dining rooms, listen to live jazz in the Basin Street Lounge at the top of the house, or even visit the bar in the Bayou Room in the basement. People love to leave their business cards at the bar. Those cards have overflowed the bulletin board next to the bar and are displayed all over the walls and ceiling and even on the bar itself. If you visit Two-Nineteen, you can leave a little piece of your own history behind!

NEW ORLEANS-STYLE BARBECUED SHRIMP

1 cup butter
1 cup margarine
½ clove garlic, minced
1½ tablespoons pepper
1 tablespoon rosemary leaves
¼ teaspoon Tabasco
¼ cup Worcestershire sauce
1 lemon, sliced
1 pound shrimp, peeled and deveined

Melt butter and margarine in a large skillet. Add garlic, pepper, rosemary, Tabasco, Worcestershire, and lemon slices. Simmer over low heat for 30 minutes. Add shrimp and cover pan. Cook over medium heat until shrimp grow firm and turn pink. Turn shrimp several times during cooking. Remove from pan and drain. Serve immediately. Serves 4.

Note: Two-Nineteen serves this recipe with warm French Bread.

OYSTERS BIENVILLE

12 fresh oysters in the shell
½ cup butter
1 slice bacon, diced
1½ teaspoons minced garlic
pinch of salt
½ teaspoon white pepper
6 tablespoons flour
1 quart milk
2 tablespoons lemon juice
¼ cup white wine
2 tablespoons minced parsley
8 ounces baby shrimp, cooked

Shuck oysters. Arrange half shells on a sheet pan. Melt butter in a large skillet. Add bacon, garlic, salt, pepper, and flour. Allow flour mixture to become a light golden brown, stirring constantly. While stirring over low heat, slowly add milk until sauce thickens. Add rest of ingredients and allow to thicken slightly. Remove from heat and cool completely.

Top each oyster with ¼ cup cold sauce. Broil oysters until topping is bubbly and golden brown. Serve immediately. Serves 4 as an appetizer.

The Farmhouse RESTAURANT
You'll savor the tradition.

285 Ridinger Street NW
Christiansburg, VA 24068
540-382-4253

This authentic farmhouse was constructed in the 1800s as part of the extensive Ridinger Estate. You can still sit in the front parlor next to the lovely old brick fireplace with its gleaming copper pots and pans and enjoy a meal surrounded by the charm of the past. The buildings have been expanded over the years to allow new generations of guests to savor this southwestern Virginia landmark.

The Farmhouse Restaurant began serving guests in 1963 under the ownership of Gene Thomas. Initially, only 75 people could be accommodated at one time. Under today's owner, Arthur Tsiamis, over 250 guests can be served in the Grand Ballroom alone. Crystal Osbourne showed us around the building. She told us that one of the most interesting changes to The Farmhouse has been the addition of the original caboose from the local Huckleberry Train—so named because it progressed slowly enough through the mountains that the passengers were able to get off, pick berries, and jump back on before it passed!

Karen, who can never resist wandering around and peeking into every nook and cranny, had a wonderful time roaming the maze of hallways, booths, and cozy alcoves for two or four or more. Most of the walls are made of rough-hewn planks, which together with the red-and-white gingham tablecloths and the antique farm implements create a wonderfully rustic atmosphere. This is accentuated by the numerous old rifles and the unique collection of antique Indian statues. You'll find barrels, pottery firkins, ceramic water jugs, metal milk cans, and, last but not least, a large showcase of primitive paintings by a local artist. If you search very carefully, you will even find that one of the outside walls of the original farmhouse is still intact inside the expanded building.

The extensive lunch menu includes seven salads and nine sandwiches, to say nothing of the burgers, steaks, and pasta dishes. The special that day was the very spicy Vegetable Beef Soup, which caught Debbie's eye. Karen chose the Maryland Crab Cake Sandwich. Both were piping hot and delicious.

The dinner menu is more upscale and even longer. The Farmhouse has long been known for its fabulous steaks. Guests can find almost every cut of steak that exists, from Filet Mignon to Boneless Sirloin, from T-Bone for one to Châteaubriand for two. Alongside these choices are Ribs, Chops, and various chicken, seafood, and pasta dishes. Our hostess told us that one of the favorites for dessert is the Grasshopper Cake. However, we thought that the Chocolate Chess Sundae—a brownie-style pie topped with ice cream, Fudge Sauce, and whipped cream—sounded pretty good, too!

This is the sort of place that guests return to again and again, sure of a warm welcome and a delicious home-cooked meal. It's best summed up on the place mats at the tables, which state, "The Farmhouse Restaurant, You'll savor the tradition."

SALMON WITH DILL BUTTER

2 8-ounce salmon fillets
3 sprigs fresh dill, chopped and divided
½ cup warm water
2 tablespoons butter

Grill fillets over medium heat until marked with grill stripes. Move once to crisscross stripes. Preheat oven to 350 degrees. Put water and half of dill in an oven-safe container large enough to hold salmon. Add fillets and poach for about 10 minutes to finish cooking. Do not overcook. In a sauté pan, combine remaining dill with butter over medium heat. Once butter is melted, plate salmon, brush with Dill Butter, and serve. Serves 2.

SCALLOPS WRAPPED IN BACON

6 large sea scallops
¼ cup white wine
¼ cup water
½ cup breadcrumbs
¼ cup fresh shredded Parmesan
3 slices bacon
½ cup buttermilk
2 lettuce leaves
additional Parmesan for garnish
2 lemon wedges

In a medium sauté pan, partially cook scallops in wine and water. Remove scallops from liquid and chill. Combine breadcrumbs and cheese. Cut bacon in half crosswise. Preheat oven to 350 degrees. Dip scallops in buttermilk, then roll in breadcrumb mixture. Roll a half-slice of bacon around each scallop. Use a toothpick to secure. Place all 6 scallops on a skewer. Bake for 7 to 10 minutes until bacon is done. (You can deep-fry instead of baking if you prefer.) Serve on lettuce leaves, sprinkle with Parmesan, and garnish with lemon wedges. Serves 2 as an appetizer.

CHAPTER 8

The New *Mill*ennium

The Inn at Gristmill Square

Early in our history, mills played a vital role. They were crucial to the survival of the early settlers, providing the ingredients for nourishment at times when food was scarce. Today, technology has made many of those mills obsolete. The ones featured in the following pages have managed to evolve yet still provide sustenance to the citizens of their communities. Their continued presence evokes the pioneering spirit and the dependence on the land upon which our country was founded.

TUSCARORA MILL
at Leesburg
AN AMERICAN RESTAURANT AND CAFE

203 Harrison Street SE
Market Station
Leesburg, VA 20175
www.tuskies.com
703-771-9300

Normally, when a restaurant visit is in order, I'm alone or Karen and I are dining together. However, on this particular occasion, an entourage of eleven accompanied me. They were teammates and parents from my daughter's softball team. All of us were in the area for a national-championship softball tournament.

Once we were seated and our drink orders were taken, silver baskets filled with slices of Focaccia arrived. All twelve of us thoroughly enjoyed multiple pieces, the excellent wait staff promptly refilling our supply. Carol Seltz, one of my cohorts in my original ladies' luncheon group, ordered the Lobster Medallions appetizer. It passed muster with everyone who sampled it. Attractively presented on a bed of Sweet Potato Polenta and garnished with a stack of Sweet Potato Hay—crisp slivers of sweet potatoes only millimeters thick—the dish was an indication of good things to come. Our entrées of Sole, Rainbow Trout, and Salmon all got

hearty approval. The Vietnamese Stir-Fry Salad was a popular choice among our group, as was the Smoked Chicken and Penne Pasta, tossed with bacon, spinach, and peas in Asiago Cream Sauce. All were superb.

We were quite tempted by the desserts. We tried the Bread Pudding, swathed in bourbon and caramel and then topped with Vanilla Ice Cream. It was a real hit. We also received an order of the Double Chocolate Torte, for which the restaurant has been frequently recognized. It was a fudgy, rich, bittersweet concoction drizzled with Raspberry Sauce. Our final selection was the Chocolate Tiramisu, a light, refreshing end to a delectable summertime meal.

We sat in what I would describe as the garden dining room. Floral murals were painted over whitewashed walls. Lush ferns augmented the cool atrium atmosphere, creating a casual, yet elegant, feel. The bar area and the other dining room are much more rustic, displaying their original beams and rough walls. A collection of quilts adds a splash of color. It was a Tuesday evening in July when we visited, and the restaurant was packed. We all agreed that this was a true indication of the restaurant's success.

The mill was built in 1899, replacing a longstanding grain mill destroyed by fire the year before. In 1917, the structure was purchased by the Saffer family, who ran the business as an old-time general store. The store was both a meeting place for townsfolk and a place where seeds, supplies, machinery, and flour were meted out. Today, it's part of Market Station, a cluster of quaint buildings in downtown Leesburg. There are shops and offices as well as the restaurant. Frequently, visitors enjoy musical entertainment performed in the courtyard. The night we visited, a troupe was rehearsing for a performance of a Broadway show to be staged later in the week. Had our schedule allowed, we would have returned to enjoy the show and another meal from the Tuscarora Mill's delicious menu.

SAUTÉED CALAMARI

½ cup olive oil, divided
1 tablespoon plus 1½ teaspoons chopped garlic, divided
4 thick slices bread
½ cup shaved Asiago cheese
1 pound calamari, cleaned and cut into ½-inch rings
¼ cup white wine
½ cup chopped fresh tomato
2 tablespoons capers
4 tablespoons pitted and chopped black olives
1 cup marinara sauce
1 tablespoon finely chopped basil

Preheat oven to 450 degrees. Combine ¼ cup of the olive oil with 1½ teaspoons of the garlic. Brush bread with oil mixture. Top with Asiago. Place on a baking sheet and bake for about 10 minutes until golden brown. Set aside. Heat a large skillet on full flame. Add remaining olive oil and heat just until smoking. Add remaining garlic and brown. Add calamari and cook 2 minutes. Add wine and cook 1 minute. Add tomatoes, capers, olives, marinara, and basil. Cook 2 minutes. Serve immediately. Serve with garlic toast. Serves 4 as an appetizer.

GLAZED PORKCHOPS

¾ cup ketchup
¼ cup plus 1 tablespoon light molasses
¼ cup bourbon
2 tablespoons Dijon mustard
1 large clove garlic, minced
6 8-ounce porkchops
salt and pepper to taste
Spiced Onion Marmalade (recipe below)

Preheat oven to 400 degrees. Spray a baking pan with nonstick cooking spray. Whisk first 5 ingredients together in a small bowl. Sprinkle porkchops with salt and pepper. Brush porkchops on each side with 1 generous tablespoon of glaze. Place in baking pan and bake for about 20 minutes. Serve with warm Spiced Onion Marmalade. Serves 6.

Gristmill Square

The Inn at Gristmill Square
VA 645
Warm Springs, VA 24484
540-839-2231

In one quick turn off US 220, cars immediately seem out of place as they wind their way past buildings of yesteryear. Cottages, the local library, tin-roofed homes, and the courthouse—all bring on bouts of reminiscing. A little farther down the road is the delightful haven known as The Inn at Gristmill Square, operated by the McWilliams family.

The inn is a delightful combination of buildings that continues to give off the aura of a community. Rather than stores and businesses, they now house lovely, spacious guest rooms for overnight visitors. The cream building with gold trim was a hardware store until the late 1800s. The light sage building with the large clock at the peak of the eaves was a country store. The miller's house now has accommodations creatively referred to as the Oat Room, the Barley Room, the Wheat Room, and the Rye Room. The old mill, the focal point of the collection, functions as The Waterwheel Restaurant.

A mill was constructed on this site around 1771, when Jacob Butler began grinding cornmeal for his hoecakes and spoon bread. From that point until 1969, a mill was in operation here. The current building, constructed in 1900, utilized an overshot wheel. In the center of the restaurant is the grain elevator. In fact, some of the shafts still open. The hopper housing the mill stone is still there, along with the screw mechanism once used to change the heavy stones.

My server, Debby, has been with the restaurant from its inception in the early 1970s. She was a wealth of information not only about the menu but also about the structure itself. After I let her guide me on my menu selections, she invited me to wander. I first poked my head in the old miller's office. It's now a cozy bar extremely popular with guests. It has space for two tables, a small bar with four barstools, and a potbelly stove. The wine is stored in the cellar of the mill along the stone walls. Diners are encouraged to go down and inspect the wide variety before making a selection for their meal.

As I climbed the steps, my Chilled Avocado Soup was being delivered to my table. It was a refreshing way to begin a meal on a hot summer night. That was followed by a lovely tossed salad dressed with a Greek-inspired vinaigrette full of feta cheese and chopped olives. My entrée, one of two trout selections on the menu, was Black Walnut Trout, served with Steamed Broccoli and a

Baked Potato. Truly, I savored every bite. Had Karen been along, I have no doubt that she would have enjoyed either the Chocolate Mousse or the Profiterole in Butterscotch Sauce for dessert. For once, I refrained, savoring instead a few more sips of my cool, authentic spring water. After all, this is Warm Springs!

PÂTÉ MAISON

1½ pounds chicken livers
1 pound lean pork
½ pound bulk sausage
1 tablespoon chopped shallots
2 tablespoons chopped fresh parsley
1 teaspoon pepper
½ teaspoon ground ginger
½ teaspoon cinnamon
1½ teaspoons salt
2 tablespoons brandy
2 tablespoons dry white wine
6 to 8 strips bacon

Place all ingredients except bacon in a food processor and process until finely blended. Line a pâté mold or loaf pan with bacon strips. These should slightly overlap and be placed across the pan so edges of bacon hang over pan. Pour meat mixture over bacon strips. Bring hanging strips over top. Place pâté pan in a second pan filled with water to cover ¾ of pâté pan. Bake in a 350-degree oven for 2½ hours. Remove from oven and place weight on top of pan (a brick covered in foil works nicely) until pâté is cooled. Refrigerate and slice thin to serve with Melba toast or cocktail bread. Serves 12.

CINNAMON MUFFINS

2 eggs
½ cup canola oil
1 cup low-fat milk
2 cups flour
1 cup sugar
1 tablespoon baking powder
1 heaping tablespoon cinnamon
½ cup raisins

Heat oven to 350 degrees. Mix eggs, oil, and milk with a wire whisk. Fold in flour, sugar, baking powder, and cinnamon. Do not beat or muffins will be tough. Some lumps will remain in batter. Stir in raisins. Grease a muffin tin with nonstick cooking spray. Fill cups about ¾ full with batter. Bake about 25 minutes until firm to the touch. Yields 12 muffins.

1 Mill Street
Staunton, VA 24401
www.millstreetgrill.com
540-886-0656

The menu at Mill Street Grill is extensive. It starts off with Oysters Rockefeller, includes traditional favorites like Potato Skins and Steamed Shrimp, and even has options like Grilled Chicken Satay. Fortunately, an Appetizer Sampler is available, so those struggling with indecision can have a bite of this and that. Had Karen been with me, I imagine that's what we would have tried. Six salads are offered, many of which come in several varieties. I opted for the Cajun Shrimp Spinach Salad drizzled with one of the house specialties, Orange Poppy Seed Dressing.

The restaurant is well known for its ribs, and my daughter was happy to provide a taste test, ordering the White Star Rib Platter, which includes both Baby Back Ribs and St. Louis Ribs. Steaks, pork, chicken, veal, pasta, and seafood are also served up in plentiful quantities. My husband reveled in the Chicken and Shrimp Bracica, served over a bed of rice.

The history of this old mill can be traced back to 1890, when Michael Kivilghan, Isaac Witz, Charles Holt, and Andrew Bowling created White Star Mills. The firm's main purpose was to construct a mill with modern machinery for the processing of wheat and corn feed, meal, and flour. The Edward P. Allis Company of Milwaukee—the largest, most successful mill builder in the world—was awarded the contract for installing the milling machines. The stone foundation was quarried closer to home—less than a mile away, in fact—and the bricks were fired locally. The beams, still in place today, are of wormy chestnut. A tidbit we found fascinating was the fact that they carry a higher fire ranking than steel beams.

Although Bowling withdrew his interest in the company seven years later, the families of the other men continued the operation until 1963. Michael Kivilghan passed away in 1942, leaving his son J. Harold Kivilghan his ownership share. Harold subsequently became the manager and immediately launched plans to modernize, updating from steam to full electrical power. The younger Kivilghan also constructed five silos that increased the wheat storage capacity to nearly a quarter of a million bushels. By the time all the improvements were made, the mill was able to churn out a thousand barrels a day. The main brand of flour milled here was sold under the name Melrose, a Southern kitchen staple for many years. Other brands such as Kansas Rocket, Dixie Biscuit, Gurley's Carolina Queen, and

White Star Feed all began here.

From 1963 until 1970, the building sat empty, slowly deteriorating. A slow, arduous restoration was undertaken by HHK Properties. It wasn't until 1980 that a restaurant opened here, using the name White Star Mill. In March 1992, owners Ron Bishop and Terry Holmes finally discovered a recipe for success—good food served with fast, fun, efficient service, all in the cozy confines of a turn-of-the-twentieth-century mill.

 PROSCIUTTO- AND PROVOLONE-STUFFED CHICKEN

2 8-ounce boneless, skinless chicken breasts
2 slices provolone
¼ pound prosciutto, shaved
6 tablespoons butter
¼ cup flour
2 teaspoons chopped garlic
scant ⅓ cup Marsala wine
½ cup chicken stock
½ cup beef stock
6 button mushrooms, sliced
½ cup julienned onion
1 teaspoon dried basil
generous pinch of oregano
¾ cup shredded Parmesan, divided
2 servings angel hair pasta, prepared according to package directions
generous pinch of parsley

Using a meat-tenderizing mallet, beat chicken until an even thickness is achieved. Place a slice of provolone on half of each chicken breast. Place prosciutto on other half of chicken. Fold over so ham and provolone are sandwiched in between. Heat a sauté pan over medium heat. Melt butter in pan. Heavily dust chicken with flour and place in pan. Cook 3 to 4 minutes. Flip and cook an additional 3 to 4 minutes, adding garlic toward the end. Add wine and simmer. Add chicken stock, beef stock, mushrooms, onions, basil, and oregano. Reduce liquid by at least ⅓ until thick. When chicken is done, add half of Parmesan to thicken sauce. Place pasta on a large plate. Place chicken in center and top with mixture from pan. Sprinkle parsley on top and garnish with remaining Parmesan. Serves 2.

THE MAIN STREET MILL PUB & GRILLE

500 East Main Street
Front Royal, VA 22630
540-636-3123

Upon being seated for lunch, we noticed that we were being watched—not by the other diners, although the restaurant was full, but by a horse and a ghostly apparition. They were both works of local artist Patricia Windrow, painted into the whimsically attractive mural that surrounds the first-floor dining room. The horse was peeking around a beam, which itself was painted to look like the real beams visible throughout the restaurant. Many actual architectural features are incorporated into the mural. Sometimes, you have to look twice to see what is three-dimensional and what is part of the scenery.

Belle Boyd was the ghost peering over Debbie's shoulder. Belle, known as "the Siren of the South," was a Confederate spy. She operated from her father's hotel here in Front Royal, gleaning strategic information that she passed to Generals Turner Ashby and Stonewall Jackson during the Shenandoah Valley Campaign of 1862. Be-

trayed by her lover, she was captured that July and sent to prison. She contracted typhoid and was sent to Europe to regain her health. After recovering, she embarked upon a successful stage career in England and wrote several books about her experiences.

The military action here enshrined Stonewall Jackson as one of history's great commanders. The blows delivered by Jackson's men temporarily paralyzed the Union army in its attempt to advance on Richmond. During one forty-eight-day stretch, Jackson drove his men hard, covering 646 miles and sending Northern forces on one wild goose chase after another. The Battle of Front Royal commenced on Friday, May 3, 1862.

The mill was built in the 1890s, long after the conflict ended. A fire in 1921 destroyed it. The structure was quickly rebuilt. It was used as a feed mill until the 1980s, at which time it was converted into a restaurant. There is no mistaking the building's original purpose, as the Proctor Biggs sign painted at the top of the mill can still be seen for quite some distance.

As we watched lunches issuing forth from the kitchen, it was quickly obvious that the Pulled Pork BBQ Sandwich was a popular choice. Debbie rarely misses a chance to enjoy barbecue. Her only disappointment with the meal was that she failed to order a side of Onion Rings to accompany her tasty selection. Karen opted for the Shrimp and Crab Chowder, served in a bread bowl. It was a deliciously successful way to find some warmth on a rainy day. The home-made Vegetable Beef Soup would have suited that purpose equally well. The Nacho Grande Platter was a popular selection delivered to several tables nearby. Judging from the size of the portion, the word *grande* was apt. The menu includes salads, steaks, pastas, burgers, and sandwiches, so there's something for everyone at this local landmark.

MAPLE-GLAZED PORKCHOPS

4 center-cut porkchops, bone in
1 cup maple syrup, divided
¼ cup honey

Marinate chops in ¾ cup of the maple syrup for 1 to 3 hours. Discard syrup. Grill chops for 5 to 7 minutes per side, depending on thickness. Combine remaining maple syrup with honey. Brush chops with mixture during grilling, reserving enough to drizzle over finished chops. Serves 4.

APPLE SPICE CAKE

1 box spice cake mix
20-ounce can apple pie filling
2 cups powdered sugar
2 teaspoons vanilla
2 to 3 tablespoons milk

Preheat oven to 350 degrees. Prepare cake according to package directions. Coat a 13-by-9-inch pan with nonstick spray. Spoon apple pie filling over bottom of pan. Pour batter over apples. Bake as directed on cake package. While baking, combine sugar, vanilla, and milk in a medium bowl. When cake is cool, drizzle over top. Cut in squares to serve. Serves 12.

CRAB MELT

1 pound crabmeat
¼ cup diced celery
¼ cup diced red onion
4 hard-boiled eggs, diced
½ teaspoon Old Bay seasoning
¼ teaspoon dill weed
½ cup mayonnaise
¼ cup sour cream
4 English muffins
8 slices tomato
8 slices cheddar

Combine first 8 ingredients in a medium bowl. Separate muffins. Top each muffin half with 1 slice of tomato, crab mixture, and 1 slice of cheddar. Broil in oven just until cheese melts. Serves 4.

at the mill

198 North Twenty-first Street
Purcellville, VA 20132
www.magnoliasmill.com
540-338-9800

When this town was invaded in November 1862, a *New York Times* reporter wrote, "Purcellville cannot be dignified with the title of village, consisting merely of a few struggling houses on the Winchester and Leesburg Turnpike." Through early 1874, things remained much the same. Purcellville was still a hamlet consisting of a blacksmith shop, a store or two, a small hotel, a few houses, and an eating establishment.

All that changed with the arrival of the Washington & Ohio Railroad. The first train pulled into the local station around noon on March 31, 1874. Several days later, Leesburg's newspaper, the *Loudon Mirror*, observed, "The running of the trains has set the little village aglow with activity. The scene around the depot on Saturday reminded us of accounts we read of towns and cities springing up as it were, in a night."

The area was still abuzz on the day I visited. Unfortunately, Karen was not along to enjoy the hustle and bustle. Members of the Purcellville Preservation Society were arriving for a luncheon meeting at the depot, which still looks as it did at the turn of the twentieth century. Right next door is the mill, built in 1905. W. H. Adams acquired it to provide farmers seed for corn, wheat, other grains, and orchard grass, on which many of the area's dairy cows grazed. After the advent of hybrid corn, Adams and his son, Contee, began to concentrate on the cleaning of seed.

In 1943, Contee Adams decided to sell the milling portion of his business to Wilkins & Rogers, which owned the successful milling operation at Hamilton Mill. An accord was reached in which Adams agreed not to sell feed and Wilkins & Rogers agreed not to sell seed. Adams subsequently moved his business across the street, and Wilkins & Rogers remained at the mill until 1967, when Contee Adams, Jr., took over his father's seed business and also bought back the mill.

The restoration of the mill began in late 2001 and was completed in February 2004. The fabulous result is the restaurant known as Magnolia's at the Mill. In the main dining room, the mill works are still plainly visible, as are the rough wooden walls. Colorful quilts hanging throughout add a splash of color, as do the interesting lights mounted above each table and along the bar.

Magnolia's is a charming, eclectic restaurant that serves items such as a Grilled Chicken Breast Sandwich with Red Onion Marmalade, Horseradish-Crusted Salmon, and Grilled Tamarind Citrus-Glazed Breast of Chicken. It has a wood-fired grill and a pizza oven and specializes in what it calls "Small Plates," a unique version of an appetizer menu. It's obvious that the staff at Magnolia's at the Mill has planted a new "seed" that will allow all of us to enjoy its truly unique "feed."

 LACQUERED SALMON

2 green onions
1 to 2 teaspoons water
1 ice cube
1½ cups mashed potatoes
wasabi to taste
2 3-ounce salmon fillets
2 to 3 teaspoons sugar
1/3 cup soy sauce

Preheat oven to 425 degrees. Blanch and shock green onions. Squeeze excess water out. Cut woody tips off. Purée the remainder in a blender with the water and ice to keep the green color. Fold into mashed potatoes. Add wasabi. Keep warm. Dust salmon with sugar. Sear salmon in a sauté pan on medium heat until sugar is caramelized. Deglaze pan with soy sauce and reduce by half. Place salmon in the oven for 3 to 5 minutes to finish cooking. Place salmon atop mashed potatoes. Drizzle with soy syrup. Yields 2 "Small Plate" servings.

GRILLED TAMARIND CITRUS-GLAZED BREAST OF CHICKEN

2 quarts chicken stock
2 cups orange juice
1 cup sugar
3 tablespoons butter
½ cup tamarind paste
3 tablespoons grated orange zest
3 tablespoons grated ginger
4 10-ounce chicken breasts
salt and pepper to taste
rice
2 cups Pineapple Chutney
½ cup macadamia nuts, roasted and chopped

Whisk together chicken stock, orange juice, sugar, butter, tamarind paste, orange zest, and ginger in a large pot. Bring to a boil. Reduce heat and simmer until reduced to about 2 cups. Season chicken with salt and pepper. Coat chicken with tamarind glaze and grill. Serve with rice and Pineapple Chutney. Garnish with macadamia nuts. Serves 4.

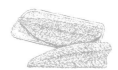

FORT LEWIS LODGE

On the Cowpasture River
Millboro, VA 24460
www.fortlewislodge.com
540-925-2314

I can honestly say that the first afternoon I spent at Fort Lewis Lodge was one of the most restful and peaceful I've had in years. I was sorry Debbie wasn't along. I whiled away a happy afternoon visiting the various buildings that make up the farm and strolling down to the Cowpasture River to check out the swimming hole. The lodge is nestled on approximately thirty-two hundred acres of mountain farmland once known as Fort Lewis Plantation.

John Lewis fled to America around 1728 to escape murder charges after an unfortunate encounter with his landlord. Since his brother-in-law, Dr. William Lynn, was part of eastern Virginia's gentry and was heavily involved in land speculation, John brought his growing family to the Shenandoah Valley and became a land agent himself. Two of his sons were surveyors. This placed the Lewis family in a prime position to acquire the best land available. Around 1750, John Lewis made a trip to the 950-acre tract he owned alongside the Cowpasture River. He

erected a crude log cabin and planted crops. By 1756, he built a small wooden stockade around the dwelling, to which nearby families could come for protection from Indian raids.

By the time John Cowden acquired the land in 1950, the fort was long gone. In its place were an 1850 gristmill, a barn, and a glazed-tile silo. After working the farm for some time and experimenting with various other ventures, John and his wife, Caryl, decided the best use of their land would be to encourage others to visit it. So they took down the barn and reused the timbers in the construction of a lodge. They also restored the gristmill. The mill has a large kitchen and dining room on the first floor and a great room on the second floor with activities for guests. The walls upstairs are covered with articles about the lodge and testimonials to the delicious meals and good hunting to be found here. I was amazed by the huge hand-hewn beams and the fabulous stenciling on the wide-plank floor upstairs. Downstairs, the kitchen is open for all to see. Arrive early and you'll spot Caryl hard at work in the kitchen creating tempting desserts and creative salads made from vegetables grown in the farm's own gardens. John can often be found manning one of the outside grills, when he's not behind the bar or doing something handy around the place.

There is one seating for dinner. Visitors are called in from the decks and pastures by the ringing of a large bell. Or, like me, they can wander across to the mill early and have a delicious glass of wine or locally produced beer while sitting on the deck overlooking the millpond or while admiring the unusual fountain—made entirely from wind instruments—next to the bar.

The dining room is informal, cozy, and comfortable. A variety of stuffed and mounted wild creatures look down from the walls. Dinners are served buffet-style here. On the night I visited, the delicious Beef Tenderloin was on the menu. I sampled the Caesar-Style Potatoes, the Green Beans with Caramelized Onions, the Fresh Tomato-Cheese Casserole, and the divine Pumpkin Muffins. The Spinach and Strawberry Salad was terrific, as was the Dilled Cucumber and Pasta Salad. To top it all off, the Almond Mocha Cake with Coffee Ice Cream proved a perfect ending to a memorable meal.

 CAESAR-STYLE POTATOES

2½ pounds red potatoes
1 small onion, diced
4 slices bacon, cooked and crumbled
1 hard-boiled egg, diced
2 tablespoons chopped fresh parsley
¼ cup vegetable oil
2 tablespoons lemon juice
2 tablespoons grated Parmesan
½ tablespoon salt
½ tablespoon Worcestershire sauce
1/8 teaspoon pepper

In a large saucepan, cook potatoes in boiling water about 20 minutes until tender. Drain and cube potatoes. In a large bowl, combine potatoes, onions, bacon, egg, and parsley. Toss gently. Combine oil and remaining ingredients, beating until thoroughly blended. Pour dressing slowly over potato mixture and toss gently to combine. Serve immediately. Serves 6.

FRESH TOMATO-CHEESE CASSEROLE

2 medium purple onions, sliced thin
6 tablespoons butter, melted
2 cups croutons
6 large tomatoes, sliced
1 teaspoon salt
½ teaspoon pepper
¾ teaspoon basil leaves, dried
3 cups Monterey Jack or cheddar, shredded

Preheat oven to 350 degrees. Sauté onions in butter in a large skillet for 5 minutes. Add croutons and sauté for a further 5 to 10 minutes. Set aside. Place tomato slices in a large bowl. Sprinkle with salt, pepper, and basil. Toss gently. Spoon half the onion mixture into a 13-by-9-inch baking dish. Arrange half the tomatoes over onion mixture. Sprinkle with half the cheese. Repeat layers. Bake uncovered for 35 to 40 minutes until hot and bubbly. Serves 8.

Old Mill Restaurant

497 Stover Avenue
Strasburg, VA 22657
540-465-5590

When General Philip Sheridan made his march through this valley during the Civil War, he torched almost everything in his path. This mill was one of only three along the charred swath that was spared. Instead, the Union forces utilized the structure to process the grain pillaged from local farms. Prior to the conflict, the fertile lands around Strasburg had produced enough that wagon trains regularly carted loads to Pennsylvania and Washington, D.C. After Sheridan's destruction, none of the large farms remained. Only small, unsuccessful, subsistence-type farmsteads were left. They were unable to generate the level of production the area had seen before the war. It took nearly a hundred years for the economy to recover.

The mill was built in 1797 and continued operating until 1926. Children were frequently dispatched with a bucket or a burlap sack to go knock on the miller's door and ask him to fill it up from the family's supply, stored in the second-story loft. In 1938,

the building was purchased by George Pappas, who converted it into a tavern open for breakfast, lunch, and dinner seven days a week. The reputation of Pappas's Old Mill Tavern was widespread. Many guests come to the restaurant today and talk fondly of Saturday nights there. Folks would drive from Luray, Front Royal, and other communities to do the jitterbug and other new dances.

The stone building with weathered wood siding looks much as it did then. A postcard from the 1940s shows little difference from today's facade. The photograph was taken by a young man who sent it off to the Wayne Paper Box and Printing Company of Fort Wayne, Indiana, where it was turned into postcards. He did the same with a photo of a local church. His intent was to sell the postcards to the locations on the front, which could in turn sell them as souvenirs. It seems he was a better photographer than a salesman. When he passed away some fifty years later, his daughter came across unsold boxes of postcards in the attic of his home. She brought them to each location and managed to complete the transactions her father had started a half-century before.

Not too long after Sarah Mauck took over the restaurant, a foreign dignitary was a dinner guest here. Also dining that evening was ninety-seven-year-old Strasburg native Julia Campbell. The dignitary had several questions about the mill, some of which

Sarah couldn't answer. So she called across the room to ask Julia Campbell. Campbell began to recount her childhood memories of the mill, such as how she had to ford the creek in the family wagon just to get here. Pretty soon, the dignitary pulled his table over to Campbell's, where she entertained him with stories of Strasburg's past. The gesture reflected everything the restaurant is— a comfortable, welcome-home kind of place.

The Sunday buffet at the Old Mill Restaurant is extremely popular. The selection and quantity of items are intended to pay homage to the local farmers. The regular menu is simpler, consisting of four or five items written on a board guests see as they enter the building. The choices change each weekend. On the Saturday evening we visited, the offerings were Vegetable Lasagna, Crab Cakes, Rib Eye, Chicken Mozzarella, and Spiced Shrimp. Sarah believes in keeping it simple and doing what you do well, a philosophy we heartily endorse!

JEAN'S POTATO WHOLE-WHEAT BREAD

3 tablespoons sugar
2 teaspoons salt
2 tablespoons butter
½ cup potatoes, mashed
1½ cups water
1 cup milk
4 cups flour
1 cup whole-wheat flour
2½ tablespoons dry yeast

Preheat oven to 350 degrees. Place sugar, salt, butter, potatoes, water, and milk in a medium saucepan and heat through. Do not boil. Remove from stove. In a large bowl, combine flour, whole-wheat flour, and yeast. Add potato mixture and combine until a soft dough is formed. Add more flour and knead again. Place dough in a greased bowl and let rise for about 25 minutes until doubled in size. Punch down dough and work into individual loaves. Allow to rise again. Bake loaves for about 1 hour until crust is brown and loaves give a hollow sound when you thump the top. Yields 8 to 10 mini loaves or 2 large loaves.

PINEAPPLE DELIGHT

20-ounce can crushed pineapple with juice
¼ cup brown sugar
¼ cup sugar
⅓ cup butterscotch schnapps
2 tablespoons cornstarch
handful of dried apricots, diced

In a noncorrosive pan, bring pineapple and juice, brown sugar, sugar, schnapps, and cornstarch to a boil. Remove from heat. Add apricots and stir well. Allow to cool. Mixture can be served over vanilla ice cream. Or as a nice winter alternative to strawberry shortcake, you can spoon it over pound cake and top it with whipped cream. Yields 2 cups.

Old Mill Tavern at the Swift Creek Mill
17401 Jefferson Davis Highway
Colonial Heights, VA 23834
www.swiftcreekmill.com
804-748-5203

Henry Randolph of Little Houghton, South Haptonshire, England, emigrated to this country around 1640. Some years later, he acquired a large tract of land in the area known as Bermuda Hundred on Swift Creek, where he subsequently erected a mill. Historic documents indicate that there has been a mill here since 1663, making this the oldest gristmill site in the country. William Bland Randolph, an heir of Henry Randolph, deeded the mill to William Rowlett on February 20, 1805. In 1852, Rowlett's heirs changed the name from Rowlett Mill to the Swift Creek Manufacturing Company.

May 9 and 10, 1864, saw a battle waged around the mill as Union general B. F. Butler's Army of the James attempted to ford Swift Creek. The Confederacy suffered heavy casualties, but the Union army did not follow up, resulting in an inconclusive outcome of the skirmish. After the Civil War, the prop-erty became a distillery. Following that endeavor, it again was used as a gristmill, taking the name Swift Creek Mill in 1929 and continuing its operations until 1956.

On December 2, 1965, the former mill opened its doors as the Swift Creek Mill Playhouse. Although renovations and additions were required to accommodate this use, the exterior stone and brick remained intact. Much of the old equipment was refurbished to accessorize the rustic building. Today, the playhouse is the last remaining dinner theater in the greater Richmond area. Posters of many of the shows performed here through the years line the old, white-washed stone walls of the restaurant.

Seated in the upstairs dining room, known as the Mill Room, we enjoyed a quiet Sunday brunch, munching on Biscuits, Cinnamon Rolls, and omelets as we marveled at the relics. Over in the far corner at the opposite side of the restaurant were the housings for the old grist stones. This was some mill in days gone by, operating with three stones.

On theater evenings, the Mill Room serves a buffet while, downstairs, the Old Mill Tavern offers perennial favorites like Veal Marsala, Crab Cakes, Chicken Cordon Bleu, and Prime Rib. The starters range from Roasted Red Pepper Soup to Oysters on the Half Shell to a salad of field greens, pecans, and strawberries, topped with the house dressing. Entrées like Duck with Apple Butter and Porkchops Stuffed with Cornbread and Apples reflect the restaurant's vision of traditional Southern flavors combined in new and appealing ways.

Before leaving, we stood at the water's edge, where ducks swam peacefully in the still water just downstream from where it rushed over the dam. It gave us pause to think of how many other people visiting the mill have enjoyed that spot as well.

 SPOON BREAD EGGS BENEDICT WITH GRILLED ASPARAGUS AND BROILED TOMATOES

2½ cups water, divided
1 cup yellow cornmeal
1 teaspoon salt
1 cup milk or buttermilk
4 eggs, beaten
2 tablespoons butter
1 pound fresh asparagus
2 medium beefsteak tomatoes
4 eggs, poached
1 to 1½ cups hollandaise sauce

Preheat oven to 400 degrees. Butter a 1½-quart casserole. Stir ½ cup of the water into cornmeal. Bring remaining 2 cups water to a boil. Add salt, then add cornmeal slowly, stirring constantly. Cook for 1 minute. Beat in milk, beaten eggs, and butter until smooth. Pour into casserole and bake for about 40 minutes until a straw inserted in center comes out clean. Allow to cool. While Spoon Bread is cooling, trim woody ends of asparagus. Grill about 5 minutes until stalks are al dente. Place tomatoes under broiler for 1 to 2 minutes. Cut Spoon Bread into 4 servings. Top each serving with a poached egg and hollandaise sauce. Serve with a side of grilled asparagus and a broiled tomato. Serves 4.

RUM RAISIN GRITS

1 cup water
1 cup rum
½ cup quick grits
½ cup sugar
½ cup raisins

Bring water and rum to a boil in a medium saucepan. Pour in grits and whisk continuously to prevent lumps. Cook over medium heat for about 10 minutes until desired thickness is reached. Remove from heat and add sugar and raisins. Stir to combine. Set aside in a warm place and allow raisins to plump slightly. Serve alongside Spoon Bread Eggs Benedict with Grilled Asparagus and Broiled Tomatoes. Serves 4.

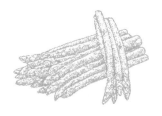

BOAR'S HEAD Inn

200 Ednam Drive
Charlottesville, VA 22903
www.boarsheadinn.com
434-296-2181

The Boar's Head Inn is located on the original site of Terrell's Ordinary, a relatively humble inn that offered meals to travelers moving west to find a better life. In the 1960s, local businessman John Rogan convinced a group of his friends to help him build the quintessential inn on the site of Terrell's Ordinary. An old gristmill on the banks of the Hardware River was carefully taken apart and reconstructed as the basis for the inn. Every fieldstone, pine beam, and plank of wood was carefully numbered so as to be sure it was placed exactly as it had been.

Built in 1834, the gristmill had prospered until the Union army marched through town. As was their custom, the soldiers tried to burn it to prevent the townspeople from supplying the Confederate army with flour and cornmeal. Many tales have been passed down of the heavy rain that day, and of the solid construction that stopped any real dam-

age from occurring. Once the army passed through and was well out of sight, the miller came out of hiding, and local trade resumed. When the war was over, a retired Confederate captain purchased the mill and ran a very successful business there for the next sixty years.

One cold and windy fall day, I sat in the Old Mill Room in a cozy seat next to the window. Debbie was dining elsewhere on that occasion. The original hand-hewn posts and beams dwarf the large room. The old wooden floors and the unique wrought-iron candlestick chandeliers add to the ambiance. The pictures of famous horses lining the walls remind visitors of Virginia's heritage of hunting and horse breeding.

This restaurant's American cuisine has earned an unparalleled AAA Four Diamond rating for the past sixteen years. Grilled Hawaiian Swordfish with Fingerling Potato Ecrasée and Sun-Dried Tomato Fondue is among the many delicious items on the menu, as is Cinnamon-Dusted Leg of Venison with Spinach and Wild Mushroom Ragout. I was particularly taken with the Sweet Potato Crêpe with Crabmeat Sage Cream and Crispy Pancetta, as well as the Warm Goat Cheese with Tapenade Crust, Poached Pear, and Fig and Ginger Dressing. Even the salads are unusual. The Radicchio and Watercress Salad with Roasted Root Vegetables, Filberts, and Mascarpone Cheese Dressing was my favorite.

Back in the days of Good Queen Bess

and Shakespeare, the Boar's Head Inn in England was renowned for the food it offered to travel-worn ladies and gentlemen. Boars' heads were used on public tavern signs to indicate that hospitality could be found within. That tradition continues today at the Boar's Head Inn in historic Charlottesville.

 SEAFOOD RAVIOLI

1 cup white wine
1 bay leaf
¼ bunch thyme
½ bunch tarragon, divided
2 black peppercorns
1 cup shallots, chopped
2 1½-pound whole lobsters
1 stalk celery, chopped
1 leek, chopped
1 carrot, chopped
1 onion, chopped
1½ cups sweet corn
2 tablespoons tomato paste
2 cups sherry
1 quart heavy whipping cream
salt and pepper to taste
12 4-by-6-inch fresh pasta sheets
24 small scallops
24 medium shrimp, peeled and deveined
1 pound lump crabmeat
½ cup combined zucchini, squash, red peppers, and yellow peppers, diced fine

In a large pot, place wine, bay leaf, thyme, half of the tarragon, peppercorns, and shallots. Add enough water to hold lobsters. Bring pot to a rolling boil. Add lobsters and cook for 10 to12 minutes. Remove lobsters and plunge them in ice water. Retain cook-

ing liquid. Extract meat from lobsters, roughly chop meat, and set aside.

In a large pot, sauté celery, leeks, carrots, onions, and corn until moisture has been removed. Add tomato paste and mix well. Add sherry and remaining tarragon. Reduce by ½. Add reserved cooking liquid and reduce by ½ to ¾. Add cream and reduce by ½. Strain through a large-holed sieve, then purée solids. Add purée back to strained liquid. Add salt and pepper.

In a large pan, bring enough water to a boil to cook pasta sheets according to package directions. In another large pan, sauté scallops, shrimp, and crabmeat. Add diced vegetables and cook thoroughly. Add sauce and lobster to pan. Stir well.

Place a cooked pasta sheet on each of 6 plates, spoon sauce and seafood over pasta, and place another piece of pasta over top. Serve immediately. Serves 6.

 POTATO-CRUSTED HALIBUT

1 medium potato, peeled
2 tablespoons butter, melted
4 6-ounce portions halibut
2 tablespoons oil
Artichoke and Fennel Confit
  (recipe on page 190)

Preheat oven to 375 degrees. Using a small ring-mold cutter about 1½ inches in diameter, cut potato into cylinders. Slice cylinders into thin circles. Dip potato circles in melted butter, then place on top of halibut, overlapping each circle so top of fish is covered.

Heat oil in a sauté pan. Add halibut to pan potato side down and gently sear until potato is golden brown. Carefully flip fish and sear bottom. Place in oven for 10 to 12 minutes until fish is firm and cooked. Serve over Artichoke and Fennel Confit. Serves 4.

 ARTICHOKE AND FENNEL CONFIT

½ onion, chopped
1 shallot, chopped
1 clove garlic, chopped
2 bulbs fennel, chopped, roots removed
4 artichoke hearts, chopped
4 sprigs tarragon, chopped
2 tablespoons oil of your choice
½ bunch chives, chopped
¼ red pepper, diced

Preheat oven to 265 degrees. In a medium sauté pan, sweat onions, shallots, garlic, and fennel. Add artichokes and tarragon and cover with oil. Cook in oven for 30 to 40 minutes. Plate and garnish with chives and red peppers. Serve immediately. Serves 4.

CHAPTER 9

Goods and Services

Southern Inn Restaurant

This chapter features restaurants housed in buildings that were once stores or warehouses. The interiors are not elaborate, since the structures' original uses were ones of function rather than style. For many of these estalishments, the buildings' original brick walls provide the backdrops for the dining areas. Oh, if those walls could talk, what tales they'd have to tell!

Heart in Hand
Restaurant ♥ Caterers
7145 Main Street
Clifton, VA 20124
703-830-4111

The cute red building next to the railroad tracks in historic Clifton is home to the Heart in Hand Restaurant. Its history began at the turn of the twentieth century, when it was the largest general store in Fairfax County. Folks came from miles around to buy, sell, and barter for just about anything. At that time, it was called Buckley Brothers' General Store. The prosperous and enterprising brothers claimed that if something existed, you could buy it from them. Their slogan was "Everything from a pin to a plow."

As was the case with many stores of that time, owners came and went. The building changed hands many times and housed numerous retail businesses over the years. It was even renamed and used as the Buckley Inn at one point, named after the successful brothers.

It still looks like a store from the outside, thanks to the traditional bow windows of a double storefront and the double-door entrance. Inside, visitors will find the original wooden floors, a brick fireplace at the back of the large dining room, and the exposed beams of the ceiling.

The Heart in Hand name was chosen by the current owners as a tribute to their fore-fathers, who worked hard with their hands through the love in their hearts. This is mentioned on the menu, so customers might understand the hard work and love that has gone into making this restaurant such a special place. Love is a theme that has found its way into all aspects of the restaurant. It is reflected in the red heart-shaped decorations in the windows, in the red roses in the red glass vases on every table, and even in the beautiful hand-stitched quilts displayed on the walls.

Debbie dined elsewhere that particular evening, and so I sat alone next to the fireplace and enjoyed the individual attention of the wait staff. The Tennessee Ham and Bean Soup is a favorite here, as are the salads, since the dressings are all homemade. I tried to choose among Rack of Lamb with Fresh Rosemary Sauce, Grilled Smoked Pork Loin with Scalloped Apples, and Southern-Style Catfish Sautéed in Cornmeal, served with a dollop of Pecan Butter. But once my server told me about the specials, I opted for the Crabmeat-Stuffed Flounder, served with assorted steamed vegetables and Mashed Sweet Potatoes.

I sat back and enjoyed the firelight as I munched on delectable, freshly baked muffins. When my flounder arrived, it was scrumptious. I would have liked to sample the desserts, but, alas, I was full, having eaten far too many muffins! So Debbie and I will visit another day to try the homemade Raspberry Ice Cream, or perhaps Geba's Iron

Skillet Pie, a creamy blend of milk chocolate heated in an iron skillet and then poured into a piecrust. What makes the meals here so delicious? It must be the love!

 OLD-FASHIONED CREAM OF TOMATO SOUP

½ cup butter
½ cup flour
4 cups milk
2½ pounds canned tomatoes, diced
1½ cups tomato juice
1½ cups Bloody Mary mix
2½ teaspoons salt
2 teaspoons pepper
½ cup sugar
2 cups heavy cream
sour cream for garnish
chopped green onions for garnish

Melt butter in a large pot. Add flour and stir to make a roux. Allow to cook for about 1 minute, stirring constantly. Do not brown. Add milk and stir until thickened. Add next 7 ingredients and bring to a boil. Reduce heat to medium and simmer for 15 minutes. Garnish each serving with a dollop of sour cream and green onions. Serves 12.

CHICKEN SUZANNE

1 cup flour
1 egg, beaten
1 cup milk
3 cups good-quality fresh breadcrumbs
6 boneless chicken breasts

½ to 1 cup light cooking oil
Herb Butter (recipe below)

Prepare 3 dipping dishes. Place flour in first dish. Beat egg and milk together in second dish. Place breadcrumbs in third dish. Dip chicken in flour, then in egg mixture, then coat thoroughly with breadcrumbs. Heat oil in a large sauté pan and sauté chicken for 2 to 3 minutes on each side until well browned. Do not overcook. Remove from pan and drain. Serve immediately with dollops of Herb Butter. Serves 6.

 HERB BUTTER

½ cup chopped green onions
½ cup chopped fresh parsley
2 cloves garlic
1 teaspoon basil
½ teaspoon oregano
1 teaspoon marjoram
1 teaspoon tarragon
1 teaspoon dill weed
1 teaspoon black pepper
dash of Tabasco
2 cups unsalted butter, softened

Place all ingredients in a food processor and mix thoroughly. Butter may be stored in a sealed container in refrigerator for at least a week. Yields 2 cups.

Note: Herb Butter is delicious on toasted French bread and can be used on steaks, hamburgers, veal scaloppine, or steamed vegetables, as well as in the chicken recipe above.

1201 East Cary Street
Richmond, VA 23219
www.TheTobaccoCompany.com
804-782-9555

The Tobacco Company Restaurant is located on the western edge of historic Shockhoe Slip in Richmond. The large brick building was once a tobacco warehouse. In the late 1860s, the cobblestone streets outside were busy with the efforts of postwar reconstruction and filled with the sounds of the tobacco business. Today, those same streets are crowded with locals and tourists enjoying the shopping and dining that the revitalization of this area has brought.

The atmosphere at The Tobacco Company Restaurant is, in a word, fun! Stepping inside the leaded-glass doors, you are immediately awed by all there is to see. An old wooden Indian seems to have the job of greeting guests as they make their way to either the first-floor bar or to the hostess desk to secure a table on one of the two upper floors. Visitors wishing to enjoy a drink have three very different choices.

There are the traditional chairs at the bar, seating in a quiet Victorian parlor complete with elaborate chandeliers and a moose head, and sleek tables in the atrium that offer a soaring view to the third story and front-row seats for the live entertainment.

Guests access the unusual dining areas at The Tobacco Company in one of two ways. Many choose to climb the wide staircase, rescued from Richmond's Saint Luke's Hospital. Others prefer the novelty of the antique elevator that delivers guests to the second and third floors. At every turn, the décor drips Victoriana. Whirring ceiling fans, period antiques, framed posters, and stained glass all enhance the feel. The spectacular brass chandelier, once situated in the lobby of the Federal Reserve Bank in Cincinnati, now hangs amid a profusion of plants in the three-story atrium.

In for a quick bite on a sunny afternoon, we chose to sit where we could enjoy the soaring view. The third-floor dining area is decorated with white wicker to give guests the feel of a Southern veranda. The second floor is more formal, with low lighting and lots of wood. It even has enclosed rooms for private dining. The second story is also where you'll find The Tobacco Company's popular dessert buffet. The choices on the day we visited were Apple Pie, Pecan Pie, Black Forest Cake, Strawberries with Whipped Cream, and three types of cheesecake.

The menu contains a wide variety of

appealing selections. The appetizers range from Portabello Montrachet to traditional Crab Cakes to Chèvre Fondue. She-Crab Soup is there, along with several salad options. Entrées such as Chicken Chesapeake (served with crab, shiitake mushrooms, and sun-dried tomatoes in Sherry Cream) and Szechuan Sea Bass (served with Asian Cucumber Salad) caught our eye. Ultimately, we chose to share the Cajun Shrimp and Crayfish, served with patties of Garlic Cheese Grits. The portion was ample and delicious. With so much to offer, it's no wonder The Tobacco Company is one of Richmond's most popular destinations.

 GARLIC CHEESE GRITS

4½ cups water
½ teaspoon salt
½ cup butter
½ teaspoon granulated garlic
½ teaspoon onion powder
1 teaspoon Mrs. Dash
1 teaspoon freeze-dried chives
1 cup grits
½ cup grated cheddar
1½ tablespoons grated Parmesan
½ cup flour
2 eggs, beaten
1 cup cracker crumbs
¼ cup oil

Bring water to a rapid boil with salt, butter, and seasonings. Gradually stir in grits. Cook for 15 to 20 minutes until all water is absorbed and grits are thickened. Stir often.

Remove from heat and stir in cheddar and Parmesan. Serve as a side dish or follow instructions below to make cakes.

Pour grits into a parchment-lined 9-by-9-inch sheet pan. Refrigerate to set up. Cut into rounds with a biscuit cutter. Dredge rounds in flour, eggs, and cracker crumbs. Heat oil in a large sauté pan over medium heat and fry cakes for about 2 minutes until golden brown on each side. Place cakes on paper towels to drain, then serve immediately. Yields 8 to 12 cakes.

CAJUN BBQ SAUCE

2 cups chili sauce
1 cup Worcestershire sauce
1 cup lemon juice
4 tablespoons granulated garlic
4 tablespoons minced parsley
4 tablespoons Liquid Smoke
2 tablespoons cayenne
2 tablespoons coarse black pepper
3 tablespoons paprika
3 tablespoons oregano
2 tablespoons Tabasco sauce
3 cups olive oil

In a large mixer bowl, blender, or food processor, combine first 11 ingredients in the order listed. Slowly add olive oil and beat until well blended. Place in a covered storage container, label the date, and refrigerate. Mix well again before using. Holds for 30 days in refrigerator. Yields 7 cups.

197 East Davis Street
Culpeper, VA 22701
www.hazelriverinn.com
540-825-7148

In 1759, sixteen-year-old George Washington was commissioned by Lord Fairfax to survey the town of Culpeper, Virginia. This brick building on the corner of East Davis Street and East Street occupies Lot 35 on Washington's original plat and is said to be the oldest commercial building in the historic downtown area. The rear portion of the structure was built around 1790, while the front was added approximately forty-five years later, around 1835. Constructed of handmade brick, hand-hewn and pegged timbers, and pine floors, the building has housed numerous businesses, including a stable and a tobacco warehouse. *Yowell Hardware Company, Inc.*, is still emblazoned on the bricks across the front of the building. The upstairs was used as an armory for the Culpeper Minute Men. It continued in service as an armory into the early 1900s.

We were seated next to the large wood-burning fireplace centered on the front wall of the restaurant. It is original to the building and was no doubt the primary source of heat for this level of the store. Looking out across the remainder of the restaurant, it was obvious that people were enjoying themselves. The majority of the tables were full, and many of their occupants lingered, engaged in lively conversation, long after the remnants of their Sunday dinners had been cleared.

Karen had difficulty choosing among the Grilled Venison Sausage, the Smoked Norwegian Salmon with Boursin Cheese Turnovers, and the Bison Fricadelles with Wild Berry Preserves. We'd had bison while working on our Pennsylvania book but hadn't had an opportunity to enjoy it since, so that was the winning selection. Debbie opted for the Red Pepper and Cilantro Bisque, served piping hot. On another visit, we'll have just as much difficulty deciding among items like Pear and Stilton Empanada, Escargot Ragout, and Roasted Rack of Lamb with Pear and Currant Marmalade.

The restaurant is owned and operated by Peter and Karen Stogbuchner. Prior to establishing themselves in Culpeper, Peter was the chef at a restaurant in Chevy Chase, Maryland, and Karen was a groundskeeper at a golf course there. The Blackberry Grilled Chicken, one of the restaurant's most popular items, came into being as a result of Karen's horticultural efforts. One summer, she grew too many blackberries and challenged her husband to come up with a creative culinary use for the surplus. The blackberries quickly went from excess to success.

After lunch, Karen gave us a tour of the

pub downstairs. During the Civil War, this lower level was used as a jail by both the Northern and Southern armies. The unique décor reflects Karen's horticultural background. Irregularly shaped tables have been fashioned from cross-sections of trees, with trunks supporting each one. Trunks also support the backbar, which is suspended from the ceiling. The bar itself was made from some of the store's original flooring. Tree trunks have been incorporated there as well. From the pub to the main dining room to the food created by chef Peter Stogbuchner and sous-chef Nathan Moates, the Hazel River Inn Restaurant is a one-of-a-kind experience.

BAKED ROCKFISH IN FENNEL AND TARRAGON HERB CRUST

4 6-ounce skinless rockfish fillets
juice of 2 lemons
sea salt to taste
3 slices white bread, ground into crumbs
¼ cup dried fennel seeds, ground
⅓ cup butter, melted
4 teaspoons tarragon
2 cloves garlic, chopped

Preheat oven to 375 degrees. Place fillets in a shallow dish. Add lemon juice and sprinkle with salt. Cover with plastic wrap and put in refrigerator to marinate for 30 minutes. In a medium bowl, thoroughly combine breadcrumbs, fennel seeds, butter, and tarragon. Add garlic and mix. Remove fillets from lemon juice and place side by side in a buttered baking dish. Spread breadcrumb mixture evenly over top and bake for about 20 minutes until fish flakes easily. Serves 4.

JUGGED HARE

2 red wine
1 bay leaf
½ teaspoon rosemary
1 teaspoon fresh thyme, chopped
1 teaspoon flack peppercorns, crushed
1 cup shallots, chopped
5 pounds rabbit, cut into pieces
5 strips smoked bacon, chopped
1 stalk celery, chopped
½ cup flour
3 cups chicken stock

Preheat oven to 375 degrees. Place fillets in a shallow pan, combine wine, bay leaf, rosemary, thyme, peppercorns, adn shallots. Marinate rabbit in wine mixture for at least 1 hour. Preheat oven to 400 degrees. Remove rabbit from marinade and place in a single layer in an overproof pan. Strain marinade and sprinkle herbs and shallots over rabbit. Set liquid aside. Sprinkle bacon and celery over and around rabbit. Sprinkle flour evenly over top of rabbit, then moisten with chicken stock. Use reserved liquid if necessary. Cook in oven for 1 hour, turning rabbit frequently. Serves 4 to 6.

105 King Street
Old Town Alexandria
Alexandria, VA 22314
www.fishmarketoldtown.com
703-836-5676

We can all thank Ray Giovannoni, fondly known around this area as "Mr. Ray," for what we know as The Fishmarket today. During the 1930s and 1940s, this building underwent several style changes in the name of modernization. However, it was Mr. Ray who recognized its intrinsic beauty and value. He renovated the old building in 1976, recapturing the ambiance of its nineteenth-century mercantile days. Ray passed away in 1998, but his spirit lives on in this place and in the hearts of its many longtime employees, many of whom have been around The Fishmarket for more than twenty years!

The building is over two hundred years old. It was constructed from bricks and cobblestone used as ballast in ships crossing the Atlantic. At that time, Alexandria was a very important port on the eastern seaboard, ranking third behind New York and Boston. Space was needed to store cargo coming into the port, and the building at 105 King Street was constructed for just that purpose. Its use continued until the War Between the States, when it was converted into a field hospital. Toward the end of the nineteenth century, ham and beef were cured here. Many of the nails from which the meat hung are still visible in the beams along the second and third floors.

Just after the turn of the twentieth century, some enterprising gentlemen utilized the space in their attempt to jump on the Coca-Cola bandwagon. These entrepreneurs attempted to create their own soft drink, CHRIP, billed as "a bird of a drink." Whether it was the flavor or the advertising, the endeavor was short lived. Later, during Prohibition, another tenant was significantly more successful with what he concocted. The beer that he brewed was better received and considerably more popular than CHRIP had been.

Today, this historic spot offers some of the best seafood around. We were seated in the dining room directly behind the lobby. Copper pots hang on the walls, and two murals depict scenes from the nineteenth century. The other dining room, to the left of the lobby, is decked out in blue and white gingham to match the stamped-tin ceiling.

Karen started with a bowl of Crab Soup, concocted with a vegetable tomato base. Debbie decided to go traditional, ordering the Original World-Famous Fishmarket Recipe Clam Chowder. Each was a wonderful way to start the meal. A Shrimp Salad Sandwich completed Debbie's evening repast, while Karen settled on the Crested Treasure Chest, a hollowed pineapple filled with Shrimp Salad. There were so many choices that we found ourselves dithering, but our waitress was patient. For those not fond of meals from the deep blue sea, there are several landlubber selections. The menu states, "We serve shrimps, a few crabs, tall people, and a lot of nice people, too!" Obviously, everyone is welcome at this local landmark.

 CLAMS CASINO

¼ cup diced green pepper
1 teaspoon pimentos
¼ cup onion, diced
⅛ teaspoon seafood seasoning
pinch of cayenne
1 tablespoon butter
24 small clams in shells
4 slices bacon, diced

In a food processor, finely grind green peppers, pimentos, and onions. Place in a small saucepan. Add seafood seasoning, cayenne, and butter. Cook about 5 minutes until a glaze appears on top. Open clams. Place cooked sauce over clams, using about 1 teaspoon for every 3 clams. Sprinkle with diced bacon. Place under broiler for about 2 minutes until bacon is cooked. Serves 8 as an appetizer.

 SHRIMP CREOLE

½ cup shortening
½ cup flour
3 cups chicken stock or fish stock
1 cup diced green pepper
1 cup diced onion
1 cup diced celery
27-ounce can whole tomatoes with juice
1 teaspoon cayenne
1 teaspoon sugar
2 pounds uncooked shrimp, peeled
6 servings white rice, cooked

Melt shortening in a large pot. Whisk in flour to make a roux. Gradually stir in stock and simmer for several minutes. Add remaining ingredients except shrimp and rice. Let simmer for about 45 minutes. Mixture should be thick. If not, combine a little cornstarch with water and add to thicken. Add shrimp. Simmer another 20 to 25 minutes. Spoon rice onto serving plates. Top with Creole mixture. Serves 6.

Withers Hardware Restaurant

260 West Main Street
Abingdon, VA 24210
276-628-1111

If you're driving through downtown Abingdon, it's hard to miss Withers Hardware Restaurant. The name is proudly spelled out in gold letters mounted against an attractive green facade. Above, two stories of red brick trimmed in the same green complete the historic building. For decades, Withers was the hardware store for Abingdon. Built in 1885, the building burned in 1917. Quickly restored, it continued to dispense tools and nails until 1982.

From that time until the present, the old store has served as a popular local restaurant, dishing up creations made with a sauté pan and a whisk, rather than lumber and screws. The cream-colored tin-tile ceiling is still here, as are the building's original brick walls. These give the eatery a warm, comfortable feel. Decorated with old metal signage advertising such companies as Revere Tires, Gould Battery, and Clifton Insurance Agency, the walls are as nostalgic as they are colorful. The old ladders used to reach the stock on the top shelves are here, too, providing a historical reminder and a bit of whimsy.

The bar on the main level has a mellow atmosphere created by the dark wood of the backbar and the attractive brass lamps dispersed along the bar's entire length. The bar was fashioned out of the store's original sales counter. The booths and casual tables in the main seating area provide a relaxed atmosphere.

The extensive menu includes appetizers ranging from Potato Skins to the Asian Sampler, which features Spring Rolls, Marinated Shrimp, and Pork Dumplings. The Black Bean Cakes—served over sautéed spinach and red onions and topped with Salsa, sour cream, and chopped scallions—are as tasty as they are unusual. The lengthy list of salads includes Bourbon Steak Salad, Fajita Salad, and Sesame Chicken Salad. The three soup choices can be ordered as a cup, as a bowl, or in combination with a salad or a half-sandwich. Lunch here is more than just sandwiches, although there are eight such offerings on the menu at all times. Pot Roast, Trout, Fried Catfish, Lasagna, and Baby Back Ribs are just a few of the choices.

When dinnertime rolls around, the menu really makes it hard to choose. The Chicken Curry in Curry-Coconut Sauce was too tempting for Karen to pass up. The dish is also available with shrimp or pork instead of chicken. Debbie decided to give the Salmon Rockefeller a go and was not disappointed. There are many other choices, such as Creamy Penne (made with smoked bacon, snap peas, and Roma tomatoes and tossed in Alfredo Sauce) and Vegetarian Orzo in Lemon Butter Sauce.

After dinner, we lingered over an excellent cup of coffee while we chatted with owner Hazel Cano-Ramos. She'd just returned from her son's wedding, for which she'd created a beautiful wedding cake. As she told us how some of the restaurant's menu items came to be, it became clear that creating is what she enjoys best. It's no wonder that one visit here definitely wasn't enough to try everything!

 SALMON ROCKEFELLER

2 tablespoons olive oil, divided
2 8-ounce salmon fillets
salt and pepper to taste
2 teaspoons finely chopped shallots
2 teaspoons minced garlic
2 tablespoons bacon, crumbled
2 tablespoons diced red onion
½ cup heavy cream
1 cup baby spinach
3 tablespoons panko breadcrumbs
2 tablespoons shaved Parmesan

Preheat oven to 425 degrees. Heat 1 tablespoon of the olive oil in a skillet. Pat salmon dry, then place in skillet. Sear salmon on both sides until golden brown. Add salt and pepper, then set aside and keep warm. In a separate ovenproof skillet, heat remaining olive oil. Sauté shallots and garlic until translucent. Add bacon and red onions and sauté for a few seconds. Add cream and spinach and simmer until sauce is reduced by half. Place salmon in the same skillet, smothering fillets with sauce. Top with breadcrumbs and Parmesan. Put skillet in oven and bake for 7 minutes. Serves 2.

Note: This dish is excellent with wild rice and sautéed vegetables.

 GINGER-SOY REDUCTION

2 cups soy sauce
2 cups honey
2 tablespoons garlic, minced
2 tablespoons shallots, minced
2 tablespoons green onions, sliced
1 teaspoon fresh ginger, minced
¼ cup sherry

Combine all ingredients in a medium saucepan. Heat over medium heat, stirring frequently, until mixture begins to bubble. Allow to come to a boil, then lower heat to a simmer until mixture is reduced by half. This sauce is excellent with seafood. Yields about 2 cups.

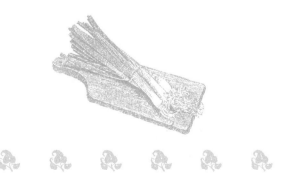

...Where The Neighborhood Comes Together

Charley's Waterfront Café
201 B Mill Street
Farmville, VA 23901
434-392-1566

Charley's Waterfront Café overlooks the Appomattox River. In the summer months, the outdoor deck is full of patrons enjoying the delicious food and unique atmosphere of this historic tobacco warehouse. We were told that five or six tons of rocks were used to create the waterfall. Guests can enjoy the deck, the tavern with its vast wooden bar, the private dining rooms, or the family-dining area, all of which have great views of the original exposed wooden beams and wooden floors. The furnishings are simple, and creative touches are provided by assorted antiques, such as the brass cash register and the unique collection of beer taps.

Current owner Tommy Graziano has been involved with Charley's since the 1980s. After graduating from Benedictine High School in Richmond in 1986, he began in the business as a dishwasher. He worked his way up the ladder until he became a partner. He was so successful that he eventually bought out his partner and former boss in 1997. We think that's quite a statement.

We sat on a triangular dais in one corner of the bar, where we enjoyed a great view of the waterfall and the pretty tubs of impatiens on the deck below. Tammy, our server, suggested we sample the Roasted Red Pepper and Crab Soup and the Hot Crab Dip. Those arrived together with freshly baked bread and Garlic and Herb Butter. We were not surprised to hear that patrons often order the soup by the gallon to go. We had just about decided to order the Grilled Scallop Kabobs with Orange Apricot Glaze and the Baked Snapper Oscar with Vegetable Rice when it occurred to us that we ought to take a look at the dessert menu before committing ourselves.

As usual, deciding was difficult, and we lingered over the menu. So we were taken completely by surprise when pastry chef Anne Simboli showed up at our table with a banquet plate full of delicious goodies for us to sample. Anne, who also teaches cooking, says that Tommy "just lets me run wild in the kitchen." She runs so wild, in fact, that her specialty, Chocolate Fantasy Cake, has won twenty-five blue ribbons in competition. We sampled the Chocolate Flowerpot, the Orange Crunch, the Snickerdoodle Cookies, the Cinnamon Pinwheels, the Chocolate Ganache Tart with Toasted Almonds, the Lemon Coconut Pie, and, last but definitely not least, the famous Chocolate Fantasy. All the desserts were wonderful, and Anne insisted that we take the ones we couldn't eat home with us for our families.

Needless to say, not many of them made it all the way home! The staff members at Charley's have a saying: "Eat Well, Drink Well, Live Well!" This is surely the place to do exactly that.

 SAUSAGE AND PENNE PASTA

10 Roma tomatoes
¼ cup fresh basil, chopped
2 15-ounce cans stewed tomatoes
2 tablespoons garlic, minced
½ cup olive oil
½ cup white wine
salt and pepper to taste
2 medium shallots, chopped
1 bunch scallions, chopped
2 pounds hot Italian sausage, sliced 1 inch thick
1 pound penne pasta
Parmesan for garnish

Place all ingredients except sausage, pasta, and Parmesan in a food processor and purée until smooth. Place purée into a large stockpot and add sausage. Cook over low heat for 1 hour, stirring frequently. Season to taste. Cook pasta according to package directions. Drain pasta and plate immediately. Top with sauce and garnish with Parmesan. Serves 8.

 FILET MIGNON
MEDALLIONS
WITH LUMP CRABMEAT

3 tablespoons olive oil, divided
2 to 3 cloves garlic, minced
2 medium shallots, chopped
¼ cup chicken stock
2 cups heavy whipping cream
2 tablespoons Parmesan, grated
1 cup flour
¼ teaspoon red pepper, crushed
1 teaspoon basil, ground
¼ teaspoon salt
¼ teaspoon pepper
2 8-ounce filets mignons
½ pound jumbo lump crabmeat

In a small bowl, combine 1 tablespoon of the olive oil, garlic, and shallots. Add salt and pepper to taste and spread mixture in an ovenproof roasting pan. Broil about 15 minutes until golden. Remove from oven and cool completely. Remove mixture from pan and drain off oil.

In a small sauté pan, heat garlic mixture on medium-high until sizzling. Stir in chicken stock and reduce until mixture is just moist. Stir in cream and reduce heat to medium. Allow mixture to reduce by half, then whisk in Parmesan slowly. Reduce heat to low and allow sauce to rest.

In a flat dish, combine flour, red pepper, basil, ¼ teaspoon salt, and ¼ teaspoon pepper. Cut filets mignons into ¼- to ½-inch medallions and dredge in seasoned flour. In a medium sauté pan, heat 1 tablespoon olive oil on medium heat. Drop in medallions and sear each side until golden. Remove from pan and set aside. Add 1 tablespoon olive oil to pan. Add crabmeat and heat thoroughly. Add salt and pepper to taste. Serve crabmeat on top of medallions and drizzle with sauce. Serves 2.

SOUTHERN INN
RESTAURANT

37 South Main Street
Lexington, VA 24450
www.southerninn.com
540-463-3612

Lexington's Main Street was once an Indian track used for hunting expeditions. Today, it is a thriving thoroughfare bustling with residents, college students, business folk, and tourists.

On June 5, 1787, James Lyle was granted two parcels of land, designated Plots 21 and 27 on the town plat. Today, Plot 21 is none other than the Southern Inn. The rules of property ownership specified that structures be built on the plots within six months of the purchase. Frame buildings were the common construction of the day, and it is assumed that Lyle built such structures on his land. Unfortunately, a fire in 1796 destroyed all sixty of the buildings. By the time the town was rebuilt, brick was the preferred material, the hope being that it would help avoid another such disaster.

Ownership has changed hands multiple times over the years. At some point, the heirs of James Lyle transferred the property to John Perry (spelled Parry in some accounts). During the 1820s, a boom time for Lexington, the property was split between Perry and James Campbell. It was then purchased by Jacob Bear. A dispute arose over the exact measurements of the parcel, the result being that more than fifty feet went missing from Bear's purchase. But it seems he was no worse off for this problem, since the property value doubled during his ownership. In 1886, a jewelry store was opened here by a Mr. Jahnke, who was quite successful. Upon his death, his will stated that his heirs should continue to operate his store. They eventually sold the property, and a restaurant opened here under the proprietorship of a Mr. Deaver.

It was in 1932 that George Macheras opened his restaurant at 37 South Main. Before the start of business, he had thirteen cents to his name. But the brisk trade brought in a grand total of seventy-five dollars during his first day in operation. The well-known sign announcing the Southern Inn's location was erected at that time and has hung there ever since. Likewise, the interior has changed little since Macheras's tenure. Straight-backed booths line one side of the dining room, and there is a simple bar on the other. Behind the bar are etched mirrors typical of the period, flanked on either side by sconces with shell-shaped globes. Additional lighting is provided along the center of the room by interesting hanging fixtures.

I slid into one of the booths and quickly decided on the Asian Pear Salad, a mixture of greens, sliced pears, red onions, walnuts, and goat cheese. It was a delicious combination that I would happily have again and again. Had Karen been with me, I have no doubt that we would have shared the Wild Mushroom Pâté, served on a bed of greens with grilled French bread and Roasted Red Pepper Vinaigrette. The Grilled Salmon Pizza and the Southwestern Pizza also sounded tempting. The Spinach and Sun-Dried Tomato Cannelloni was served at the next booth and got rave reviews. Had I saved room for dessert, I would have had a hard time choosing between the Pineapple Upside Down Cake and the S'mores Cheesecake. Another time, perhaps.

After the death of George Macheras, the Southern Inn Restaurant went through some rough times. Now, under the expert guidance of chef George Huger and his wife, Sue Ann, "the walls are alive again," as Mrs. Macheras has proclaimed.

VIRGINIA GOLD ASIAN PEAR CHUTNEY

2 tablespoons chopped fresh ginger
1 tablespoon chopped garlic
1 large scallion, minced
1 jalapeño pepper, minced
1 star anise
2 teaspoons mustard seed
1½ cups rice wine vinegar
1 cup sugar
1 tablespoon finely diced red bell pepper
1 tablespoon finely diced yellow bell pepper
2 tablespoons finely diced red onion
2 cups diced Virginia Gold Asian pears
1 teaspoon kosher salt
2 sprigs fresh mint leaves, chopped
2 sprigs fresh basil, chopped

Combine first 8 ingredients in a medium saucepan. Simmer over medium heat until almost dry. Combine remaining ingredients except mint and basil in a medium bowl. While ginger mixture is still hot, strain reduction from saucepan over ingredients in bowl. Allow chutney to sit for at least an hour. Garnish with mint and basil. Yields about 3 cups.

15 South King Street
Leesburg, VA 20175
703-777-7246

There is some confusion about when the building that houses The Green Tree was built. Some documents say 1767, and others say 1794. Whatever the true date, this is an old building that has seen many owners and businesses pass through its portals. Originally a tavern and perhaps an inn as well, it has also housed a goldsmith shop, a hardware store, a package store, a feed store, and a restaurant. It even housed the first A & P grocery store in the area.

The atmosphere nowadays is unmistakably colonial. The main dining room is located in what used to be the courtyard. Boasting wide-plank floors and floral walls displaying hunting pictures, it is the more formal of the two rooms. Debbie couldn't accompany me on this visit, and I chose to eat in the taproom. The polished wooden tables and ladder-back chairs were cozy and comfortable. I found the brick floor and the roaring fireplace warm and inviting.

The recipes at The Green Tree are historic in their own right. The staff spent months researching at the Library of Con-gress and the National Archives to amass what has become a fabulous selection of eighteenth-century recipes. Each was garnered from diaries or old letters discovered during the research.

At dinnertime, The Green Tree serves elegant eighteenth-century cuisine. For lunch, guests enjoy fine traditional cuisine. And for the less adventurous, there is a wide range of more modern choices. I couldn't wait to try the Green Herb Soup, featuring twenty-one different herbs and spices. Friends had recommended the Salmagundi, which is the original tossed salad, reputed to have been served at Monticello. Eventually, I opted for the soup and Welsh Rarebit, a dish I hadn't had since I was a child. It consists simply of a rich, creamy cheese served over toast points.

Listed on the menu are a large number of eighteenth-century drinks that all sound extremely interesting. Russian Tea—a strong tea brewed with cinnamon sticks, pineapple, cloves, Oriental spices, and brown sugar—caught my eye. Artillery Punch was another drink of interest. Made from whiskey, wine, tea, gin, orange juice, brandy, and champagne, it is alternately referred to as "the Shrew's Downfall." It is said that after two glasses of this potent brew, a man will become completely immune to complaints, snide remarks, unsolicited advice, and suggestions against his best interest.

Do save room for one of the delicious desserts. The Bread Pudding with Rum Sauce and the Rum and Black Walnut Pie came highly recommended, as did the Lemon Flummery and the Bourbon and Caramel Custard Pie. The Green Tree calls itself "a purveyor of fine comestibles to the gentry." To my mind, there is no doubt that whatever your background—genteel or otherwise—you'll certainly enjoy the comestibles here.

CURRY SAUCE

2 tablespoons oil
1 onion, diced
½ bunch celery, diced
1 carrot, diced
pinch of granulated garlic
pinch of ground ginger
pinch of white pepper
pinch of black pepper
pinch of red pepper
ground coriander to taste
2 tablespoons parsley flakes
ground cumin to taste
2 cups curry powder
¾ cup chicken stock
2 cups white wine
6¼ cups water, divided
4 cups whipping cream
2 tablespoons cornstarch

In a large sauté pan, heat oil and sauté onions, celery, and carrots until onions are translucent. Add garlic, ginger, white pepper, black pepper, red pepper, coriander, parsley, cumin, and curry powder to the pan. Stir well to combine. Add stock, wine, and 6 cups of the water. Bring to a boil and reduce by ⅓. Just prior to serving, add cream.

Stir to combine. Check consistency. If thickening is required, combine cornstarch and remaining ¼ cup water to make a slurry. Add slurry drop by drop to sauce, using only enough to thicken sauce to desired consistency. Stir well. Yields 8 cups.

CHEESE PIE

5 eggs
¾ cup half-and-half
¾ cup whipping cream
9-inch piecrust, prepared
3 slices cheddar
3 slices ham, cooked
10 slices bacon, cooked
3 slices Swiss cheese
3 slices provolone

Preheat oven to 325 degrees. In a medium bowl, whip together eggs, half-and-half, and whipping cream until light and frothy. Place the following into piecrust in order: 1 slice cheddar, ham to cover cheese, bacon to cover ham, Swiss cheese to cover bacon, and remaining cheddar and provolone on top. Fill pie to the top with egg mixture; there will be some egg mixture left over. Bake for 10 minutes. Remove pie from oven and pierce top in several places. Add remaining egg mixture and return pie to oven for 25 minutes. When pie is cooked, it will be very pale. If required, pie may be browned slightly under broiler. Serves 6 to 8.

The Wharf

119 King Street
Old Town Alexandria
Alexandria, VA 22314
703-836-2836

She-Crab Soup is on the menu here. It's one of the foods that always brings back memories of my childhood, though not because it was part of a traditional holiday meal or because my mother always made it. It's one of the dishes my father always looked forward to eating when we were on vacation at Myrtle Beach, South Carolina. So each time I see it listed on a menu, I have fond thoughts of childhood summers.

Given a restaurant named The Wharf, it's not surprising that a great many of the menu items are seafood. Oysters on the Half Shell, Maine Mussels, Littleneck Clams, New Orleans Oyster Loaf, and Fried Calamari are among the myriad seafood choices. For those not fond of seafood, items such as Chicken Piccata, Lamb Chops, and Prime Rib are also available.

This was one of our "divide and conquer" days, since Alexandria has so much history and so many restaurants to offer. Karen was elsewhere as I was seated in the dining room for an early lunch. Since we live far enough inland that enjoying fresh seafood wonderfully prepared is not a regular

occurrence, my mouth watered as I considered my choices. Ultimately, it was the novelty of the Shrimp Salad BLT that got my attention. Served on an ample French loaf, it was a unique variation of a tried-and-true classic.

In 1749, surveyor John West, Jr., plotted the beginnings of what was to become Alexandria. George and Lawrence Washington, John Carlyle, and William Ramsey were some of the early investors here. Less than fifty years later, Alexandria boasted well over ten thousand tons of home-owned shipping vessels, which created an acute need for warehouses, a better harbor, and new wharves. To meet this need, a landfill project was undertaken that created an additional block of waterfront. Although the dates are sketchy, the site that The Wharf occupies is thought to have been filled sometime around 1790, and the building erected between that time and 1800.

One of the first businesses to flourish at this location was Miller Company, importers and dealers of china, crockery, and the like. Believe it or not, the elevator at the front of the restaurant was installed during its tenure. Ownership changed hands through the years, sometimes due to debt. During a 1911 sale, the Miller Company was awarded thirty-five dollars for its claim to the elevator, although it had given up ownership of the building years before.

In 1970, Herbert Bryant, who used the space to store feed and grain, purchased the building, complete with elevator. After a period of vacancy and gradual decay, renovations began. An effort was made to retain as much of the eighteenth-century structure as modern building codes would allow. The original stone and bricks are still in place, and all of the original columns and beams remain intact. Although The Wharf hasn't been around quite that long, the strength of its reputation since opening in 1973 indicates that it well deserves to be housed in a building with this kind of history.

 PAN-SEARED YELLOWFIN TUNA

4 8-ounce high-quality tuna steaks
kosher salt and cracked black peppercorns to taste
¼ cup peanut oil
Eastern Shore Blue Crab Succotash (recipe follows)

Preheat a heavy cast-iron skillet. Season tuna generously with kosher salt and peppercorns. Add peanut oil to skillet and sear fish on 1 side for approximately 2 minutes. Reduce heat to medium, flip tuna, and continue cooking for 1 minute. Place tuna in the middle of each of 4 plates on a bed of Eastern Shore Blue Crab Succotash. Serves 4.

 EASTERN SHORE
BLUE CRAB SUCCOTASH

¼ cup unsalted butter
1 tablespoon minced shallots
2 cups sweet corn
1 cup frozen lima beans
½ red bell pepper, diced
1 teaspoon minced garlic
2 teaspoons Old Bay seasoning
½ pound jumbo lump crabmeat
¼ cup heavy cream
salt and white pepper to taste

Melt butter in a large sauté pan. Add shallots and cook for about 1 minute. Add corn, lima beans, and red pepper. Cook for 1 minute over medium-high heat. Add garlic and Old Bay and stir until well mixed. Add crabmeat and cream and toss until heated through, being careful not to break up lumps of crabmeat. Season to taste and divide among 4 heated plates. Serves 4.

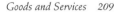

WHERE THE FUN HAS JUST BEGUN...

STELLA'S

FINE FOODS & SPIRITS

Stella's Second Story
57 Market Street
Onancock, VA 23417
757-789-7770

In our travels to date, the village of Onancock is definitely one of the most picturesque towns we've visited. One lovely Victorian home after another lines Market Street as you make your way from US 13 to the center of town. Our original purpose was to check out Hopkins & Brothers General Store, built in 1842, our philosophy being that you never know what you might find. Located on Onancock's waterfront, the store provides everything a fisherman might need.

Fortunately, on the way in, the bright interior of Stella's caught our eye. So we retraced our steps and found ourselves seated in the downstairs dining room of this casual eatery. The original tin ceiling in this former hardware store is phenomenal. The top third of the wall is ornately covered as well. This Victorian feature is in stark contrast to the original narrow slat paneling, now painted a brilliant vermilion. A variety of watercolors, some of which are for sale, are dis-

played, adding further color to the expansive interior.

The downstairs is considered the preferred family-dining area. The upstairs, although not for adults only, is designed for adult enjoyment. There's a tin ceiling there, too, but a thirty-foot bar dominates the room. In the back corner is a game room complete with a pool table and a dartboard. Next to the game room is an area with soft leather couches and chairs. Boasting a view of the harbor, it's a place where local residents can come to relax. A bookshelf lines one wall, its shelves full of books that patrons are free to take and to return whenever they've finished. It's an interesting approach.

The menu offers a great deal of variety. The seafood selections include Fried Shrimp, Clam Strips, Fried Oysters, Mini Crab Cakes, Conch Fritters, Crab Salad, and a Crab Sandwich. Many of these are served basket-style with French Fries and Coleslaw. We shared an order of Mini Crab Cakes, served with three dipping sauces—Cocktail, Tartar, and Spicy Mayonnaise. We enjoyed every morsel. The lengthy list of sandwiches ranges from Cheesesteak to those made with deli meats to Italian choices such as Chicken Parmesan. For lighter appetites, salads are available. And there's a section of hand-tossed pizzas. One of them is called Lance's Favorite. According to the menu, Lance, one of the owners, likes his pizza with Sun-Dried Tomato Pesto, blue cheese, asparagus, and a five-cheese blend. The other owner, Bob, has his dish—Bob's Homemade Lasagna—listed under the Italian section. Stuffed Shells and Baked Ziti are among the other Italian offerings.

When we met the owners, both were wearing shorts, as were the majority of patrons. So kick back and relax. It's what Lance and Bob want you to do!

 CAESAR SALAD DRESSING

¼ cup anchovy paste
¼ cup balsamic vinegar
½ cup lemon juice
¾ cup grated Parmesan
1/3 cup puréed fresh garlic
2 tablespoons Worcestershire sauce
2 cups olive oil

Place all ingredients in a blender and process until thoroughly combined. Yields about 4 cups.

 CHESAPEAKE PIZZA

fresh or frozen dough for one 12-inch pizza
1 clove fresh garlic
½ cup Bloody Mary mix
oregano to taste
basil to taste
½ to 2/3 cup shrimp, cooked, peeled, and deveined
½ to 2/3 cup crabmeat
½ to 2/3 cup bay scallops
1 cup shredded mozzarella
½ cup shredded Romano
½ cup , shredded Parmesan

Preheat oven to 450 degrees. Prepare crust as required and place on a lightly greased pizza pan. Cut garlic clove in half. Rub crust thoroughly with garlic, then mince clove and sprinkle over crust. Cover crust with Bloody Mary mix. Sprinkle oregano and basil on crust. Generously cover crust with seafood. Combine the 3 cheeses in a small bowl. Sprinkle over pizza. Bake for 15 to 20 minutes until cheese is bubbly and crust is golden. Serves 2.

313 East Water Street
Charlottesville, VA 22902
434-977-1518

The downtown mall in Charlottesville contains a delightful mix of historic buildings that have been restored or renovated over the past decade. The brick-paved pedestrian area is lined with fountains and outdoor cafés, creating a relaxed atmosphere. Visitors can be seen sipping drinks in the shade of the old oak trees and tripping from boutique to museum with shopping bags in hand.

One of the most intriguing places we've ever visited takes up almost a whole city block at the mall. The Old Hardware Store is a favorite of locals and visitors alike. Erected in 1895, this landmark building contains not only a restaurant but also a collection of stores, including a candy shop, a bookstore, a jewelry story, a fabulous art gallery, and much, much more. We were so excited that we actually visited twice!

There is so much to see that it's hard to know where to begin. In the central dining area, customers can sit in comfortable booths amid the high walls covered in shelves, drawers, and cabinets. It's easy to imagine what they looked like when they were full to the brim with nuts, bolts, and assorted tools of the day. The vintage advertising signs add to the décor. If you want to climb nearer to the original ceiling, there's a small circular staircase that leads upstairs to the art gallery.

We were told that the original store was in continuous operation from 1895 to 1976. One of the largest stores in the area, it employed a significant number of sales staff, clerks, and laborers. At the Water Street end of the store, the clerical offices have been turned into dining rooms. The old, cumbersome adding machines and typewriters used by the clerical workers are still there, adding interest for patrons today.

Noted for its generous portions, the restaurant is always well patronized. The ten-page menu offers an extensive selection of offerings. A discerning diner can find anything he or she might desire, from salads, spuds, crêpes, knishes, pierogies, and blintzes to sandwiches, pastas, wraps, and quiches. The entrées include Mesquite-Grilled Chicken, Barbecued Ribs, Fried Fish, and a wide variety of burgers and seafood dishes. No visit to this establishment would be complete without a trip to the Pickle Bar and its vast selection of pickles in various sizes, from the tiniest vinegar-coated crunchy bite to something that would make a whole meal by itself.

We were in the mood for dessert, which

will come as no surprise to our readers. The Old Hardware Store offers a wide selection of pastries, sundaes, cakes, and pies. Karen opted for the deliciously dense Double Chocolate Truffle Cake and an Orange and Strawberry Smoothie. The Southern Pecan Pie was more to Debbie's taste, although she was tempted by many of the treats from the old-fashioned soda fountain.

We were as charmed by the table condiments sitting in individual toolboxes as we were by the store itself. If variety is the spice of life, then this is surely the place to find it!

TRICIA'S TREASURE

3 slices bacon
1 onion roll
4 ounces roast turkey, sliced
1 slice cheddar

Fry bacon in a small sauté pan until crisp but not burned. Remove from pan and pat dry to remove fat. Split onion roll in half. Place on cookie sheet. Top bottom part of bun with turkey, bacon, and cheddar. Place under broiler to melt cheese and warm bun. Serves 1.

MAC'S HOLE IN ONE

3 or 4 slices Roma tomato
1 bagel
1 cup chicken salad
1 slice sweet red onion
1 slice muenster cheese

Spray a baking sheet with nonstick cooking spray. Preheat oven to 350 degrees. Roast tomato slices for about 10 minutes. Slice and toast bagel. Top half of bagel with chicken salad, onion, tomato, and cheese. Place under broiler to melt cheese. Place other bagel half on top and serve. Serves 1.

CHAPTER 10

B is for Bistro

Julep's New Southern Cuisine

IThe French word *bistro* is interchangeable with the
Italian word *trattoria*. Both signify an eating place where the
menu tends to be regional and the customers are typically
from the neighborhood. The food is uniquely local in flavor, well prepared,
and accompanied by local wines and other beverages. The atmosphere is casual,
inviting, and occasionally robust, as if the customers are visiting friends at
someone's home. Be adventurous and enjoy!

Caroline's

"A Dining Experience"

301 East Main Street
Abingdon, VA 24210
276-739-0042

Abingdon's Plumb Alley runs right behind Caroline's. It was at the east end of this little thoroughfare, just in front of the cave, where wolves attacked dogs belonging to Daniel Boone. From that incident arose the community's first name—Wolf Hills. Later, the town became known as Black's Fort. It was christened Abingdon in 1778. It is the oldest town in southwestern Virginia.

The building that houses Caroline's was constructed much later, right around the turn of the twentieth century. Originally, it was a drugstore and a pool hall. Chef Eric Riffe told us that the building housed the Abingdon General Store until Caroline's took over the space. Salmon and Rib Eye are popular entrée choices, while Chicken Stuffed with Prosciutto and Boursin and New Orleans Barbecued Shrimp please more daring palates. Burgers can be ordered with toppings of either blue cheese or applewood bacon and Vermont cheddar. The list of sandwiches caught Debbie's eye. She struggled to choose among the

French Onion Chicken Sandwich, the Salmon Club, and the unusual Vegetable Reuben. Ultimately, the Shrimp Taco won the debate, a soft taco deliciously stuffed with lettuce, tomatoes, cucumbers, and shrimp. Karen went straight for the dessert menu, surveying the table behind us for opinions, since the people there had ordered one of everything. She narrowed her choices to the rich but delicious Chocolate Mousse, the Pecan Tart, and the nut-encrusted Chocolate Cake. Once a chocoholic, always a chocoholic. She selected the cake and enjoyed it down to the last crumb.

This little bistro offers not only great food but interesting artwork as well. On the main floor, the general store's original shelves line an entire wall. Painted a neutral taupe, the shelves now display wonderful pottery rather than tins of crackers, yard goods, and jars of candy. A second, smaller set of shelving was situated near our table. We browsed it while waiting for our food. Had we not been on the front end of a week-long trip when we visited, we certainly would have purchased some of these unusual wares. Upstairs, you'll find an art gallery and intimate dining tables for two. The two-month exhibit when we visited featured monotype, a medium that combines the traditions of printmaking and painting. Here, Karen was foiled because a piece she desperately wanted to purchase had already been sold.

The restaurant was quite busy the night we visited. The main floor was bustling, couples were seated in the gallery, and several tables of four enjoyed al fresco dining. Our favorite table—complete with a cushion-covered window seat—was nestled in one of the front display windows. Another not-to-be-missed architectural feature is the columns, painted an attractive shade of grape.

An essay displayed on the wall at Caroline's states that the community has long been known for its history, refinement, and culture. This establishment is one that will carry that tradition into the future.

STUFFED PORTABELLO MUSHROOMS

2 to 3 tomatoes, diced
½ cup white wine
1 cup chicken stock
4 cloves garlic, minced
2 tablespoons sun-dried tomato paste
1 to 2 cups sourdough bread croutons
1 cup diced Gorgonzola cheese
fresh herbs (basil, oregano, thyme, chives) to taste
3 green onions, sliced thin
4 portabello mushroom caps
¼ cup crumbled Asiago cheese

In a medium saucepan, stew tomatoes in white wine, chicken stock, and garlic. Reduce natural juices down to half the original amount. Add enough tomato paste to thicken slightly. Place hot tomatoes in a stainless-steel bowl. Add croutons until mixture reaches the consistency of stuffing. Fold in Gorgonzola, fresh herbs, and green on-

ions. Stuff mixture into mushroom caps. Sprinkle with Asiago. Broil about 4 minutes until mushrooms soften slightly and cheese melts. Serves 4 as an appetizer.

PAPAYA CHUTNEY

3 cups diced red onion
4 cups diced papaya
water as needed
1 cup rice wine vinegar
1 cup sugar
salt to taste
vinegar to taste

Sauté onions in a medium skillet until caramelized. Add papaya and cook over low heat about 30 minutes until soft. Add water as needed to prevent sticking and burning. When papaya is soft, add rice wine vinegar and bring to a simmer. Add sugar and reduce until mixture is almost dry. Season with salt and vinegar. Yields about 3 cups.

Note: Chef Carl Eskridge suggests tasting throughout the cooking process so desired flavor is achieved. Chicken stock may be substituted for water and apples for papaya. A dash of cayenne may be added for a little bite or various nuts for texture.

new southern cuisine

1719-1721 East Franklin Street
Richmond, VA 23223
www.juleps.net
804-377-3968

Julep's is a great place to visit any time of year, but especially on a cool fall evening. The old-fashioned street lamps at the corner of East Franklin Street bounce light off the whitewashed walls and onto the striped awning at the ground floor of the building. The candles in the windows and the glorious floral window boxes make a very pretty picture.

We sat in the window on the ground floor and enjoyed the cozy, intimate atmosphere. The lighting was subdued and the service discreet and efficient. The lower floor of the restaurant has exposed brick walls and a large curved staircase to the right of the long, dark wooden bar. We particularly liked the oversized artwork by J. Blowers overlooking the lower dining area. Upstairs is a more private dining area lit by hurricane lamps and strategically placed spotlights that highlight the exposed ceiling beams and woodwork.

Owners Amy and Bill Cabaniss are very proud of this lovely building that they helped to restore, and rightly so. Reputed to be the oldest commercial building in Richmond, it has enjoyed a rich and varied past. Constructed in 1817 by Charles Whitlock as a lumber house, it has been the site of a candle and soap factory, a brewery, a produce market, and a locksmith shop, among other businesses. Local rumor has it that the locksmith came home one day and caught his apprentice in flagrante delicto in the stairwell with none other than the locksmith's own wife! The locksmith shot the apprentice. Unfortunately, local history did not record what happened to the wife!

The food here is as interesting as the history. Chef Eric Cohen serves up a fresh take on Southern cuisine. Karen sampled the Fire-Roasted Red Pepper and Blue Cheese Soup, followed by the Peppercorn-Encrusted Tuna with Cilantro Emulsion. Both were delicious, as was Debbie's Venison Ossobuco. Another time, we might have chosen the Butterleaf Lettuce Salad with Blackberries, Sweet Potato Crisps, and Sweet Poppy Seed Vinaigrette or the Fire-Seared Jumbo Sea Scallops with Crushed Pecans in Red Currant Barbecue Sauce.

We were nicely sated and about to take our leave when Amy Cabaniss insisted that we sample dessert. Since we almost never leave dessert untasted, we were a pushover. The Frozen Grand Marnier Soufflé with White Chocolate Ganache and Orange Coulis was sensational. Julep's is also reputed to serve a fabulous Bananas Foster, which is one of our favorite desserts. Whatever your choice here, it's bound to leave you wanting to return again and again!

VENISON OSSOBUCO

olive oil to lightly coat pot
salt and pepper to taste
10 6-ounce portions venison
1 medium onion, chopped
3 medium carrots, chopped
2 stalks celery, chopped
1 cup white wine
1 teaspoon chopped garlic
2 tablespoons tomato paste
8 cups venison or beef stock

Preheat oven to 350 degrees. Heat oil in a large braising pot. Salt and pepper the venison and sear it until golden brown on each side. Remove meat from pot and set aside. Place onions, carrots, and celery in pot and sauté until tender. Deglaze pot with wine and scrape up all the stuck-on bits from bottom. Add remaining ingredients and return venison to pot. Bring to a boil, cover, and place in oven for 1½ to 2 hours until fork tender. Remove from oven. Remove venison from pot and set aside. Strain remaining liquid through a fine strainer. Return liquid to pot. Reduce sauce to desired consistency. Season to taste. Serves 5.

Note: Julep's serves this dish with stone-ground grits and seasonal greens.

SAUTÉED BLUE MUSSELS WITH BRAISED FENNEL

¼ bulb fennel
2 tablespoons olive oil, divided
salt and pepper to taste
10 to 15 mussels
1 tablespoon finely diced red pepper
1 teaspoon minced shallots
1 teaspoon minced garlic
½ cup anisette liqueur
½ cup water
1 tablespoon chopped parsley
¾ tablespoon butter
toast points

Preheat oven to 350 degrees. Place fennel in a cast-iron skillet and drizzle with 1 tablespoon of the olive oil. Season with salt and pepper. Cover with foil and place in oven for about 2 hours until very tender. Remove from oven and reserve.

Heat remaining oil in a sauté pan. Cut fennel crosswise into thin strips. Add fennel, mussels, and red peppers to pan and sauté for about 30 seconds. Add shallots and garlic and sauté another 15 seconds, being careful not to let garlic burn. Remove pan from flame and deglaze with liqueur. Return to flame and allow alcohol to burn off. Add water. Add parsley and butter, swirling pan until butter is melted into sauce. Add salt and pepper. Serve in bowls with toast points. Serves 2 as an appetizer.

l'étoile

817 West Main Street
Charlottesville, VA 22903
434-979-7957

Since the 1940s, the building at 817 West Main Street in Charlottesville has housed some type of restaurant. Many locals know the spot as Buddy Buddy's, a burger-and-beer joint. Others remember its ten-year stint as the Cotton Exchange, so named to reflect its early history as a cotton warehouse. The building is located along the railroad tracks just across the street from the train station. The cotton was off-loaded by cranes and brought in through archways located near today's deck area. Ultimately, the cotton was shipped by horse- or mule-drawn wagon down the street to the woolen mills.

During the 1970s, the site was a revolving door for restaurateurs, none of whom gained any longevity. We're glad, some thirty years later, that the door has finally stopped spinning now that proprietors Mark and Vickie Gresge and chef Christopher Poole have moved in. The restaurant has focused on developing a distinctive Virginia cuisine utilizing regional products. Signature dishes such as Duck over Pearl Barley, Catfish Provençale, and Chicken and Sausage Roulade are just a few of the menu selections utilizing local ingredients.

Had we come at dinnertime, we may have started with a wedge of Baked Brie (topped with Spiced Apple Compote, clove honey, and toasted almonds) or the Oven-Roasted Bacon-Wrapped Sea Scallops. The entrées include Polish Pierogis (stuffed with Parmesan-flavored potatoes and served with Roasted Corn and Squash Stew) and Whole-Grain Mustard- and Herb-Crusted Lamb Chops (accompanied by Black Currant Veal Reduction and served over Truffle-Scented Mashed Potatoes). The other choices are equally creative.

We arrived at l'etoile for a late lunch. The restaurant was crowded even at that hour. Downstairs, the dining room is painted a cheery mustard. Upstairs, the rooms are equally colorful, painted coral and maize. We thought the sage-green room in which we were seated the most interesting, thanks to its bumpy bricks and angular walls. The guests proved as eclectic as the food, ranging from university professors to students to housewives to business professionals. We chatted easily with the woman at the next table, in Charlottesville on business. She'd walked past the day before on her way to her conference and decided to experience the little bistro before returning to Minnesota. She ordered Rutabaga Soup, which was the soup du jour. Served with a thick slice of homemade Buttermilk Pepper Cheese Bread, it was quite tasty, she said. We opted for two varieties of chicken salad. The Coconut Curry Chicken Salad was a special of the day, while the Tarragon and Roasted Walnut Chicken Salad is a mainstay on the menu.

The restaurant is well known not only for its soups but also for its homemade cakes and cookies. We were debating whether to order the Apple Butter Cake, the Three-Layer White Cake iced in Chocolate Ganache, the Coconut Cake, or the Chocolate Brownie Cake when our waiter delivered Christopher Poole's version of Virginia Bread Pudding. The contrasting flavors of the ganache and dried cranberries were incredibly unique and enjoyable. As a restaurant, l'etoile—"the star"—has certainly earned its name.

 GRILLED RACK OF LAMB WITH WILD MUSHROOMS AND SWEET POTATOES

4 sweet potatoes
2 tablespoons olive oil
salt and freshly ground pepper to taste
2 tablespoons vanilla
4 tablespoons butter, divided
¼ pound green beans
2 racks of lamb
¼ pound wild mushrooms, chopped
1 cup veal stock, warmed

Preheat oven to 350 degrees. Brush potatoes with oil and season with salt and pepper. Place in oven for 40 minutes. Peel and whisk potatoes with vanilla, salt and pep-

per, and 2 tablespoons of the butter. Set aside. Blanch green beans in boiling water for 3 minutes. Place in ice water, then drain. Season lamb with salt and pepper. Place on a hot grill flesh side down for 10 minutes. Turn over and cook for 5 more minutes. While lamb is cooking, heat remaining butter in a saucepan until just about brown. Add beans and mushrooms. Stir constantly, so as not to burn. Divide potatoes evenly at center of 2 plates. Place mushrooms and beans at an angle on top of potatoes. Fan racks of lamb around potatoes. Spoon veal stock onto plates. Serves 2.

 ROASTED PUMPKIN BISQUE

1 tablespoon olive oil
1 tablespoon unsalted butter
1 cup chopped onion
½ cup diced carrot
½ cup chopped celery
2 cloves chopped garlic
1 Granny Smith apple
1 teaspoon ground fresh ginger
1 sweet potato, peeled and chopped
1 cup white wine
½ teaspoon salt
½ teaspoon nutmeg
½ teaspoon cinnamon
½ teaspoon white pepper
3 cups roasted pumpkin
6 cups vegetable stock
2 cups heavy cream

Heat oil and butter in a large saucepan. Add onions, carrots, and celery. Sauté 5 minutes over medium-low heat. Add garlic, apples, ginger, and sweet potato. Add wine and spices. Sauté for 3 minutes. Add pumpkin and stock. Stir well and bring to a low simmer for 30 minutes. Turn heat down and let sit for 20 minutes. To purée, use a hand blender, as hot soup in a blender can be dangerous; it may blow the lid and cause burns. After puréeing, return soup to pot. Add cream. Reheat but do not boil. Serves 6.

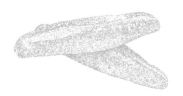

 VIRGINIA BREAD PUDDING

3 baguettes
6 eggs
1 cup sugar
1 quart half-and-half
1 cup water
½ cup bourbon
1 cup chocolate chips
½ cup dried cranberries
pinch of salt
1 tablespoon vanilla
whipped cream, if desired
chocolate sauce, if desired
caramel sauce, if desired

Preheat oven to 350 degrees. Cut baguettes into ¼-inch cubes and place in a large mixing bowl. In another bowl, whisk eggs and sugar together until well combined. Add half-and-half, water, and bourbon. Pour liquid into bowl with bread. Mix with your hands. Add chocolate chips, cranberries, salt, and vanilla. Mix well. Pour into a greased baking dish and bake for 25 minutes. Serve warm with your choice of toppings. Serves 12.

650 Zachary Taylor Highway
Flint Hill, VA 22627
540-675-1111

I'm not sure if there are actually four and twenty blackbirds situated around the dining room, but there are quite a few birds of all descriptions on display. Several blackbirds sit perched atop an antique china cabinet, and a lone blackbird is near the front door. The remainder of the birds can be found in the posters and framed artwork hanging on the walls—the very walls that are painted lime green. Lime green with fuchsia trim. The bright, bistro atmosphere creates a fun, slightly funky ambiance in a building that started its life as a carpentry shop. A photo near the stairs shows that very little has changed on the exterior since that time. However, I'm sure the carpenter would be amazed to see the checkered chair cushions in various combinations of yellow, blue, green, and fuchsia, as well as the bold print curtains hanging at the windows. Even the fresh rose trio accenting each table is bursting with color.

During the 1940s, the structure became a general store. It has subsequently served as the local Democratic Party headquarters,

a doctor's office, a beauty shop, a real-estate office, and a country restaurant. In 1990, after the building was purchased by Vincent DeLouise and Heidi Morf, it continued to function as a restaurant, but with an emphasis on fine dining in a definitely unstuffy environment. Through the years, Four and Twenty Blackbirds has won numerous awards, including being named one of *Zagat*'s top forty Washington/Baltimore area restaurants and one of *Washingtonian* magazine's hundred best restaurants each year since 1993. That probably explains why the eatery has hosted such notables as Brooke Shields, Clarence Thomas, Robert Duvall, and Jackie Onassis.

The menu is intriguing. Since Karen was elsewhere, it meant I actually had to make a definitive decision, rather than ordering mine and trying hers, too. Always in the mood for mango, she would have chosen the Grilled India-Spiced Shrimp with Fresh Mango Chutney as her appetizer. The Roasted Vegetable Potstickers with Thai Coconut Lemon Grass Sauce was equally appealing to me. The entrées on the evening I visited ranged from Pan-Seared Duck Breast with Grapefruit Marmalade to Asian-Marinated Pork Tenderloin with Five-Spice Apples to Grilled Wild Rockfish with Chili Corn Bacon Relish. After consulting my server, I settled on the most unusual item on the menu, the Wild Mushroom Bread Pudding, served with Smoky Red Bell Pepper Sauce and Lemon-Thyme Mustard

Grilled Vegetables. It was a choice I'd readily make again. Sated, I reluctantly passed on dessert, although I would have gladly experienced the Warm Italian Blood Orange Cream Crêpes with Pistachio Nut Anglaise or the Golden Pineapple Dumpling, served with Banana Caramel Soup and Coconut Ice Cream.

Just before I departed, Vincent DeLouise escorted me downstairs to see the second dining room. I was amazed at how different the ambiance was. Regulars of the restaurant have their individual preferences. Some choose the quiet coziness of the downstairs room, where the rough stone walls contrast with the yellow floral fabric. Others choose the robustness of the colors upstairs. Of course, the quality of the food and the professionalism of the service are identical in the two settings.

COUNTRY HAM AND SHIITAKE MUSHROOM TIMBALE

½ pound shiitake mushrooms, sliced
6 tablespoons butter, divided
½ medium onion, chopped fine
3 eggs
1 egg yolk
1 cup milk
2 cups cream
½ teaspoon nutmeg
1½ teaspoons dry mustard
salt and pepper to taste
½ pound country ham, cooked and julienned
1 cup walnuts, chopped rough

2 tablespoons walnut oil
4 to 5 cups mixed salad greens
1½ cups sherry vinaigrette or vinaigrette of your choice

Preheat oven to 375 degrees. Sauté mushrooms in 2 tablespoons of the butter until golden brown. Remove from sauté pan. In same pan, melt an additional 2 tablespoons butter and sauté onions until golden. Remove from heat. In a medium bowl, whisk eggs, egg yolk, milk, cream, nutmeg, mustard, and salt and pepper together. Add onion mixture. With remaining 2 tablespoons of butter, grease 6 parchment paper circles and put into 6 buttered timbale or custard cups. Divide mushrooms and ham among cups. Pour custard over top. Place cups in a baking pan ⅓ full of hot water. Bake for 20 to 25 minutes until a knife inserted in center comes out clean. Remove from water. Sauté walnuts in walnut oil. Sprinkle with salt. Toss greens with vinaigrette. Arrange on 6 plates. Unmold warm custard onto greens and sprinkle with walnuts. Serves 6.

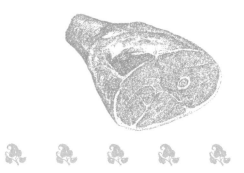

128 East Davis Street
Culpeper, VA 22701
540-825-4264

On our first trip to Culpeper, we walked up and down Davis Street, enjoying the signs of a thriving community. It was then that we noticed It's About Thyme. Unfortunately, it was a Sunday, so we had to wait until our next visit to experience the unique cuisine and ambiance.

It seems that until the mid-1990s, the building at 128 East Davis Street had always housed a store. A photo from 1899 in *The Pictorial History of Culpeper* show this locale as W. J. Shotwell's Grocery. The cornerstone reads 1907, but whether this reflects a major renovation to the facade or a complete overhaul of the building resulting from fire is unclear. However, a change is evident in the exterior appearance from that photo taken in 1899 to ones from the early 1900s. Sometime prior to the 1920s, Florsheim Shoes occupied the property. In the following decade came Deckelman's, a haberdashery. Changes continued through the years. A gourmet shop opened here in 1984. It's About Thyme took over in 1995.

Amazingly, despite all the changes in use and ownership, the original copper-panel ceiling remains. From the ceiling hang handmade lighting fixtures reflective of the store's period of origin. The facade remains true to its 1907 appearance, painted to reflect the history of downtown Culpeper. The mosaic tiles along the storefront were common to many, many stores of the period. What has been added are the fabulous murals that flank both walls of the café. The scenes depict Lake Como, Italy, and the hotel at Bellagio, giving the interior a Mediterranean flair.

The restaurant was quite full when we arrived on a Saturday afternoon in late February. The sun was shining, and a touch of spring was in the air. The gentleman seated at the table next to ours leaned over and introduced himself as we chatted about the town. He was obviously a regular, ordering without even looking at a menu. Karen selected the Portabello Mushroom Sandwich, while Debbie chose the Bruschetta. The Pear Salad, consisting of pears roasted in cinnamon and honey over mixed greens with prosciutto, blue cheese, and walnuts, was a popular choice. Also delivered to quite a few tables was the Roast Pork, stuffed with dried apricots and cherries. On another visit, we'll try some of the other options, including the Chicken and Sausage Gumbo, the Artichoke and Onion Soup, and the Puff Pastry Ham and Swiss Sandwich.

The list of desserts is lengthy, so making

a decision was difficult. How does one choose among Citrus Cheesecake, Chocolate Hazelnut Cheesecake, Coconut Cream Tart, Hazelnut Biscotti Gelato, Flourless Chocolate Tart, and Carrot Cake? We ultimately took our server's recommendation and enjoyed the Upside Down Gingerbread Pear Cake and the Orange Sherry Cake. Upon finishing our meal, we stepped out into the sunshine to do some shopping, having every intention of continuing what had already become an enjoyable day.

CONNIE'S COSMO

3 ounces Jose Cuervo
1 ounce Cointreau
1 ounce lime juice
2 splashes cranberry juice
2 twists lime

Using a shot glass, measure Jose Cuervo, Cointreau, and lime juice. Add cranberry juice. Chill. When ready to serve, shake well to combine. Serve in 2 martini glasses with twists of lime. Serves 2.

GREEK LEMON CHICKEN SOUP

1 whole chicken
2 quarts water
2 tablespoons chicken base, powdered
¾ cup long-grain rice
4 eggs
5 tablespoons fresh lemon juice

In a large pot, gently boil chicken in water until done. Remove chicken to cool. Add chicken base to water to make stock. Remove 1 cup of stock and set aside. Bring remaining stock to a boil and add rice. Cook about 10 minutes until rice is done. While rice is cooking, beat eggs and lemon juice in a glass or stainless-steel bowl until frothy. Slowly add reserved chicken stock to egg mixture, whisking constantly. Remove pot from heat. Slowly whisk in egg mixture. Remove chicken meat from carcass. Add bite-sized pieces to individual bowls for serving. Fill bowls with broth and serve. Serves 8.

DEB'S KEY LIME PIE

½ cup plus 2 tablespoons butter
2 cups graham cracker crumbs
2 tablespoons sugar
2 cans sweetened condensed milk
1 cup Key lime juice
7 egg yolks

Preheat oven to 350 degrees. Melt butter and add to crumbs and sugar in a medium bowl. Using fingers, blend well. Press into an 8-inch springform pan to cover bottom and ⅓ of the way up sides. In a separate bowl, whisk together sweetened condensed milk, lime juice, and egg yolks. Pour into crust and bake for 15 minutes. Cool. Yields 1 pie.

203-205 Mason Avenue
Cape Charles, VA 23310
757-331-3005

We approached Cape Charles down a long avenue of the most beautiful crape myrtles we had ever seen. The town's water tower looks just like the top of a lighthouse. It even has false windows hanging on one side to further enhance the lighthouse image. The wind was blowing slightly from the northwest, evidenced by the large seagull weather vane perched on the chimney of the Harbor Grille near the bottom of Mason Avenue. The two-story structure, constructed of red and white bricks, contains a double storefront with a door to the upstairs apartment set in the middle. We could have opted to sit roadside amid a plethora of floral topiaries and watch the world go by. Instead, we went inside to check out the specials on the chalkboard set into the center of the bar.

The grille is long and thin, as former stores are wont to be. The original tin-tile ceiling has been painted a smoky navy, and the slatted walls are white. We loved the look of the galvanized-metal-topped tables and the pub-style chairs. In one corner, a baby grand piano has had a countertop added to it, turning it into a very attractive table with high stools. Colorful posters, utilitarian lighting, and a yellow and black tile floor complete the look. The Harbor Grille has a very definite style and feels friendly but chic.

We pondered the menu while Spanish guitar music played gently in the background. There are a lot of items to choose from. We counted ten different freshly baked breads, including a Raisin-Pecan Loaf, an Asiago Loaf, a Portuguese Batard, and a Crusty Baguette. Eventually, Debbie opted for Mom's Famous Double-Mustard Mayo Apricot Almond Chicken Salad on a flaky croissant with a side of al dente Sun-Dried Tomato Pasta Salad. Karen, who loves sushi, chose Julie's Sesame-Coated Seared Rare Tuna Carpaccio with Wasabi Mayonnaise, Pickled Ginger, and Soy Sauce. Both were extremely good. Julie Delsignore, who owns the Harbor Grille, is famous for her Coconut Cream Pie, so we couldn't leave until we'd sampled a slice. It certainly lived up to its reputation! The filling, more a light and fluffy coconut mousse than a custard, was complemented perfectly by the toasted pieces of coconut.

While we were there, we checked out the old picture of the New York, Philadelphia & Norfolk Railroad track near the harbor. The town of Cape Charles was created in 1884 to be the southern terminus of the newly formed NYP & N Railroad and to be the transfer point for barges and steamers taking freight and passengers across Chesapeake Bay to Norfolk.

William L. Scott, a congressman from Erie, Pennsylvania, was the first to propose this rail-sea link. He was so keen on the idea that, even prior to the harbor being dredged and any railroad track being laid, he purchased the land in question and started to lay out a town. Seven avenues running east and west were named for famous Virginians, and six streets running north and south were named for fruit trees.

Today, if you walk to the end of Mason Avenue and climb to the top of the long, grassy sand dune, you can see a wonderful panoramic view of the bay. Remember to turn around and take a look at the two Sears, Roebuck & Co. mail-order houses from the 1920s for yet another slice of history.

DEVILED CRAB CAKE SANDWICHES

2 8-ounce cans crabmeat
2 eggs
10 dashes Tabasco sauce
1 tablespoon Old Bay seasoning
½ cup mayonnaise
¼ cup chopped celery
¼ cup chopped onion
2 tablespoons Worcestershire sauce
1½ tablespoons lemon juice
1 tablespoon parsley
1 tablespoon cilantro
2 large buns

In a large bowl, combine all ingredients except buns. Form mixture into 2 balls and flatten into patties. Grill until hot all the way through. Place on buns. Top with tartar sauce, salsa, remoulade sauce, or other condiment of your choice. Serves 2.

BRONZING SEASONING

1¼ cups Cajun Seasoning (recipe below)
1 tablespoon brown sugar
2 tablespoons olive oil

Combine all ingredients in an airtight container. Mix well. Use as a rub for tuna, chicken, burgers, crab cakes, fresh fish, or other meat of your choice. Store in refrigerator for future use. Yields about 1 cups.

CAJUN SEASONING

¼ cup garlic powder
¼ cup onion powder
¼ cup paprika
¼ cup thyme, dried
3 tablespoons red pepper, ground
1½ tablespoons black pepper

Combine all ingredients in an airtight container. Mix well. Use for blackening meat. Yields about 1¼ cups.

CAFFE BOCCE

330 Valley Street
Scottsville, VA 24590
434-286-4422

Not too long ago, the town of Scottsville was featured in a PBS documentary entitled, *The James River*. This community at the northernmost portion of the waterway was founded in 1744. Thus, the town of Scottsville is thirty-two years older than the United States. Scottsville was the first county seat of Albemarle County. History notes that Peter Jefferson, brother of Thomas, was one of the original magistrates.

The town was prominent in the Revolutionary War, as the Marquis de Lafayette made a successful strategic ploy here. Scottsville was also involved in the Civil War. Both George Armstrong Custer and William T. Sherman stayed at local historic properties during the conflict.

Because of its location on the waterfront, the town was originally called Scott's Landing. Thomas Jefferson's Monticello is just twenty miles away. As he designed and supervised the construction of the University of Virginia, building materials came through this port and then were hauled by wagon to the site of the fledgling college. Even the well-recognized marble pillars that give the campus its air of grace and gentility arrived from Europe via Scottsville. It continued as a hub for east-west commerce throughout the nineteenth century.

Caffe Bocce is located in a storefront dating to 1911. The original brick walls and stamped-tin ceiling remain in place, giving the eatery a nostalgic feel. Owners Chris Long and Marcia Miller have old photographs of the street as it existed in the early 1900s. One photo even depicts the Sclater Hardware Store next door, complete with piles of chicken wire and wheeled plows. A group of men is standing on the steps of the store watching the photographer. It's clear from this photograph how well preserved the downtown business area is. Little except the owners has changed in all that time.

The menu here is anything but turn-of-the-twentieth-century, though. Appetizers such as Rice-Flaked Diver Scallops in Orange-Ginger Foam and Crispy Fried Shrimp, Chicken, and Portabello Dumplings with Salmon Mousse and Mango Purée are part of an up-to-date cuisine. Items such as the Avocado, Fennel, and Hearts of Palm Salad make even the salad course a difficult choice. Half of the entrées listed on the menu are pasta selections. The Farfalle with Jumbo Lump Crab and Asparagus tossed in Ginger Sherry Cream sounded quite tasty, as did the Grilled Salmon with Pear Applesauce.

For a slightly more casual menu, the restaurant also offers Bar Bocce. There without Debbie for Sunday brunch, I sat near the bar and chose the French Herb Omelet with Oven-Roasted Potatoes. It was a delicious combination from chef Marcia Miller, who sat and talked to me as I ate. She is self-trained but is continually taking master classes to be sure she stays on the cutting edge. The cuisine is a delightful combination of traditional Italian and classic French cooking. The small menu reflects the chef's desire for every item to be her very best offering. No wonder people travel for miles to eat at this establishment. The only disappointment of the meal was not being able to sample every appealing item on the list!

WON TON PRAWNS WITH WATERMELON MANGO SALSA

1 mango, skinned and chopped fine
2 tablespoons coriander leaves, chopped
½ cup finely chopped cucumber
½ cup diced watermelon
1 tablespoon lime juice
½ chile pepper, seeded and chopped fine
32 prawns, cooked and peeled
32 won ton wrappers

In a medium bowl, place mango, coriander, cucumber, watermelon, lime juice, and chile pepper. Stir thoroughly to combine. Place salsa in an airtight container in refrigerator until ready to serve. Place each prawn diagonally on a won ton wrapper. Roll, then seal wrapper with water. Deep-fry for 2 to 3 minutes until golden brown. Remove won tons from oil and drain on paper towels. Serve immediately with salsa. Serves 8 as an appetizer.

SCALLOPS WITH RAVIOLI AND WILD MUSHROOMS

½ cup butter
1 cup shallots, diced
20 Diver scallops
1 cup wild mushrooms, sliced
1 cup sherry
1 cup veal stock
½ cup heavy cream
16 ravioli
whipped cream for garnish

In a large sauté pan, melt butter and allow to brown slightly. Add shallots and sauté until golden. Add scallops and mushrooms. Increase heat to high and sauté for about 4 minutes until scallops are opaque. Remove scallops and mushrooms from pan and set aside. Add sherry to deglaze pan. Be sure to scrape up all the brown bits with a spatula. Reduce liquid until only 2 tablespoons remain. Add veal stock and cream and reduce for 2 to 3 minutes. Add ravioli to pan. When ravioli are cooked, remove from pan and plate. Add scallop mixture. Add sauce over plate. Garnish with whipped cream. Serves 4.

La Petite Auberge
311 William Street
Fredericksburg, VA 22401
540-371-2727

La Petite, as this restaurant is affectionately known, is a sight to behold from the outside. The warmth of its yellow walls contrasts nicely with the deep blues of the large awning and the gingham tablecloths on the tables along the sidewalk. On a cold January evening, it made me think of summers in the south of France with warm bread, pungent cheeses, and cold wine. It was too cold to remain outside, so reluctantly I went inside to eat.

There are three dining areas inside—a small, private room, a cheery bar area, and a large room at the back. The bar is full of red-gingham-topped tables, exposed brick walls, and an eclectic collection of paintings. It was very full when I visited, so I opted for the rear dining room. Thanks to its high exposed-timber roof and whitewashed fencing along the walls, the room is rather elegant. The large carriage lamps on the side walls and the tiny votive candles on each table produce a subdued lighting that brings an intimacy to each table in the room. The

upper walls are covered in large oil paintings that range in subject matter from glorious sunsets to misty mornings, from landscapes to portraits. Art lovers will find much to admire.

Constructed in 1880, this building first housed McKracken's, a liquor store. Ladies of the day crossed the street rather than walk past such a questionable business. Eventually, the property was sold and became a much more respectable hardware store.

I was sorry Debbie couldn't join me that evening. At La Petite, the menu is fairly long. The thirteen appetizers range from Tomatoes Auberge to Prosciutto di Parma with Marinated Red Peppers and Artichokes. Of the entrées, the Blackened Mahi-Mahi with Bananas and Spring Onions or the Tournedos au Poivre Vert would have been my choice. However, there were twenty items on the specials listing the night I dined, so I decided to select two items from that menu.

The Country Pâté with Armagnac and Prunes was most enjoyable, served with freshly sliced tomatoes, baby gherkins, and a large dollop of mustard. The rolls were warm and delicious, straight from the oven. Alternating between the cold pâté and the warm bread, I would have been happy to dine on those two alone. I followed with Duck Confit with Grilled Toulouse Sausage and Lentils. This was an unusual but tasty combination, and the lentils were particularly good. I finished with the highly recommended Rum Cake, served with a large scoop of Vanilla Ice Cream. This is certainly a restaurant where guests can enjoy a unique experience each time they visit.

JACKIE'S RITZ CRACKER BUTTER-FRIED OYSTERS WITH SPICY CABBAGE STEW

20 oysters, shucked
2 cups flour
10 to 12 eggs, beaten
3 cups Ritz crackers, crumbled
½ cup butter, divided
1 medium cabbage, cored and quartered
salt and pepper to taste
cayenne to taste
4 slices prosciutto, julienned
4 tablespoons lemon juice, divided
parsley for garnish
cocktail sauce

Drain oysters and dredge them in flour. Coat oysters with beaten egg, then with cracker crumbs. Place oysters on a flat cooking pan lined with wax paper until needed.

In a large sauté pan, heat ¼ cup of the butter until foamy. Season cabbage quarters with salt and pepper and cayenne. Add cabbage and prosciutto and sauté until just cooked. Add 2 tablespoons of the lemon juice and toss ingredients thoroughly. Set aside and keep warm.

In another large sauté pan, heat remaining ¼ cup butter until foamy but not brown. Add oysters 1 by 1 and cook for 3 to 4 minutes on each side until golden brown. When done, add rest of lemon juice and toss gently.

To plate, arrange ¼ of the cabbage on each of 4 plates and place 5 oysters on top of cabbage in a row. Garnish with parsley and serve with cocktail sauce. Serves 4.

CHAPTER 11
Carry Me Back . . .

Mansion House Restaurant

Plantations were a way of the South throughout much of this
country's early history. The Civil War altered that lifestyle irrevocably.
However, the best elements of that time—its grace and gentility—
live on in these properties for us to enjoy today.

Maple Hall

3111 North Lee Highway
Lexington, VA 24450
540-463-2044

As you drive north on Interstate 81, it's hard not to notice the lovely three-story, red-brick, white-columned home just off Exit 195. Its stately appearance gives travelers along this busy thoroughfare a glimpse into the elegance that once defined the antebellum South.

The home was built by John Gibson to meet the needs of his growing family. Gibson married Grace M. Taylor in June 1829. By 1849, they were blessed with ten children, so not surprisingly, they needed additional space. Owning land six miles north of Lexington, Gibson decided to build a new home there. Before construction started, he looked around at other homes to decide what he wanted. He focused on the Thompson home, a two-story brick residence quite envied at the time. According to his great-granddaughter, Meta Gibson Short, John Gibson never wanted to be outdone. He christened the Gibson estate Maple Hill Farm, and the plantation house became known as Maple Hall.

Maple Hall was handed down to the Gibsons' eldest son, John Alexander. In the years before the Civil War, it was a popular destination for young people. Girls came beautifully dressed with handsome beaus for a waltz or other popular dance, as the older generations enjoyed the music and festivities. Descendants continued to live here until the summer of 1984, when the Peter Meredith family purchased the home and fifty-six surrounding acres. The Merediths fully restored the mansion. A year later, Maple Hall joined the Alexander-Withrow House and the McCampbell Inn in being designated the Historic Country Inns of Lexington.

Each guest room at Maple Hall is individually decorated with period antiques. Ten of the sixteen rooms even have working fireplaces. In the Southern tradition, shaded patios and porches provide rocking chairs for guests to relax. For those interested in more active pursuits, a fishing pond, a tennis court, a swimming pool, and a variety of walking trails are to be found amid Maple Hall's rolling landscape.

The late-afternoon sunshine shone across the beautiful Blue Ridge Mountains and glistened through the autumn colors the day we visited. Our footsteps crunched along a gravel path strewn with leaves as we made our way from the parking area. En route to the sunroom, we got a glimpse of the two main dining rooms, both decorated with subdued elegance. Karen ordered the Lobster Bisque—one of chef Richard Dytrych's signature dishes—and the Sausage Rolls, delicious sausage pâté in puff pastry. The Chicken Spanakopita that Debbie chose was scrumptious. We ordered a piece of the Fourteen-Layer Chocolate and Raspberry Torte and a piece of the Dang Good Pie to take with us. Much later that evening, when we enjoyed them in our hotel room, we agreed that everything about Maple Hall was pretty dang good!

🦞 LOBSTER BISQUE 🦞

2 tablespoons oil
1 tablespoon chopped garlic
1 tablespoon chopped shallots
4 carrots, chopped
4 large stalks celery, chopped
1 medium onion, chopped
3 bay leaves
1 tablespoon thyme
½ tablespoon whole peppercorns
1 lobster cavity
½ cup sherry, divided
1 tablespoon lobster base
1 cup tomato purée
16 cups (1 gallon) water
½ cup butter
½ cup flour
1 tablespoon paprika
3 cups heavy cream
¼ pound lobster meat with juices
salt and pepper to taste

Heat oil in a large pot. Add garlic, shallots, carrots, celery, and onions and cook until onions are transparent. Add bay leaves, thyme, peppercorns, and lobster cavity. Sauté until vegetables turn brown. Use ⅓ cup of the sherry to deglaze pan, then add lobster base, tomato purée, and water. Reduce stock to 12 cups, skimming top layer of oil as mixture reduces. While stock is reducing, melt butter in a saucepan. Add flour, blending with a wire whisk to make a roux. Add paprika, stirring vigorously with whisk. Set aside. Strain stock through a fine sieve, reserving liquid. Return stock to heat and add roux. Strain through a sieve again and return liquid to pot. Add cream, lobster meat and juices, remaining sherry, and salt and pepper. Heat through. Serves 6 to 8.

🦞 YANKEE POT ROAST 🦞

2- to 3-pound boneless chuck roast, trimmed
2 tablespoons vegetable oil
1 bay leaf
1 teaspoon salt
1 teaspoon pepper
1 teaspoon paprika
¼ teaspoon cayenne
2 cloves garlic, minced
3 cups beef broth
2 carrots, shredded
2 medium onions, quartered

Preheat oven to 350 degrees. Brown roast on all sides in hot oil in a large Dutch oven. Add remaining ingredients. Cover and simmer for about 2½ hours until roast is tender. Serve with au jus. Serves 6.

Prospect Hill
The Virginia Plantation Inn

2887 Poindexter Road
Trevilians, VA 23093
540-967-0844

It's hard to believe that the magnificent yellow-and-white plantation house known as Prospect Hill was originally a barn. The Roger Thompson family was forced to take up residence here in 1732 after its log cabin burned. Just a year later, Richmond Terrill assumed ownership and began shaping the homestead into a plantation. Thomas Jefferson was a neighbor, as his beloved Monticello is just down the road.

The year 1840 saw the home pass into the hands of William Overton. During his tenure, he added two wings and a spiral staircase. Fortunately for the Overtons—and for us—the home was not burned during the Civil War. However, the family was forced to continue its operations without labor or capital, eking out an existence over the next sixteen years. Gradually, like many plantation owners, they took advantage of a resource they did have—Southern hospitality—by opening their grand home to guests.

Visitors can choose to experience Prospect Hill by enjoying dinner or being an over-night guest at the inn. Rooms are located in some of the plantation's restored outbuildings, which include the slave quarters, a log cabin, the overseer's house, the summer kitchen, the smokehouse, the carriage house, and the groom's quarters. Unlike many inns, Prospect Hill utilizes the Modified American Plan, in which a sumptuous breakfast and the prix fixe dinner are included in the room rate.

For the last twenty years, the epicurean experience at Prospect Hill has begun in exactly the same way. Originally, the innkeeper's bell announced the start of a dinner prepared by Mierelle Sheehan, who was a proprietor of the inn, along with her husband, Bill. Today, it signals the beginning of a five-course candlelight dinner prepared by their son, Michael, who is continuing the family tradition with his wife, Laura. The menu changes regularly but is always of the highest quality, utilizing the freshest regional ingredients. For example, your starter might be Grilled Chilean Sea Bass over Saffron Rice with Red Beet Vinaigrette and Basil Chiffonade, followed by chilled Cucumber Fennel Soup. The entrée could be Seared Beef Tenderloin Medallions with Spicy Sweet Red Onion Confit, served with Stone-Ground Yellow Grits and Haricots Verts. We were treated to an appetizer of Garlic Sautéed Shrimp over Angel Hair with Basil Cream Sauce, followed by flavorful Roasted Sweet Potato Plantain Soup. Roasted Tenderloin of Beef with Sweet Australian Pepper and Button Mushroom Glaze was the entrée of the evening.

Dessert is something to be eagerly anticipated. Given choices such as Sabayon Glacé with Fresh Berries and Almond Canolis with Amaretto Mascarpone Cream, served with fresh Apricot Coulis and drizzled with dark chocolate, everyone is sure to leave with a smile on their face!

CUMIN SEED ISRAELI COUSCOUS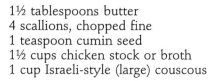

1½ tablespoons butter
4 scallions, chopped fine
1 teaspoon cumin seed
1½ cups chicken stock or broth
1 cup Israeli-style (large) couscous

Melt butter in a saucepan and sauté scallions for about 1 minute over medium heat. Add cumin seed and continue 1 minute more until soft. Add broth, bring to a rolling boil, and add couscous all at once, stirring until broth boils again. Cover and remove from heat. Let stand 5 minutes. Fluff with a fork and serve. Serves 4 to 6.

 CRAB MOUSSE ROULADE

1 pound crabmeat, picked
2 eggs
½ cup puréed squash
3 scallions, chopped
½ cup cracker crumbs
1 tablespoon Old Bay seasoning
1 tablespoon lemon juice
7 sheets phyllo dough
½ to ¾ cup shredded Parmesan
½ to ¾ cup ground pecans

Preheat oven to 350 degrees. Combine crabmeat, eggs, squash, scallions, cracker crumbs, Old Bay, and lemon juice. Set aside. Separate first sheet of phyllo and lightly spray with cooking spray. Sprinkle with Parmesan and cover with a second sheet of phyllo. Spray and sprinkle with nuts. Alternate cheese and nuts for remaining sheets. Mold crab mixture into a row on long edge of phyllo facing you. Roll all 7 sheets to form a tube around crab. Transfer to a greased pan. Bake about 15 minutes until golden brown. Cut into 1-inch strudels. Serves 4.

CLIFTON

Clifton Inn
1296 Clifton Inn Drive
Charlottesville, VA 22911
www.timeandplacehomes.com
434-971-1800

We waited by a crackling fire in the lovely sitting room until we were summoned to dinner. The cheery yellow walls of the sitting room were attractively offset by the black and white fabrics of the draperies and upholstery. A grand piano sat at one end of the room, practically dwarfed by the enormity of the space. Yet because of its décor, the room was comfortable, inviting, and homey.

Dinner was served on the veranda, which featured white-painted brick and wall sconces creatively enclosed in birdcages. Crisp white linens, fresh flowers, and graceful candles on the tables completed the air. A fire flickered away nearby, allowing guests to feel as if they were dining al fresco without experiencing the nip in the late-autumn air.

Upon being seated, we were presented with an amusé of Savory Cheesecake. Just the merest bite, it was a portent of things to come. The Acorn Squash Soup with Smoked Trout and Green Apples topped the list of starters, followed by choices such as Butter-

nut Squash Ravioli with Tarragon Wild Mushroom Consommé. Karen enjoyed the Venison Loin with Brown Butter Sweet Potato Purée, Morel Mushrooms, and Plum Jus, while Debbie found the Grouper en Papillote exceptional.

When not one but three chocolate offerings are available, dessert is not to be missed. For those who don't love chocolate, many other selections are available. We, however, shared the Chocolate Marquis—which consisted of Chocolate Terrine, Chocolate Mousse, and Chocolate Roulade—down to the very last bite.

Although the menu changes regularly, many other things have remained consistent over the years. The house was built by Thomas Jefferson's son-in-law, Thomas Mann Randolph, once the governor of Virginia and a member of the Virginia House of Delegates and the United States Senate. Married to Martha Jefferson, Randolph struggled with the challenge of having one of America's greatest men as his father-in-law.

Knowing that Randolph was deeply in debt, Thomas Jefferson bypassed him in his will, leaving his beloved estate to his grandson. Jefferson feared that Randolph would sell the holdings to pay off his creditors. This snub so angered Randolph that even though his wife was acting as hostess at Monticello, he refused her invitations to join her, staunchly remaining at Clifton for several years.

The Civil War saw the family of Colonel John Singleton Mosby sheltered here. Known as "the Gray Ghost of the Confederacy," Mosby took great risks to deliver supplies and provisions to the house while avoiding Union troops nearby.

The home remained a private residence until 1985. Since that time, it has served as an inn, receiving national recognition for its service and culinary excellence. We toured the guest rooms before leaving. Each one was as charming as the next. Whether you're looking for a terrific meal, beautiful gardens, a sense of history, or a place of tranquility, Clifton has a bit of it all.

SWEET GREEN CHILE CORNBREAD

1 cup whole milk
1 teaspoon lemon juice
½ cup butter, melted
4-ounce can mild green chiles, chopped
2 large eggs
1½ cups cornmeal
¾ cup all-purpose flour
½ cup sugar
1¼ teaspoons baking soda
½ teaspoon salt

Preheat oven to 375 degrees. Butter a 9-inch-square baking dish. In a large bowl, combine milk and lemon juice. Allow to stand for 2 minutes. Add butter, chiles, and eggs and beat with a mixer. In a separate bowl, combine cornmeal, flour, sugar, baking soda, and salt. Combine wet ingredients with dry ingredients. Pour into baking dish and bake for 20 to 30 minutes until top is golden brown. Serves 9.

MANGO BOURBON BBQ SAUCE

2 tablespoons butter
2 cloves garlic, chopped fine
1 medium yellow onion, diced
2 cups chicken stock
1½ to 2 cups ketchup
juice of 1 lemon
1 ripe mango, peeled and diced
2 shots bourbon
2 chipotle chiles
1½ tablespoons Hoisin sauce
2 tablespoons Old Bay seasoning
1½ teaspoons cayenne
3 tablespoons apple cider vinegar
2 tablespoons Worcestershire sauce
salt and pepper to taste

Melt butter in a large saucepan. Sauté garlic and onions over medium heat for 3 to 4 minutes until onions are translucent. Add stock, ketchup, and lemon juice. Bring to a boil over high heat, then lower temperature to a slow simmer. Add remaining ingredients. Keep sauce covered while simmering for 25 minutes, checking every few minutes. Adjust seasonings to taste. Remove from heat and allow to cool slightly. Place contents into a blender and blend until completely smooth. Empty sauce into an airtight container and refrigerate. Remove from refrigerator 25 minutes prior to use. If you prefer a chunkier sauce, skip the part where the sauce is blended. Yields 3 to 4 cups.

L'Auberge Provençale
White Post, VA 22663
540-837-1875

Chef Alain Borel's kitchen expertise has been featured on The Discovery Channel and *Great Chefs of the East* and in such magazines as *Glamour, Food & Wine,* and *Bon Appétit*. He has also lectured about his craft at the Smithsonian and has been invited to cook at the world-famous James Beard Society in New York City. So when guests sit to dinner at L'Auberge Provençale, they're in for a treat.

All of the choices on the prix fixe menu are mouth-wateringly appealing. For the first course, choosing among Citrus-Marinated Venison, Warm Rosemary Goat Cheese Tart with Provençale Vegetables, and Foie Gras with Caramelized Apples and Calvados is difficult, to say the least. Since Dover Sole was on the menu, the choice became slightly easier. It's also one of Debbie's favorites, and I knew she'd be disappointed she missed it.

When dessert rolls around, how does one decide among Sun-Dried Blueberry Crème Brûlée, Cornucopia of Sorbets, Citrus French Cream in Rhubarb Soup, and Cinnamon Raisin Apple Crisp in Phyllo, served with Pistachio Ice Cream and Blonde Caramel and Dark Chocolate Sauces?

The room in which I sat featured vari-ous shades of orange. The tiny individual tea lights at each table created a warm glow, as the light bounced off the white-painted woodwork, the highly polished wooden floors, and the copper pans displayed on the wall. There are several dining rooms here, all lovely. The staff members are well trained and are anxious to ensure that your every need is met.

In the early 1730s, Lord Fairfax contracted with George and Charles Washington to survey the area surrounding his Virginia home. The survey extended as far as what is now West Virginia. The white post placed in this small town gave birth to the community's name. The marker still remains in its original position today.

Following the survey, John Bell received a local land grant of 880 acres for the sum of thirty-three shillings. Upon his death, his property, known as Mount Airy, passed to his son and daughter-in-law, Samuel and Jane Bell. The couple became known as great wool growers.

In 1865, Colonel John Mosby and his Confederate raiders visited this site, as did other Union and Confederate troops. Fortunately, they were most interested in the spring at the end of the property, from which they could drink and water their horses. Bullets, belt buckles, and other memorabilia from the war have been found here. During renovations in the early 1980s, Alain and Celeste Borel discovered a letter from a freed slave to her sister in Front Royal. For some reason, the letter was never mailed, but the Borels found ancestors of the two and passed it on to them. Interesting history, a beautiful setting, and exquisite cuisine—who could ask for anything more?

ORIENTAL-STYLE QUAIL

½ cup soy sauce
½ cup plus 1 teaspoon sesame oil, divided
1 tablespoon minced garlic
1 tablespoon grated fresh ginger
2 shallots, sliced fine, divided
1 tablespoon chopped fresh cilantro
½ stick lemon grass, chopped
4 boneless quail
1 small red pepper
1 small yellow pepper
1 zucchini
1 yellow squash
1 star anise, crushed
1 cup white wine
1 cup veal jus
salt and pepper to taste

Preheat oven to 425 degrees. Combine soy sauce, ½ cup of the sesame oil, garlic, ginger, and half of the shallots to make a marinade. Add cilantro and lemon grass. Place quail in liquid. Refrigerate for 2 to 3 hours, turning occasionally. Cut peppers, zucchini, and yellow squash Chinese-style. In a saucepan, sweat remaining shallots in a little sesame oil until soft. Add anise and wine. Reduce. Add veal jus and simmer for 5 minutes. Strain. Place peppers, zucchini, and yellow squash on a roasting tray and brush with oil. Season with salt and pepper. Roast in oven for about 15 minutes until cooked. Remove quail from marinade and pat dry. Sear in a hot frying pan or on a grill. Place in a roasting pan and roast for 3 to 4 minutes. To serve, mound roasted vegetables in bowls or on plates. Cut quail in half and lay on top. Drizzle sauce over quail. Serves 4.

Willow Grove Inn

A Virginia Plantation
ca. 1778

14079 Plantation Way
Orange, VA 22960
www.willowgroveinn.com
540-672-5982

Willow Grove has withstood the test of time to remain as elegant today as when it was constructed. It started life as a modest frame dwelling for William Clark in 1778. In 1820, Clark's son began to remodel the house, adding a Classical Revival brick wing that increased its size considerably. The addition is similar in style to several of the pavilions at the University of Virginia. This is not surprising, since many of the workmen labored at the university immediately prior to working on the manor house.

The house was not noticeably damaged during either the Revolutionary War or the Civil War. It is said that American generals Anthony Wayne and John Peter Muhlenberg camped on the grounds during the Revolution. In 1862, the house came under siege by Union soldiers for a short time. General U. S. Grant, attempting to advance across the nearby Rapidan River, stopped here to meet with his company commanders to discuss strategy. Workers on the property have dug up buttons and belt buckles from soldiers'

uniforms. Surprisingly, a cannonball was discovered lodged in the eaves of the manor house.

The Clark family continued in residence until the turn of the twentieth century, when the property was sold to the Lyne family. According to my server, many of the Lynes still live in Orange and the surrounding area. Often, one or another of them visits Willow Grove and recounts stories from when they were children. In the Dolley Madison Room, guests enjoy seeing the window etchings made by the Lyne girls with their diamond rings.

Very little has changed here over the years. The building was lucky to have owners who preserved the main architectural features of the property, such as the pine flooring and the staircases. Even the gardens are much as they were in Victorian days, featuring bulbs, boxwoods, and flowering shrubs that were popular then. Many mature trees surround the property—including, of course, the willows for which the plantation was named.

Each of the three dining rooms has its own atmosphere. Guests often choose to dine on the veranda overlooking the beautiful gardens. The more casual Clark's Tavern was originally the root cellar. Now, it boasts large hand-hewn beams added in the nineteenth century. Upstairs, visitors can enjoy a more formal dinner in the Dolley Madison Room, which features one of the most fabulous crystal chandeliers I have ever seen.

I was sorry Debbie wasn't there to enjoy it with me.

The food is every bit as delicious as the rooms are elegant. The chef serves regional Virginia cuisine using vegetables and herbs grown on the property, whenever possible. Every mouthful was a delight, from the Brandied Lobster Bisque with Diced Shrimp to the Salad of Mixed Baby Field Greens with Virginia Peanut Vinaigrette to the Fresh Horseradish and Mustard Seed Crusted Tenderloin of Black Angus Beef with Shiraz Reduction. The highlight of the evening, however, was the Red Wine-Poached Pear with Whipped Cream and Reduced Red Wine Syrup, which was unbelievably good. Whether you visit for the romance, the history, or the fabulous food, you are sure to be delighted.

 LOIN OF FALLOW FIELDS VENISON

2 carrots
½ large onion
1 shallot
1 large clove garlic
5-pound loin of venison
1 tablespoon olive oil
2½ cups red wine
¼ cup red wine vinegar
2 bay leaves
1 teaspoon sea salt
6 black peppercorns

Peel and chop carrots, onion, shallot, and garlic and place in a dish deep enough to hold venison. Add oil, wine, vinegar, bay leaves, salt, and peppercorns and stir to combine. Place venison in marinade and refrigerate for at least 8 hours. Remove from refrigerator and discard marinade. Preheat oven to 350 degrees. Roast venison for about 2½ hours until meat thermometer measures about 120 degrees. Do not overcook. Venison should be served medium-rare. It is a very lean meat and gets dry if overcooked. Remove from oven and allow to sit for 10 minutes. Slice to serve. Serves 8 to 10 generously.

 LEMON VERBENA SORBET

3 to 4 cups lemon verbena leaves
2 cups sugar
5 cups water

Chop verbena leaves. Place verbena, sugar, and water in a medium saucepan. Bring mixture to a boil. Reduce heat to low and simmer for 5 minutes. Let cool. Chill in refrigerator at least 8 hours. Strain mixture. Freeze according to instructions on ice cream freezer. Yields 4 cups.

DARK CHOCOLATE PISTACHIO TERRINE

2 pounds semisweet chocolate
1 cup heavy cream
2 tablespoons brandy
½ cup pistachios, shelled
fresh whipped cream

Cut chocolate into small pieces and place in a mixing bowl. Add cream and place over simmering water until chocolate is melted. Remove bowl from heat and add brandy and pistachios. Pour into a 1-quart mold and refrigerate for at least 8 hours. Serve with whipped cream. Serves 16.

MINI CHOCOLATE COFFEE WALNUT MUFFINS

2 cups walnuts
1½ cups chocolate chips
1 cup butter
1 cup brown sugar
1 cup sugar
5 tablespoons instant coffee
4 teaspoons vanilla
4 eggs
3¼ cups all-purpose flour
1 teaspoon salt
2 tablespoons baking powder
1⅓ cups milk

Preheat oven to 350 degrees. Coarsely chop walnuts and chocolate chips. In a medium bowl, cream together butter, brown sugar, sugar, coffee, and vanilla. Beat in eggs. In another bowl, combine flour, salt, and baking powder. Add flour mixture and milk alternately to the butter mixture, beating after each addition. Fold in chocolate and walnuts. Spoon into greased mini-muffin pans and bake for 12 to 15 minutes. Yields 3 dozen mini-muffins.

3601 Ironbound Road
Williamsburg, VA 23188
www.kitchenatpowhatan.com
757-220-1200

Two empty demitasse cups that only moments before had contained White Chocolate and Dark Chocolate Crème Brûlée were all that was left of our leisurely meal at The Kitchen at Powhatan Plantation. We kept peering into the petite crockery, hoping for more.

Our meal began with a plate of Cheese and Crostini delivered promptly to our table upon arrival. We could have made a meal on that alone. After contemplating choices such as the Crab Spring Roll, the Lobster Gazpacho with Avocado Cream, the Baby Spinach Salad, and the Herb-Crusted Chicken, Debbie finally chose the Pan-Roasted Quail, served atop an Ancho Chile Corn Cake. The quail had a wonderfully smoky flavor, almost as if it had been prepared over a fire, as it would have been in the kitchen's early days. Karen ordered the New Zealand Rack of Lamb, which was wonderfully prepared and presented. The intimate restaurant was full both upstairs and down, and we heard pleasant murmurings throughout the dining room.

In the 1600s, this site functioned as one of the very earliest plantations. The land was patented by Richard and Benjamin Eggleston, who arrived in Virginia in 1635. The plantation's name is a reference to nearby Powhatan Creek, which lies west of the property and meanders through territory that was once part of the Powhatan Indian Confederation.

Descendants of the Eggleston family continued to live in the area for quite some time, even after the property was conveyed to Richard Taliaferro as a result of his marriage to Elizabeth Eggleston, a granddaughter of the original settlers. According to architectural historians, it was Taliaferro, a master architect, who built the manor house at Powhatan Plantation. The style and size of the home reflect the prosperity of the plantation during his tenure.

In 1827, Dr. Thomas Martin bought the property. Martin's son, William, had to endure it when Union forces set fire to the home in 1862. The fire gutted the interior. A cannonball is still embedded in the chimney, affirming General George McClellan's visit.

The Kitchen was once the site of the bakery that served the plantation. As was common, it sat apart from the main house in an attempt to prevent potential fires from spreading to the dwelling. The parking lot for the restaurant is to the left of the manor house, while The Kitchen is to the right. This affords guests the pleasure of strolling through gardens bordered by white picket fences before arriving at the restaurant. Two round tables set with pewter and candles allow for outdoor porch seating on balmy evenings.

The setting and scale of The Kitchen are such that it's easy to feel like Alice stepping into a life-sized dollhouse. Once you're through the door, two attentive wait staff in period dress will see to your every need. Our cozy table by the fireplace was the perfect place to enjoy a wonderful evening meal.

BABY SPINACH SALAD

6 to 8 cups baby spinach, stemmed
¼ cup walnuts, toasted
½ cup Roquefort or blue cheese crumbles
5 fresh figs, halved

Wash spinach. Drain and pat dry. Arrange spinach on salad plates. Top with remaining ingredients and serve with a dressing of your choice. Serves 5.

PEAR VINAIGRETTE

2 to 3 sweet, ripe pears, peeled and seeded
¼ cup white balsamic vinegar or rice wine
  vinegar
¾ cup olive oil or grape seed oil
1 teaspoon sugar

Combine all ingredients in a blender until smooth. Yields about 2½ cups.

BITTERSWEET CHOCOLATE CRÈME BRÛLÉE

4 cups heavy whipping cream
1 cup sugar, divided
12 ounces bittersweet chocolate
8 egg yolks

Preheat oven to 300 degrees. Bring cream and ½ cup of the sugar to a boil in a nonreactive pan. Remove from heat, add chocolate, and allow to stand 3 minutes to melt chocolate. Whisk smooth. Whisk yolks in a bowl, then whisk in chocolate mixture. Strain into a 2-quart gratin dish. Set gratin dish inside a roasting pan. Place pans on middle oven rack. Add warm water to bottom of roasting pan to about half the depth of gratin dish. Bake about 1 hour until set. A thin knife or toothpick inserted in center should emerge clean. Remove baking dish from roasting pan; leave pan of water in oven to cool. Chill custard. To caramelize top, blot any moisture from top of chilled custard. Sprinkle evenly with remaining sugar. Place under preheated broiler to caramelize. For individual desserts, use shallow individual gratin dishes or ramekins, set individually in roasting pan, and follow directions as above. Serves 8.

High Meadows Vineyard Inn & Restaurant

55 High Meadows Lane
Scottsville, VA 24590
434-286-2218

Peter White, born in Scotland, came to America in the 1820s. Upon arriving, he purchased forty-four acres of land that once belonged to Scottsville's founder, John Scott. White was quite successful, undertaking the original survey of the town and becoming Scottsville's first druggist. He used the traditional Federal two-over-two floor plan in constructing a home for his wife, Elizabeth, and their two children. According to that popular style of the times, cooking and eating took place on the lower level, adult activities and sleeping were in the middle level, and children were given the third-story dormer area. Porches ran the full length of both the north and south sides of the home.

The family resided here for almost thirty years before Peter White's death just before the Civil War. Elizabeth stayed on until the property was sold to Charles Harris in 1881. Harris was a successful Scottsville merchant and the owner of the James River Canal Warehouse. Feeling that the existing home was too simple, he and his wife embarked on the construction on a new, more elaborate Victorian country house just ten feet in front of the old one. During the building process, the Harrises lived in the old structure, though they had every intention of tearing it down once the new house was complete. The carpenters and masons tried to convince them otherwise, commenting on the quality of the hand-carved wood mantels, the double-fired brick, and the heart-pine floors in the old home.

Once the Victorian house was finished, Helen Harris refused to move in, stating that she wouldn't relinquish "seven excellent rooms in the old house for a few fancy new ones." The standoff continued for more than five years, husband and wife living in two separate homes with an open porch in between. Finally, Charles Harris constructed an enclosed breezeway between the two houses, creating a one-of-a-kind structure. All of the Harris children were married here. Most took their vows in front of the marble-ized slate mantel in the music room.

A sumptuous breakfast on par with the surroundings is available to overnight guests of the inn. While Karen journeyed down the road a bit, I enjoyed the inn's Sunday brunch. The chef offers a wide array of menu items ranging from Biscuits and Gravy to Spinach Salad Sunny Side Up. Quiche and Huevos Rancheros are also on the menu, alongside Chesapeake Eggs Benedict, Charred Rare Beef Salad, and Chilled Asparagus Tips. Guests can order an entrée along with a side, or they can choose any four items from the menu to be shared at the table. My omelet of spinach, sun-dried tomatoes, and Gruyère was perfectly prepared, as were my Cheddar Cheese Grits.

When dinner starts with choices as appealing as Grilled Shrimp with Peach Salad and Key Lime Caesar Salad, then is followed by entrées like Roast Rack of Lamb in Kiwi-Spearmint Velouté, guests are obviously in for quite a treat. The special wine-tasting dinners held throughout the year are accompanied by live jazz music.

High Meadows has been recognized as the Virginia Wine Restaurant of the Year and has been selected for *Gourmet* magazine's hall of fame. Such honors are a testament to the gastronomic delights served here.

OYSTERS IN THYME CREAM WITH GARLIC CROUTONS

1 loaf leftover bread
1 tablespoon minced garlic
¼ cup olive oil
¼ cup butter, melted
2 cups heavy cream
1 cup whole milk
2 sprigs fresh thyme
2 tablespoons minced thyme leaves
10 peppercorns
1 bay leaf
1 whole clove
2 slices smoked bacon
10 baby carrots, minced
2 tablespoons minced leek
1 stalk celery, diced fine
2 dozen fresh oysters, shucked
pepper to taste
1 teaspoon Thai fish sauce (a little salt may be substituted)
red or yellow bell pepper for garnish, chopped

Cut bread into large cubes. Combine garlic, olive oil, and butter. Brush bread cubes with olive oil mixture. Bake on low heat until crisp. Combine cream, milk, thyme, peppercorns, bay leaf, and clove in a medium saucepan and reduce by ⅓. Cook bacon until crisp. Add carrots, leek, and celery and sauté until tender. Add oysters and cook just until edges curl. Season with pepper and Thai fish sauce. Remove peppercorns, bay leaf, and clove. Discard. Place croutons in 2 bowls. Ladle oyster mixture over croutons. Garnish with red or yellow bell pepper. Serves 2.

AMARETTO CHEESECAKE

¼ cup butter, melted
1 cup graham cracker crumbs
4 8-ounce packages cream cheese, softened
1⅔ cups sugar
5 eggs
1 teaspoon vanilla
1 cup amaretto

Preheat oven to 350 degrees. Combine butter and graham cracker crumbs. Press mixture into a 9-inch springform pan. Bake for 10 minutes. In a large bowl, combine cream cheese and sugar, mixing well. Add eggs 1 at a time, blending well with each addition. Add vanilla and amaretto and mix well. Pour into prepared crust. Line pan with aluminum foil and bake in a water bath for 1 hour and 20 minutes. Turn off oven and allow cheesecake to stay in for another hour. Cool to room temperature. Remove sides of pan. Place cheesecake in refrigerator to chill thoroughly. Serves 16.

Mansion House Restaurant
at
Historic Carradoc Hall

Holiday Inn at Historic Carradoc Hall
1500 East Market Street
Leesburg, VA 20176
703-771-9200

We had admired the lovely exterior of this mansion many times when driving past along busy US 7, which runs along the front of the property. The pale yellow facade and massive front pillars stand today as they did when the home was constructed. Reports vary as to exactly when that occurred. Some records date the construction as early as 1747, while others suggest the early 1800s— about the same time that many other such mansions went up throughout Loudoun County.

In the early 1700s, Captain Willoughby Newton purchased the tract of land on which the mansion now stands. After his death in 1767, the property remained in the family. It is believed that Joseph Newton and his wife, Nelly, were the owners at the time the home was built. After their passing, their daughter and her husband, Dr. William Harper, came into possession of the estate.

The Harper family had strong ties to General George Washington. Captain William Harper, the father of Dr. William Harper, was a Revolutionary War soldier who crossed the Delaware with Washington and also fought at Trenton, Monmouth, Brandywine, and Germantown and endured the famous winter at Valley Forge. In 1793, Captain Harper and his artillery company were present as General Washington laid the cornerstone of the United States Capitol. They were also in attendance in an official capacity at Mount Vernon when Washington was laid to rest. Two brothers-in-law of Captain Harper, members of the 106th Virginia Regiment, were selected to convey Washington's casket to his tomb.

The Harper family retained ownership until 1978. The original tract was gradually divided among the various heirs. However, the Harpers always remained on the land, leading what descendants have called "a not wealthy but comfortable life."

Through its history, the property has been known by a variety of names—the Home Farm on Goose Creek, Oak Grove, and even California, because of a copper mine located on the land. The best-known name was Carradoc Hall, derived from a popular 1800s tonic that was 90 percent alcohol.

We were seated in the larger dining room. The hardwood floor was covered with area rugs. A family that had gathered at the large table in front of the fireplace just before we arrived was reflecting over a day of area sightseeing.

We considered appetizers of Baked Goat Cheese, Ale-Battered Quail, and Savory Bread Pudding, made with asparagus. All seemed to reflect the home's original era. Karen ultimately selected the Asiago Polenta, topped with tomatoes, while Debbie warmed herself with a bowl of hearty Onion Bisque. A Portabello Mushroom Salad and a Spinach and Pear Salad rounded out our meal. Entrées like Portabello Mushroom Lasagna, Roasted Vegetable Strudel, Porkchops with Tart Apple Ragout, and Coriander- and Honey-Basted Quail all sounded appealing, giving us just the excuse we need for a return visit.

APPLE AND SAGE SPOON BREAD

1 cup thinly sliced apple wedges
2 tablespoons olive oil
1 tablespoon chopped fresh sage
2 cups apple cider
1 cup yellow cornmeal
¼ cup butter at room temperature
¾ cup milk
1½ teaspoons salt
¾ teaspoon pepper
3 large eggs, separated

Preheat oven to 400 degrees. Lightly grease a 6-cup soufflé dish. In a medium-sized heavy saucepan, sauté apples in oil over medium heat until browned. Add sage and stir. Add cider and bring to a boil. Gradually whisk in cornmeal until mixture is very thick. Remove from heat. Stir in butter, milk, salt, and pepper. Cool 10 minutes. Mix in egg yolks. Beat egg whites in a medium bowl until stiff but not dry. Fold half the eggs whites into lukewarm cornmeal mixture, stirring gently. Repeat with remaining egg whites. Transfer mixture into prepared dish. Bake for about 35 minutes until puffed, golden on top, and set in center. Serve hot. Serves 4.

ROASTED LAMB WITH CRANBERRY MUSTARD SAUCE

2 pounds bone-in lamb or 3 lamb racks
salt and pepper to taste
3 cups cranberry juice
1 cup chicken stock
½ cup dried cranberries
3 tablespoons whole-grain mustard

Preheat oven to 350 degrees. Season lamb with salt and pepper. In a sauté pan, brown lamb on all sides. Pour in cranberry juice to deglaze pan. Remove lamb from sauté pan and place in a roasting pan. Roast in oven for 25 to 30 minutes to medium doneness. While roasting, reduce cranberry juice over medium heat to ¾ cup. Add stock, cranberries, and mustard. Simmer until thickened and smooth. Remove lamb from oven and slice into 4 equal portions. Drizzle with sauce. Serves 4.

1763 INN

10087 John Mosby Highway
Upperville, VA 20184
www.1763inn.com
540-592-3848

Many visitors ask about the name of this establishment, wondering if the building really is that old. The answer is yes. The original section of the main building, constructed in the Federal two-over-two style, dates back to 1763. In 1775, Lord Fairfax deeded the land to George Washington as payment for survey work. The document that completed the transaction hangs in the appropriately named George Washington Dining Room.

It's hard to imagine that these fifty beautiful acres were the site of fierce fighting during the Civil War. With strategic Ashby Gap nearby, this area was coveted by both the Union and Confederate armies. At one point, Union soldiers stored horses behind the building until they were driven off by advancing Confederate troops. It's not surprising, then, to find in the sitting room a large collection of memorabilia, much of it gathered from the surrounding land. When the Kirchner family purchased the property in 1970, the front door still bore the scars where Yankee soldiers had kicked it in.

Uta and Don Kirchner began restorations with the intent of creating a country getaway for themselves. By April 1986, the property had evolved from being a home away from home to a country inn and restaurant. During its first ten years of operation, the inn was expanded to include a total of eighteen guest rooms—four in the main house, two in the cottage, seven in the restored stables, four in log cabins, and one in the carriage house.

Early on, the restaurant specialized in German cuisine, with Uta preparing her favorites. Although a German Sampler still appears on the menu, the choices have been expanded to appeal to guests' ever-changing palates.

On the night I visited, Karen was just down the road, enjoying some English pub-style fare. I started my meal with a light salad made with varieties of cress and topped with roasted onion. It was delicious in its simplicity. The Roasted Onion Tart, the Char-Grilled Eggplant Salad, and the Roasted Duck Salad on the list of starters all sounded appealing as well. After choosing my entrée of Barbecued Atlantic Salmon with Grapefruit Avocado Relish, I wandered a bit, marveling at the wide-plank floors covered with large rugs woven in muted colors. Horse paintings throughout the inn hinted at the area's ties to fox hunting, steeplechasing, and other such events. Old photos displayed here and there revealed that, in many ways, little has changed here in more than two hundred years.

I returned to my seat to enjoy my view of the pond, replete with an island gazebo and resident swans, just as my meal was served. I enjoyed the unique mixture of grapefruit and avocado. As I ate, I mused over one relic in particular, a photo of a young girl born in 1899. An article from 1989 displayed beside the picture announced the birthday party of Marie Agnes Buckner Gibson, who grew up in this house. That party, fittingly held at 1763 Inn, was attended by the many people whose lives she had touched. Just thinking of how many others have lived and celebrated their special events here since 1763 brought me a smile.

FENNEL-CURED SALMON

1 pound salmon
1 cup kosher salt
½ teaspoon pepper
½ cup sugar
4 cups fennel tops
2 tablespoons coriander seed, roasted
5 tablespoons fennel seed, roasted
¼ cup lemon vodka
2 teaspoons Pernod
¼ cup olive oil

With a razor, make ½-inch-deep cuts randomly on skin side of salmon. Turn salmon over so flesh side is up. Place in a pan and sprinkle a layer of salt and pepper on it, followed by sugar. Place half the fennel on top of that, along with half the coriander seed and fennel seed. Combine vodka and Pernod and drizzle half of mixture over herbs. Flip salmon and repeat the process. Pour olive oil over salmon and place another pan on top of fish. Place a weight (an unopened half-gallon of milk works great) on top of pan to form a press. The weight keeps the fish in the marinade.

Keep in refrigerator for a minimum of 3 days, turning salmon every other day. The longer you cure, the stronger the flavor will be. When ready to serve, remove salmon from pan and scrape off herb mixture. Carve into thin slices and serve. Serves 8 as an appetizer.

11500 West Huguenot Road
Midlothian, VA 23113
804-378-0600

When Melissa Wood, marketing representative for Ruth's Chris Steak House, first contacted us, we told her that we normally don't include restaurants affiliated with national chains. Fortunately, she was persistent, explaining that this location is independently owned and has a great history. She faxed us some background information on Bellgrade Plantation, and we were sold!

We enjoyed our time here, immersed in stories as we dined on Chop Salad and Filet Mignon. Ruth's Chris restaurants are known for their steaks, and this locale is no exception. Rib Eye, Porterhouse, T-Bone, New York Strip—the restaurant has a cut for everyone. Or guests can enjoy the salmon, lobster, chicken, lamb, or veal entrées. For dessert, we were tempted by the novelty of the Caramelized Banana Cream Pie.

The restaurant is situated in a one-and-a-half-story farmhouse built in 1732. For almost a hundred years, it saw families come and go. In 1824, Edward Cox sold the property to Edward Friend. During the Friend family's residence, the farm was expanded to approximately a thousand acres. To ac-commodate their expanding family, the Friends extensively remodeled the farmhouse, adding wings, moving the front door and fireplace, and adding a front porch and columns. At that time, the property became known as Bellgrade Plantation.

In 1840, the estate was sold to a forty-three-year-old French bachelor by the name of Robiou. In search of a wife, he settled on the fourteen-year-old daughter of a prominent attorney and landowner named Wormley. The couple moved into Bellgrade. However, just a few weeks after their wedding, Robiou returned home unexpectedly and found his bride in the arms of the nineteen-year-old who was her former suitor. Incensed, he threw his young wife out of the house and demanded a divorce. Angered and humiliated by Robiou's behavior, Wormley convinced the young boyfriend to help him exact revenge on his son-in-law. The two of them surprised Robiou one night as he returned home, fatally shooting him. Both were arrested and jailed. The young man was released, having been duped by the older, more influential Wormley. Wormley's case ended in a mistrial after he used his judicial influence to provide whiskey to the jury. However, the case gained so much notoriety that the judge retried him. Wormley was found guilty and sentenced to hang. In the months that followed, he appealed his conviction. Meanwhile, his daughter, now a widow, married her beau and moved back to the plantation. Wormley eventually lost his appeal and was hanged with six thousand people in attendance. Less than two weeks later, his daughter died as a result of falling down the front stairs of the mansion. Not surprisingly, the ghosts of Robiou and the girl have been sighted many times.

The Civil War brought more interesting events to the halls of Bellgrade. We invite you to discover those tales for yourself during your visit.

 BBQ SHRIMP

20 16- to 20-count shrimp
1 tablespoon canola oil
1 tablespoon plus 4 teaspoons chopped green onions, divided
2 tablespoons dry white wine
1 teaspoon chopped fresh garlic
4 tablespoons Worcestershire sauce
1 teaspoon Tabasco sauce
½ teaspoon cayenne
½ teaspoon paprika
1 cup butter

Wash shrimp under water, then peel shells. Discard. Devein shrimp with a paring knife and wash under water. Place on a baking sheet and put in refrigerator. Heat a large cast-iron skillet over high heat. Add oil and shrimp. Cook just until done. You may have to do this in batches, depending on size of skillet. Remove shrimp and set aside. Add 1 tablespoon of the green onions and cook for 1 minute. Add white wine and reduce by half. Add garlic, Worcestershire, Tabasco, cayenne, and paprika. Shake pan well. Cook for 1 minute. Reduce heat to low. Cut butter into small chucks and slowly add to pan, shaking fast to melt butter. Continue until all butter is melted. Add shrimp back into pan and toss well to coat with butter. Divide shrimp evenly among 4 small serving plates with deep rims. Ladle sauce from skillet over shrimp. Sprinkle each with 1 teaspoon green onions. Serve immediately. Serves 4.

 STEAK SALAD

4 to 6 ounces beef tenderloin tips, seared medium-rare
6 cups mixed field greens, washed and chilled
1 medium vine-ripened tomato, cut into chunks
1 small red onion, sliced and separated into rings
3 tablespoons chopped fresh parsley
3 tablespoons chopped fresh chives
½ cup crumbled blue cheese
4 slices bacon, cooked and crumbled
½ cup fried onion rings, crumbled
salt and pepper to taste

Thinly slice beef and set aside. Divide greens among 3 large, chilled salad plates. Divide next 7 ingredients into thirds and layer on top of greens. Add salt and pepper and toss briefly. Add beef. Top with dressing of your choice. Serves 3.

CHAPTER 12
History Repeats Itself

The Mount Vernon Inn Restaurant

For us, there is nothing more exhilarating than discovering a two-hundred-year-old structure that was soundly built and has been lovingly maintained. Unfortunately, longevity can't be taken for granted. Wars, natural disasters, and neglect often intervene. In the pages that follow, we feature not original buildings but reconstructions that stand in honor as modern testaments to the structures that came before them.

Mariah's at Tower Hill
Bed/Breakfast & Inn

3018 Bowden Landing
Cape Charles, VA 23310
www.towerhillbb.com
757-331-1700

Mariah's at Tower Hill was recommended to us as we chatted with local residents Ray and Joan Dueser while lingering over dessert at an establishment in Willis Wharf. Never ones to ignore a fervent endorsement, we detoured to Cape Charles. There, we met Barbara, the local antique dealer. She gave us directions, then regaled us with stories about playing at Tower Hill as a young girl.

The original house at Tower Hill was built by Peter Bowdoin. Eleven years in the making, it was finally completed in 1746. During the 1800s, the house passed in and out of the Saunders family. James and Maria Saunders purchased it in 1839. When Nancy Garrett, a modern-day descendant of the Saunders family, heard about the supernatural events at Tower Hill, she just knew "old Maria's at it." Garrett has a photograph of an oil painting of Maria Saunders in which Maria's dark hair is tucked into a ruffled white bonnet. Heavy lids hide her deep-set brown eyes. Her expression is indefinable. Are her lips set in a stern frown, or is that a smirk hinting at her enigmatic behavior in the years to come?

Although it was unusual for colonial homes in these parts to be built of brick, it's thought that the durable material was chosen for Tower Hill due to the structure's open exposure to the bay. Though many homes in the area were built along creeks to provide early access to navigation, this location along King's Creek is thought to have been particularly significant, since the house was built with a basement. There's a theory that a tunnel ran from the basement to the creek, and that it was used to smuggle goods past the Cherrystone Creek Customs House, located farther up the coast.

The new structure is a replica of that original dwelling, which sat empty—except for grazing goats—from 1960 until it burned in the late 1990s. Fortunately, the brick and masonry survived, so the reconstruction could follow the original design. Today, Tower Hill functions as an inn with a full-service restaurant named in honor of Maria Saunders. Five bedrooms accommodate overnight guests. Heart-pine flooring salvaged from an old mill helps to create the ambiance of Tower Hill's past.

The ambiance of Tower Hill's present is created partly by the aromas and flavors that flow from proprietor Tim Brown's kitchen. Appetizers such as Tuna Tartare, Peppercorn Bourbon Molasses Rabbit Loin, and Pan-Fried Jumbo Scallop over Vegetable Ragout are just a few of the scrumptious ways to begin your meal here. Entrées like Pistachio-

Encrusted Pork Tenderloin, Venison Tenderloin Wellington, and Sweet Potato-Encrusted Red Snapper continue the list of gastronomic pleasantries. What more could anyone want? Well, maybe the desserts, which are on a par with the rest of the meal!

SPICY MAHI-MAHI WITH BLOOD ORANGE BASIL CREAM

4 6-ounce portions mahi-mahi
¼ cup blackening mix
½ cup olive oil, divided
1 red onion, julienned
½ cup white wine
2 blood oranges, sectioned
1 cup heavy cream
2 sprigs basil, chopped fine
salt and pepper to taste

Preheat oven to 350 degrees. Dredge mahi-mahi on 1 side in blackening mix. Heat cup of the olive oil in a sauté pan. Place fish seasoned side down in hot oil. Cook for 3 minutes, then flip. Place in oven for 3 to 5 minutes. While fish is cooking, sauté onions in remaining oil. Cook until onions are caramelized. Reserve for garnish. Deglaze sauté pan with white wine. Reduce. Add oranges and cook for 2 minutes. Add cream and reduce until mixture thickens and coats the back of a spoon. Toss in basil and season with salt and pepper. To serve, plate fish, spoon sauce over top, and garnish with onions. Mariah's serves this with Herbed Buttered Grits and seasonal vegetables. Serves 4.

CHOCOLATE COCONUT DECADENCE

1 cup coconut
½ cup almonds
1¾ cups butter, divided
3 eggs
3 egg yolks
2 pounds plus 12 ounces semisweet chocolate, divided
2 cups heavy cream
4 tablespoons corn syrup
2 tablespoons white chocolate, melted

Preheat oven to 350 degrees. Grind coconut and almonds. Melt 4 tablespoons of the butter. Combine with coconut mixture. Press into a 9-inch springform pan and bake for 4 to 5 minutes. Cool. Whip eggs and egg yolks until light and fluffy. Melt 2 pounds of the chocolate and all but 2 tablespoons of the butter. Fold eggs and chocolate together. Spread on top of coconut layer. Bake for 5 to 7 minutes until mixture is a fudgelike consistency. Cool. Shave the remaining 12 ounces of chocolate into a mixing bowl. Heat cream, remaining butter, and corn syrup just until mixture starts to boil. Pour over chocolate in mixing bowl. Mix until smooth. Pour over other chocolate layer. Drizzle with white chocolate. Refrigerate. Serves 16.

Brugh Tavern

Virginia's Explore Park
Milepost 115, Blue Ridge Parkway
Roanoke, VA 24014
540-427-2440

The Brugh family immigrated to America in the late 1700s. After initially settling in York County, Pennsylvania, the Brughs sold their land there and moved south to Virginia. Around 1790, they purchased a tract of several hundred acres near Troutville. They built a large house that was almost certainly a copy of the home they had owned in Pennsylvania. On December 12, 1809, Daniel Brugh became the first in his family to apply for a tavern license. But he certainly wasn't the last. The Brugh Tavern served the general public as an ordinary for many decades.

In the early days, taverns were important social centers for all who lived close by. They were places where news was exchanged, where traveling peddlers sold their wares, and where locals met to transact business. The Brugh Tavern was highly successful. Over the decades, the surrounding area became a small commercial center that included a sawmill, a gristmill, a distillery, and

even a large threshing barn. According to records of the Virginia Department of Historic Resources, the tavern was "one of the earliest and most interesting houses in Botetourt County." Its history clearly illustrates the slow transmission of German ethnicity to the Blue Ridge.

The tavern is a three-story building on a full stone basement. Guests usually entered on the first floor and were invited to store their weapons in the large gun closet in the central hallway. The tavern was well known for its spacious rooms with plaster walls and a painted chair rail. The kitchen was located in the basement, which had an enormous corner fireplace and a well. The innkeeper himself lived on that level so he could keep a close eye on all the foodstuffs in the large stone cellar.

Virginia Explore Park acquired the Brugh Tavern in 1998. At that time, the tavern was carefully disassembled, labeled, and reassembled at the park. It was dedicated on Tuesday, April 28, 1998. Visitors to the park can now dine at the Brugh Tavern and enjoy the historic atmosphere of this original German structure. The wide front porch leads inside to spotless wooden floors and tables lit by pewter sconces and candelabra. The large brick chimneys at both ends of the house remind guests of days gone by.

The tavern continues to serve the public today by offering delicious meals, many of them from painstakingly researched historic recipes. Notable examples of these are the delicious Hashed Beef with Toast Wedges and the unusual Fried Cucumbers. Among the other favorites are the Homemade Lemon Iced Pound Cake and the Jumbles, which are yummy cookies flavored with caraway seeds. Whatever your choice, it's difficult to sit at the Brugh Tavern and not reflect upon the thousands of travelers who have visited before you!

FISH CHOWDER

1 pound small red potatoes quartered
2 teaspoons olive oil
4 tablespoons bacon, chopped
1 small red bell pepper, cut into ½-inch pieces
1 small green bell pepper, cut into ½-inch pieces
1 small onion, diced fine
2 or 3 cloves garlic, chopped
3 tablespoons flour
2 cups milk
½ teaspoon salt
¼ teaspoon cayenne
¼ pound baby shrimp
¼ pound scallops
½ pound cod or haddock fillets, cut into 1-inch pieces
¼ cup heavy cream
2 tablespoons sherry
salt and Tabasco sauce to taste

In a medium pot, cook potatoes in boiling water just until tender. Drain and set aside. In a large skillet, heat oil over medium heat. Add bacon and brown lightly. Add peppers, onions, and garlic and cook until peppers are tender. Add flour, stirring into vegetables. Add milk, salt, and cayenne. Bring to a boil. Add all the shellfish and fish. Stir gently and reduce heat to a simmer. Cover and continue to cook about 5 minutes until fish is opaque. Stir in potatoes, cream, and sherry. Adjust seasoning with salt and Tabasco if necessary. Serves 6.

JUMBLES

¾ cup butter or margarine
1½ cups sugar
4 cups flour
1 tablespoon caraway seeds, crushed slightly
2 extra large eggs
½ cup milk, warmed

Preheat oven to 400 degrees. In a medium bowl, cream together butter or margarine with sugar. In a separate bowl, combine flour and caraway seeds. Add eggs to butter mixture alternately with flour mixture. Beat well. If mixture is too dry to handle, add warm milk until a firm dough is formed. Roll dough into 1-inch balls. Place dough balls on well-greased cookie sheets. Use the bottom of a glass dipped in sugar or flour to flatten the balls. You may also make long rolls and twist them into knots, dipping them in sugar before placing on cookie sheets. Bake for 7 to 9 minutes until edges brown slightly. Do not overcook, as cookies will be very hard. Remove from oven and allow to cool. Yields about 3 dozen cookies.

THE MOUNT VERNON INN

The Mount Vernon Inn Restaurant
George Washington Parkway South
Mount Vernon, VA 22121
703-780-0011

The Mount Vernon Inn Restaurant is located on land that was once part of the Mansion House Farm, one of five farms on George and Martha Washington's 8,077-acre plantation, known as Mount Vernon. The estate, now 500 acres, has been owned and operated since 1853 by the Mount Vernon Ladies' Association. The restaurant sits just outside the gates of this national treasure, providing sustenance for travelers as the Washington family did so many years ago.

Martha Washington was a renowned hostess. A seemingly endless parade of visitors was welcomed to her table. Many were famous, like the Marquis de Lafayette, while others were strangers who came to pay homage to George Washington as a beloved and respected leader. The household ledger for the year 1785 reflects at least 423 dinner guests! Those fortunate enough to break bread with the Washingtons frequently commented on the gracious hospitality and the bounty of the meal. Although the food was plentiful, records indicate that it was not par-

ticularly fancy. Boiled meat was typical, served in hearty portions. Most of the fish and meat was caught and cured right on the estate. The Washingtons also served a wide variety of fruits and vegetables harvested from the ample gardens on the property. The kitchen staff is said to have been in constant readiness for large parties of guests. The frequency of such occurrences is implied in a letter written by Washington shortly after his retirement from public office: "Unless someone pops in, unexpectedly—Mrs. Washington and myself will do what I believe has not been done within the last twenty years by us,—that is to set down to dinner by ourselves."

Although the Mount Vernon Ladies' Association took possession of the property in 1853, it was many years before visitors were again able to partake of meals prepared here. Tourists can thank Colonel James Hollingsworth, who established a precedent by operating a small food concession out of the Washington family kitchen in 1872. The Gibbs family continued that tradition through the next decades. In 1892, the electric trolley brought visitors from Alexandria and Washington. Mr. Gibbs established a tearoom in the trolley terminal, a venture that lasted until 1929.

In 1932, the dedication of the new George Washington Parkway was accompanied by the construction of a new concession building. At that time, the food operations were overseen by the National Park

Service. Over the next 50 years, those operations were handled by numerous parties and known by many different names. In 1981, the restaurant came into the possession of the Mount Vernon Ladies' Association.

The décor and menu, both traditional colonial, recapture the spirit of hospitality provided by George and Martha Washington. In deference to the weather on the chilly January afternoon of our visit, we chose comfort food for our midday meal. Both the Roasted Vegetable Gratin and the Potted Roast were appealing. Ultimately, Debbie chose the Fried Green Tomatoes Au Gratin and a mug of Peanut and Chestnut Soup. Karen settled on the Colonial Turkey Pye, which was topped with a homemade Buttermilk Biscuit. It was a meal of which the Washingtons would have been proud.

SALMON CORN CAKES

2 cups water
1 cup dry white wine
1 fresh bay leaf
4 whole peppercorns
2 sprigs parsley
a few celery leaves
2 ½-pound salmon steaks
1 cup fresh corn kernels, cooked
½ cup finely chopped shallots
½ cup finely diced red pepper
½ cup finely diced celery
¼ cup fresh cilantro leaves, chopped
½ cup nonfat plain yogurt, drained in a fine
   strainer
½ cup light mayonnaise
¼ cup mustard
dash of Tabasco sauce
salt and pepper to taste
1 egg plus 1 egg white, beaten lightly
1½ cups cracker crumbs, divided
4 tablespoons olive oil, divided

Combine water, wine, bay leaf, peppercorns, parsley, and celery leaves in a shallow 8-inch pan. Slowly bring to a boil. Reduce to a simmer and add salmon. Simmer for 7 to 10 minutes until salmon is just cooked through. Remove with a slotted spatula, drain, and cool slightly. Flake salmon into a bowl; do not break it up too much. Discard skin and bones. Add corn, shallots, red peppers, celery, and cilantro. Fold together gently. In a separate bowl, combine yogurt, mayonnaise, mustard, and Tabasco. Fold into salmon mixture. Season with salt and pepper. Gently fold eggs and ¼ cup of the cracker crumbs into salmon. Form into 8 large or 12 medium patties. Coat on both sides with remaining cracker crumbs. Cover and refrigerate for up to 1 hour. Heat 2 tablespoons of the olive oil in a nonstick skillet over medium heat. Cook a few cakes at a time about 3 minutes per side until golden. Add more oil to skillet as needed. Serve immediately. Serves 8.

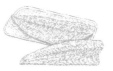

THE KING's ARMS

King's Arms Tavern
Duke of Gloucester Street
Colonial Williamsburg
Williamsburg, VA 23185
757-229-2141

In the February 6, 1772, issue of the *Virginia Gazette*, Mrs. Jane Vobe informed the local populace that she had just opened a tavern "at the sign of the King's Arms" and that she would "be much obliged to the Gentlemen who favor me with their company." The name of the tavern was a clear signal that it was her intention to maintain an operation in the tradition of the leading public houses back in England. Jane Vobe was determined to run a tavern where all the best people gathered. At the time, the King's Arms and other taverns in the area were local gathering places where news from abroad could be discussed. Many taverns provided rooms for politicians to debate independence.

The change to an American government had little impact on the day-to-day running of the tavern. It continued just as before, but with a new name to reflect the current political thinking. When the political climate changed from one where most Virginians remained loyal to the king to one where most Virginians wanted independence, the King's Arms was renamed Mrs. Vobe's. Just like in colonial days, all tavern keepers were required to be licensed and to post a list of their maximum prices for food, drink, and lodging. Guests today will see that this tradition remains.

When reproducing the tavern, historians relied upon many artifacts discovered at the current site, as well as some sketches of the tavern found on a few insurance policies from the late eighteenth century. The current King's Arms is comprised of two houses. The Purdie House, which makes up the eastern part of the tavern, was originally owned by local printer Alexander Purdie. He was also the local postmaster, appointed by Ben Franklin.

The eleven dining rooms contain a mix of reproduction furniture in styles popular with the Virginia gentry. The public areas have swagged draperies, framed prints, maps, and wallpaper. The brass sconces and pewter candlesticks are also indicative of a tavern patronized by affluent and influential customers.

The bill of fare at the tavern features the grilled and roasted meats that are the hallmark of fine British cooking, for guests with discriminating tastes. The Peanut Soup is terrific, as are the Oysters Randolph with Mustard-Herb Glaze. Entrées range from Roasted Half Chicken with Scuppernong Raisin Sauce and Cornbread Dressing to Filet Mignon Stuffed with Oysters to Cavalier's Roasted Rack of Lamb with Mustard and Aromatic Fresh Rosemary to Roast Prime Rib of Beef with Claret Jus and Horseradish. Don't forget to sample the delicious Sally Lunn Bread or the seasonal Tavern Batter Bread. And be sure to save room for a piece of Williamsburg Pumpkin Pie while enjoying a piece of Williamsburg history.

FILET MIGNON STUFFED WITH OYSTERS

6 6-ounce, 1½-inch-thick beef tenderloin filets
12 medium oysters, shucked
salt and freshly ground black pepper to taste
3 tablespoons unsalted butter, divided
6 slices bacon
1 teaspoon fresh parsley, chopped fine

Insert a sharp knife into side of each filet. With a short sawing motion, make a deep pocket without puncturing opposite side. Set aside. Season oysters with salt and pepper. In a small skillet over medium-high heat, melt 1 tablespoon of the butter. Add oysters and cook 1 to 2 minutes, only until edges begin to curl. Drain on paper towels.

Stuff each filet with 2 oysters. Wrap a slice of bacon around each filet and secure with a toothpick. Broil or sauté to desired doneness, 5 to 7 minutes on each side for medium-rare. In a small saucepan, heat remaining butter until lightly browned. Stir in parsley and pour over filets. Serves 6.

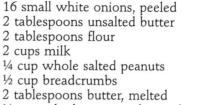

CREAMED ONIONS WITH PEANUTS

16 small white onions, peeled
2 tablespoons unsalted butter
2 tablespoons flour
2 cups milk
¼ cup whole salted peanuts
½ cup breadcrumbs
2 tablespoons butter, melted
¼ cup salted peanuts, chopped coarse

Preheat oven to 400 degrees. Butter a 1-quart casserole dish and set aside. Cook onions in boiling salted water until tender. Drain and set aside. Melt unsalted butter in a small saucepan over medium-high heat. Add flour and stir about 3 minutes until well blended and lemon colored. Pour in milk, increase heat to high, and bring to a boil, stirring often. Reduce heat to medium and cook for 5 to 7 minutes until smooth and thickened.

Place onions in casserole and pour sauce over top. Add whole peanuts and stir. Combine breadcrumbs and melted butter. Add chopped peanuts. Sprinkle mixture over top of casserole and bake about 15 minutes until lightly browned on top and bubbly. Serves 4 to 6.

Christiana Campbell's

TAVERN

Waller Street
Colonial Williamsburg
Williamsburg, VA 23187
757-229-2141

My first experience at Christiana Campbell's predated the writing of this book. In fact, it came almost twenty years to the day before we arrived in Colonial Williamsburg on our "official visit." Both of us had enjoyed the richness of Williamsburg history on prior visits with our families. I have fond memories of the Nunley family's excursions. But what I remember most from that very first time is the Fried Chicken at Christiana Campbell's. Though the menu is more upscale today than it was then, I've been told that many tourists and staff members agree that the chicken simply is the best.

For lunch, guests at this tavern can select from appetizers such as Colonial Ale-Steamed Shrimp, Welsh Rarebit, and Warm Crabmeat, Artichoke, and Spinach Dip. The range of entrées at midday includes Plantation Pye, Pickled Beef Brisket, Salmagundi (the eighteenth-century version of a chef salad), and Seasoned Crab Cakes, to name just a few. Biscuits and Sweet Potato Muffins accompany each of the selections. For dinner, seafood dishes like Baked Shrimp Randolph, Heart-Baked Cod, and Flounder Dressed with Crawfish are featured.

In Mrs. Campbell's day, few females frequented taverns, primarily because women rarely traveled. If they did, their first choice of accommodations was typically with family members. Failing that, they would seek out a lodging house. Only if absolutely necessary would they patronize a tavern, since no allowances were made for the modesties of the fair sex. However, tavern keeping was one of the few acceptable occupations for women of the era. Mrs. Campbell found it necessary to embark on that endeavor after her husband died early in their marriage. She had grown up the daughter of John Burdett, a Williamsburg tavern keeper. After her marriage, she moved to Petersburg. By the time she returned to her hometown, she was a widow with a baby and a toddler to support. She leased tavern space until she was able to purchase her own. Mrs. Jane Vobe was actually the first tavern keeper at this location. When Mrs. Vobe moved on to run the King's Arms Tavern up the road, Mrs. Campbell took proprietorship here.

Christiana Campbell's Tavern contains seven rooms on three floors. Archaeological research has shown that the structure had a very interesting feature. Located in today's downstairs dining room was once an indoor winter kitchen, a rare feature in the days when most cooking was done away from the main house for fear of fire. Another unusual feature is the full front porch. Inside, cream-and-red-checked curtains adorn the windows and colonial woodwork accents the simple cream walls. Pewter accouterments and simple candlesticks in hurricane lamps sit on each of the wooden tables. Upstairs, the rooms that were once the sleeping quarters are now bright dining rooms with lovely views.

While dining, today's guests are entertained with period music performed by strolling balladeers. This was a common practice of the day. In the long evenings, guests actually entertained each other. Some traveled with their own instruments. At some taverns, visitors could plunk down a penny to rent an instrument to play for the evening.

OYSTER FRITTERS

6 tablespoons flour, plus extra for dredging
⅔ cup lukewarm water
2 tablespoons vegetable oil, plus extra for frying
1 tablespoon finely chopped parsley
2 egg whites, beaten to soft peaks
24 medium oysters, shucked and drained
salt and freshly ground pepper to taste
dipping sauce of your choice
lemon wedges for garnish

In a large bowl, combine 6 tablespoons flour, water, 2 tablespoons oil, and parsley. Whisk until smooth. Stir about ¼ of the egg whites into mixture to lighten. Gently fold in the rest. Fill an electric deep-fat fryer or large skillet with enough oil to measure 1 to 1½ inches deep. Heat to 375 degrees. Dip oysters in dredging flour and drop into batter. Transfer batter-dipped oysters to hot oil and fry for 1 to 2 minutes, turning, until golden brown. Sprinkle with salt and pepper. Drain well on paper towels and serve warm with dipping sauce of your choice. Garnish with lemon wedges. Serves 4.

SEAFOOD MUDDLE

2 tablespoons vegetable oil
2 large onions, sliced thin
2 medium carrots, peeled and chopped fine
1 stalk celery, sliced thin
1 clove garlic, minced
16-ounce can tomatoes, drained, seeded, and chopped
2 medium potatoes, diced into ½-inch cubes
6 cups clam juice or fish stock
salt and freshly ground black pepper to taste
pinch of saffron threads
12 small clams (preferably Little Neck), scrubbed
1 pound lean fish (cod, flounder, bass, or snapper), cut into 2-inch pieces
½ pound medium shrimp, peeled, deveined, and halved
12 small mussels, rinsed, beards removed
¼ cup fresh finely chopped parsley

Heat oil in a large kettle or soup pot over medium-high heat. Add onions, carrots, and celery. Cook, stirring often, for 3 to 5 minutes until softened. Add garlic and cook 1 minute longer. Stir in tomatoes and potatoes.

Reduce heat to medium-low, cover, and cook about 10 minutes until potatoes are slightly softened. Add a few tablespoons of clam juice or fish stock to prevent scorching, if necessary. Pour in clam juice or fish stock and increase heat to high. Bring to a boil, reduce heat to medium, and season with salt and pepper. Add saffron and continue simmering for 10 to 15 minutes until potatoes are completely cooked. Add clams and cook about 5 minutes until they start to open. Add fish, shrimp, and mussels. Cook about 10 minutes until fish is opaque, shrimp are pink, and clams and mussels are fully opened; discard any that remain unopened. Season again with salt and pepper. Sprinkle with parsley. Serve hot in warmed bowls. Serves 4 to 6.

SWEET POTATO MUFFINS

¼ cup butter
½ cup sugar
1 egg
½ cup canned sweet potatoes, mashed
¾ cup all-purpose flour
1 teaspoon baking powder
⅓ teaspoon salt
½ teaspoon cinnamon
⅓ teaspoon nutmeg
½ cup milk
⅓ cup pecans or walnuts, chopped
¼ cup raisins, chopped

Preheat oven to 400 degrees. Grease 1½-inch muffin tins. Cream butter and sugar together. Add egg and mix well. Blend in sweet potatoes. Sift flour with baking powder, salt, cinnamon, and nutmeg. Add alternately with milk. Do not overmix. Fold in nuts and raisins. Fill muffin tins ⅔ full. Bake for 25 minutes. Yields 3 dozen mini-muffins.

Shields TAVERN

Duke of Gloucester Street
Colonial Williamsburg
Williamsburg, VA 23185
757-229-2141

Mr. Shields was a meticulous man. He kept detailed books about his establishment. It is lucky for visitors to Williamsburg that he did. His records were so complete that Shields Tavern was completely outfitted based on Mr. Shields's inventory of the items purchased for the house. The tavern is light and airy, with white paint and English prints on the walls. Views of St. James, Pall Mall, the River Thames, and other parts of London and its environs create an old-time feel. The furniture is sparse, just a few select period pieces adorning each room. The myriad fireplaces are mostly unlit. But pay particular attention to the large fireplace in the main dining room, which has a huge spit for roasting meat. The pewter sconces on the walls allow guests to dine in romantic candlelight. There are many dining rooms at the tavern. Visitors can eat outside, inside, or even in the basement. A huge fireplace complete with spit is downstairs.

Entertainment is offered at Shields Tavern. Diners enjoy the strolling troubadours who visit during the evenings. Mr. Shields himself was an accomplished oboe player. He actually kept an oboe behind the bar for use by his customers. But it was not often that a guest at his establishment could outplay him.

The delicious meals served here are based on classic recipes handed down from eighteenth- and nineteenth-century cooks. The menu reflects seasonal changes, as the chef strives to use the very freshest ingredients from local farms, nearby rivers, and, of course, Chesapeake Bay. Guests can partake of lunch and dinner at Shields Tavern. Starters include Melon with Shaved Virginia Ham and Ginger Vinaigrette, Spinach and Endive Salad with Glazed Pecans, Apples, English Blue Cheese, and Warm Cider-Bacon Vinaigrette, and Fried Oysters dipped in buttermilk and cornmeal and served with Tomato-Caper Remoulade.

Visitors who turn the menu over will learn some important facts about the food served in eighteenth-century Virginia. For example, capers, persimmons, and anchovies were very commonly used. Veal and beef were the most popular meats, closely followed by pork, chicken, and turkey. But venison was probably eaten only by the upper classes.

Today's menu reflects the tastes that were common then. Among the excellent entrée choices are Chicken and Dumplings,

Glazed Roast Loin of Pork with Creamy Roasted Garlic Polenta, and Roasted Duckling with Pecan Rice and Ginger-Apricot Brandy Glaze. Our favorite choice is Mr. Shields Supper. This meal consists of Pan-Roasted Chicken Breast with Surry County Ham, Roasted Mushrooms, Baby Spinach, Whipped Potatoes with Tarragon Butter Sauce, Crayfish Soup, and Pumpkin Bread Pudding with Vanilla Custard Sauce. We have eaten here often, and we suggest you do the same.

VEAL COLLOPS WITH LEMON, CAPERS, AND CREAM

6 6-ounce thin veal cutlets
salt and freshly ground black pepper to taste
¼ cup unsalted butter
1 small shallot, minced
1 teaspoon grated lemon peel
1 tablespoon finely chopped fresh parsley
½ cup dry white wine
¼ cup chicken stock
2 tablespoons lemon juice
½ cup heavy cream
2 tablespoons capers, drained and finely chopped

Pound cutlets as thin as possible between layers of waxed paper with a mallet or heavy rolling pin. Season with salt and pepper. Melt butter in a large skillet over medium-high heat. Working in batches, add as many cutlets as will lie flat in skillet. Cook about 1 minute on each side until lightly browned. Transfer to a warmed platter and cover loosely with foil to keep warm. Continue until all the cutlets have been cooked.

Pour out all but 1 tablespoon of fat from skillet. Add shallots and cook for 2 to 3 minutes until softened, stirring often. Add lemon peel and parsley. Pour in wine and increase heat to high. Boil for 3 to 5 minutes until reduced by half, stirring to deglaze pan. Pour in chicken stock and lemon juice and bring back to a boil. Cook for about 3 minutes until liquid is reduced by half again. Add cream and bring back to a boil. Reduce for 3 to 5 minutes until liquid is thick enough to coat the back of a spoon. Stir in capers and season to taste. Spoon sauce over cutlets and serve immediately. Serves 6.

CHOWNING'S TAVERN

Duke of Gloucester Street
Colonial Williamsburg
Williamsburg, VA 23187
757-229-2141

Unlike the more upscale taverns just down the street, Chowning's was established to cater to the tastes of working men of the late 1700s. Ales and grogs were the beverages of choice, and modern-day versions of these are still available. Not surprisingly, the specialty drinks feature rum in combination with a variety of fruit juices.

When Josiah Chowning announced the opening of his tavern in the *Virginia Gazette* in October 1766, his menu choices most likely centered on items that were readily available, such as fresh fish and fowl. Significant efforts have been made so that the options today are in keeping with those of more than two hundred years ago. Guests can still order a Turkey Leg or sate their appetites with Old-Fashioned Brunswick Stew. Smoky Beef Brisket and Smoked Turkey are served in heaping quantities on an interesting Pretzel Bun. We were surprised to see Barbecued Ribs on the menu but were

told that diaries from 1774 mention pit-style barbecue.

Chowning's Tavern was reopened to the public in 1941, becoming the first of Colonial Williamsburg's operating taverns. The white-painted exterior accented by black shutters and the moss-covered slate roof have changed little since then. The tavern was reconstructed on an eighteenth-century foundation, but researchers have since discovered that a store and a dwelling occupied this site, while Josiah Chowning ran a tavern nearby.

Why the tavern was named for Chowning is puzzling. Lacking the capital to buy the tavern, he rented it instead. Some sources believe that he attempted to sell his nearby farm in order to raise enough money to keep his business afloat. Since that farmland was part of his estate at the time of his death, it seems that he either changed his mind or was not able to complete the sale, although no one really knows. Consequently, only eighteen months after Chowning's opening proclamation, another enthusiastic individual announced that he had "opened tavern in the house formerly occupied by Mr. Chowning."

The interior of the tavern is fashioned after English alehouses. You'll find dark wood, plank tables, bench seating, and high-backed booths in the Tap Room. In the other downstairs dining room, the white walls are trimmed with dark brown wood trim. Just inside the front door are numerous advertisements, as was the style of the eighteenth century. Also posted, by court order, is a price list of items available at the tavern. In bygone days, should a tavern keeper be found not displaying such a list, zealous patrons could report him or her and expect to receive a shilling as a reward.

In the evening, guests are treated to light fare, balladeers, and eighteenth-century games. Although neither of us has had the opportunity to experience it, we've been told that it's a rollicking good time. Next visit, we won't miss it!

BARBECUED RIBS OF SHOAT

¼ cup sugar
¼ cup coarse salt
1 teaspoon allspice
1 teaspoon freshly ground black pepper
1 teaspoon ginger
½ teaspoon cinnamon
½ teaspoon cayenne
6 pounds lean pork spareribs, cut into sections
2 cups Barbecue Sauce (recipe follows)

Combine first 7 ingredients in a small bowl. Use your fingers to rub mixture into spareribs, thoroughly coating all surfaces. Wrap each section in plastic and refrigerate overnight.

Build a charcoal fire with a drip pan placed in center. Oil grates and let coals burn to gray ash. Cook ribs on grill for about 1 hour, turning every 10 minutes. Brush and baste ribs with Barbecue Sauce every time you turn them. After about 45 minutes,

check to see if ribs are thoroughly cooked by pulling apart 1 of the sections. If they do not separate easily, cover with foil and check again after 15 minutes. Cut ribs into individual pieces to serve. Serves 6 to 8.

 BARBECUE SAUCE

2 cups ketchup
1 cup distilled white vinegar
½ cup dark brown sugar, packed
1 large onion, chopped fine
2 cloves garlic, minced
2 tablespoons Worcestershire sauce
½ teaspoon Tabasco sauce
salt and freshly ground black pepper to taste

Combine all ingredients in a large nonreactive saucepan. Bring to a boil over high heat. Reduce heat to medium-low and simmer, partially covered, for about 30 minutes, stirring often until thickened and dark colored. Strain and cool to room temperature. Yields 2 cups.

Gabriel Archer Tavern
The Williamsburg Winery Ltd.
5800 Wessex Hundred
Williamsburg, VA 23185
www.williamsburgwinery.com
757-258-0899

The Williamsburg Winery is an unexpected oasis at the end of a suburban street. We arrived for a late lunch, winding our way slowly through a vineyard ready for harvest. Wessex Hundred is the name of the farm, in addition to being part of the address. During colonial days, *hundred* was a term used to describe a parcel of land sufficient to support one hundred families, regardless of its actual acreage. The original settlement was known as Archer's Hope or Jockey's Neck. One of the early settlers here was Joachim Andrus, who is said to have been one of the "Ancient Planters," having come to the colony prior to 1616.

Although there are no surviving records, it is assumed that this farm was subject to the Actes of 1619, laid down by the House of Burgesses. The Twelfth Acte of that decree mandated that each settler plant at least ten vines for the purpose of winemaking. Later records show that the property was owned by John Johnson and subsequently by his heirs. For a time, it continued to be used for agricultural purposes, but it was eventually allowed to grow over.

In 1781, M. Desandrouin, the cartographer for the French army during the Revolution, mapped the area. His work shows plantation buildings on this property, which then belonged to the Reverend William Bland, who is thought to have acquired it in the mid-1760s. Bland was a graduate of William and Mary who served at Bruton Parish Church and was later rector of the Church on the Main.

Skipping ahead almost two hundred years, we find that Virginia had only eleven wineries in the early 1980s. Since the tobacco industry was waning, the state offered tax incentives to individuals willing to undertake alternate agricultural endeavors. About that same time, Patrick and Peggy Duffeler were in the market for some land on which to retire. They were also interested in commemorating the efforts of those who came before them and in re-creating Virginia life of the eighteenth century. The Virginia Department of Agriculture encouraged them to pursue viticulture, and the Duffelers began planting vineyards in 1985.

The winery and its support buildings were constructed in seventeenth- and eighteenth-century architectural styles. Gabriel Archer Tavern was built in 1987 on the footprints of an old farm shed. Today, some of that flavor exists in the burlap-covered walls and plank flooring. Guests at the winery can have a bite to eat while sampling the wines made on the premises. There are nineteen different wines from which to choose, as well as tasty luncheon items such as Turkey and Smoked Gouda with Cranberry Chutney and Mustard Sauce. We opted to share the French Country Platter of selected pâtés, cheeses, and sausage to go with a glass of Plantation Blush and a glass of Gabriel Archer Reserve. The combination was perfect.

We recommend eating first and then taking the tour. Having sampled the wares, it made us all the more appreciative of the creative genius that goes into each bottle. Today, the number of Virginia wineries has grown from eleven in the early 1980s to more than eighty. The Williamsburg Winery is the largest of them all. Cheers!

BALSAMIC VINAIGRETTE

1½ cups balsamic vinegar
½ cup garlic, chopped
½ cup whole-grain mustard
1 tablespoon salt
2 tablespoons coarsely ground black pepper
½ cup raspberry Merlot
3 cups olive oil

Combine all ingredients in an airtight container and shake well. Refrigerate. Shake again before using. Yields about 5 cups.

MARINATED VIRGINIA HAM

1 pound Virginia ham
½ teaspoon freshly ground black pepper
½ cup vodka
juice of 1 lemon
1 teaspoon fresh dill

Cut ham into thin slices, then into small pieces about 1 by 1½ inches. Spread on a platter and sprinkle pepper over top. Pour vodka over ham. Squeeze lemon juice over top. Add dill. Allow 30 to 45 minutes for ham to marinate. Serve cold as an appetizer. Serves 4 to 6.

VENISON STEW

3 tablespoons vegetable oil
2- to 3-pound hindquarter venison roast
salt and pepper to taste
2 bay leaves
4 carrots, peeled and cut into 2-inch pieces
1 large onion, cut into 2-inch pieces
3 stalks celery, cut into 2-inch pieces
½ pound bacon or ham, cut into chunks

Heat oil in a large skillet over high heat. Place roast in skillet and sear on all sides. Fill a large Dutch oven or stockpot with enough water to cook roast. Add salt and pepper and bay leaves. Cover and simmer for 4 to 6 hours. Cool overnight. Add vegetables and bacon or ham. Simmer again for 3 to 4 hours. Serves 6 to 8.

Inn
at
KELLY'S
FORD

16589 Edwards Shop Road
Remington, VA 22734
540-399-1779

Not long after 1725, J. P. Kelly patented a tract of land along the Rappahannock River sixty miles southwest of where Washington, D.C., lies today. By 1773, the Kelly family owned the property on both sides of the river. Since that time, the area has been known as Kellysville or Kelly's Ford. From those early days until the Civil War, Kelly's Mill and other of the family's businesses were the center of trade in this part of Culpeper County. Business was further enhanced by the canals along the river, which provided a means of transportation for goods.

In December 1848, the first bridge to span the river was completed. The area around Kellysville grew into the largest manufacturing complex in Culpeper County. About a hundred men worked at Kelly's Mill, which turned out a hundred barrels of flour per day. The community boasted a cloth factory and a general store, owned by Granville Kelly. It also had a blacksmith shop, a wheelwright shop, a copper shop, a sawmill, and a shoe shop.

Early in the summer of 1862, as the Civil War encroached on the area around Kelly's Ford, Granville Kelly dismantled his looms and machinery in hopes of keeping them safe from the approaching Federal troops. Shipped to Lynchburg, they didn't return. Though he eventually rebuilt the mill complex on a smaller scale, the hustle and bustle of Kellysville was never quite the same. The mill lingered until it was felled by a flood in 1936.

Today, the ruins of the canals, mill, and Civil War fortifications can still be seen. The Kellys' home, built in 1779, was renovated in 1999 as part of the Inn at Kelly's Ford. Both the thirty-two-seat main dining room and the more casual Pelham's Pub are built on a portion of the foundation of the original house.

It was a quiet evening when we visited. A fire roared in the fireplace. As we watched the sun set across the farmland, we kept an eye open for the herd of deer and the bald eagle that our server, Christine, spoke vividly about. To start, we shared a plate of Country Pâté with Black Pepper. The list of entrées was appealing. We chose the Trout Stuffed with Crayfish Lobster Sauce and the John Dorey with Crabmeat. The Shrimp in Tomato and Curry Sauce, the Grilled Swordfish with Honey Sauce, and the Lamb Chop with Sage Au Jus would have been equally satisfying. Trying to choose among Marquise Cake, Three-Berry Tart, Almond Cake, and Blueberry Crème Brûlée was a welcome challenge. Crème brûlée is one of the dishes for which we've acquired a taste since we began writing, so Blueberry Crème Brûlée it was.

In addition to its restaurant and guest rooms, the inn also houses a conference center and an equestrian center. With so much to offer—and so much history, too—this is more than just an inn. It's a destination.

HALIBUT WITH FENNEL

3 tablespoons unsalted butter
2 shallots, minced
4 7-ounce halibut fillets
1 bulb fresh fennel, julienned
juice of 2 lemons
salt and pepper to taste

Preheat oven to 375 degrees. Butter a shallow baking dish. Sprinkle shallots over bottom. Top with halibut. Arrange fennel strips over fish. Dot with remaining butter. Sprinkle with lemon juice and salt and pepper. Bake for 10 minutes. Remove from oven and baste fish with cooking juices. Return to oven and cook 10 additional minutes until done. Fish will appear white at the bone. Season to taste and serve. Serves 4.

TURNIPS DAUPHINOISE

3 tablespoons unsalted butter
2 pounds small white turnips, peeled and sliced thin
1¼ cups heavy cream, heated
fresh thyme leaves to taste
salt and pepper to taste

Preheat oven to 350 degrees. Butter a shallow earthenware casserole dish. Arrange turnip slices in the casserole and dot with butter. Pour hot cream over turnips. Sprinkle with thyme and salt and pepper. Cook for about 45 minutes until turnips are tender and cream is thickened. Serves 4.

Old Chickahominy House

1211 Jamestown Road
Williamsburg, VA 23185
757-229-4689

Just down the road from the College of William and Mary in Williamsburg is the Old Chickahominy House, affectionately known at "the Chick." It's a popular place for breakfast and lunch with locals and visitors alike. The Chick was originally located along the Chickahominy River a short distance away but was moved to this mid-eighteenth-century house in the restored section of Williamsburg. The large front porch invites visitors to sit awhile and wait for a table.

Sometimes, the wait is the most interesting part of a visit to this old house. Before enjoying a real plantation meal in an eighteenth-century dining room, many visitors like to browse the excellent American and English antiques on display. There is a large selection of unique furniture, prints, crystal, silverware, candelabras, handcrafted items, and cards. This is a fine place to find a curiosity to take home to remind you of your trip to Virginia.

Guests have three well-appointed dining rooms to choose from. We sat in the larg-est, a big, square room with plain wooden tables and worn wooden floors. The colonial décor was continued in the cream and tan paint, the floral tapestry swags at the window, and the large brass candlesticks. Hung around the walls were several large oil paintings, portraits of folks from times gone by. The wainscoting, paneling, and mantelpieces were brought from Carter's Grove Plantation House nearby.

We sat in the high-backed rush chairs and contemplated our choices for breakfast. Traditional Southern cuisine is served here. Visitors most often select the Plantation Breakfast, which includes Virginia Ham, Country Bacon, Sausage, Eggs, Grits, and Biscuits. On the morning we visited, Miss Melinda's Pancakes, named for the original owner, were also very popular. Debbie opted for the Eggs and Cheese with Biscuits, while Karen devoured the Creamed Ham on Biscuits. The Biscuits are large, flat, and rectangular but extremely tasty with Virginia Ham or even just butter. Besides the usual coffee, tea, and hot chocolate, the Chick also serves a Rebel Cocktail, an interesting concoction of tomato juice and beer that will brighten anyone's morning.

For luncheon, the Brunswick Stew sounded delicious, as did the Homemade Chicken and Dumplings. Visitors whose tastes don't incline toward colonial fare might try the Deluxe Hamburger Plate, the Bacon, Lettuce, and Tomato Sandwich, or the Julienne Salad Bowl before sampling the selection of homemade pies. The service here is swift, efficient, friendly, and knowledgeable. The food is always freshly made and in such demand that patrons can now purchase Brunswick Stew by the quart or a Wallace Edwards Ham to take home. On many levels, this visit was a truly delicious way to start our day!

 VIRGINIA HAM STRAWS

2 cups flour
2 teaspoons baking powder
½ teaspoon paprika
⅛ teaspoon red pepper
½ cup butter, softened
1 egg
½ cup milk
¾ cup ground Virginia ham

Preheat oven to 350 degrees. Sift flour, baking powder, paprika, and red pepper 3 or 4 times into a medium mixing bowl. Cut in butter. Add egg, milk, and ham and combine until mixture forms a dough. Roll dough very thin on a floured pastry board. Cut dough into strips about ¼ inch wide and 4 inches long. Lay strips in rows in a buttered baking pan about ¾ inch apart. Bake for about 10 minutes until pale brown. Serve with salads, soups, or even breakfast coffee. Yields 6 dozen straws.

 TIDEWATER QUICHE

9 inch piecrust
¼ pint fresh medium oysters
2 tablespoons butter
4 thin slices Virginia ham, julienned
¼ cup finely chopped scallions
10-ounce package frozen spinach, thawed and drained
¼ cup grated mozzarella
¼ cup grated Swiss cheese
3 eggs
1½ cups light cream
¼ teaspoon nutmeg
¼ teaspoon freshly ground pepper
thinly sliced tomatoes for garnish
paprika for garnish

Preheat oven to 375 degrees. Place pie weights in piecrust and bake for 10 minutes. Remove from oven, remove weights, and set aside. Drain oysters and pat dry with paper towels. In a medium sauté pan, melt butter and sauté ham and scallions until tender. Stir in spinach until warmed through. Place mixture into partially baked piecrust. Add oysters and cover with mozzarella and Swiss. Beat eggs in a small bowl. Stir in cream, nutmeg, and pepper and mix well. Pour over cheeses. Garnish with tomato slices and sprinkle with paprika. Bake in upper third of oven for 25 minutes. Remove from oven and allow to rest for 5 minutes before cutting. Serves 8.

Restaurant Index

Recipe Index

Sesame Honey Salad Dressing, 22
Sesame Soy Vinaigrette, 67
Tahini Vinaigrette, 4

Marinated Carrots, 42
Potato Cauliflower Curry, 149
Turnips Dauphinoise, 274
Veggie Chessie's Pasta, 67

Venison
Loin of Fallow Fields Venison, 243
Venison Medallions with Sweet Potato
    Purée, 107
Venison Ossobuco, 219
Venison Stew, 272

Walnuts
Mini Chocolate Coffee Walnut Muffins,
    244
Smoked Chicken and Walnut Spread, 151
Walnut Crêpes, 87

Zucchini
Zucchini Bread, 129